Bougainville
1943–1945

Bougainville 1943–1945

The Forgotten Campaign

HARRY A. GAILEY

THE UNIVERSITY PRESS OF KENTUCKY

Publication of this volume was made possible in part
by a grant from the National Endowment for the Humanities.

Copyright © 1991 by The University Press of Kentucky
Scholarly publisher for the Commonwealth,
serving Bellarmine University, Berea College, Centre
College of Kentucky, Eastern Kentucky University,
The Filson Historical Society, Georgetown College,
Kentucky Historical Society, Kentucky State University,
Morehead State University, Murray State University,
Northern Kentucky University, Transylvania University,
University of Kentucky, University of Louisville,
and Western Kentucky University.
All rights reserved.

Editorial and Sales Offices: The University Press of Kentucky
663 South Limestone Street, Lexington, Kentucky 40508–4008

Cover photo: "These men have earned the bloody reputation as being skillful jungle fighters. They are U.S. Marine Raiders, gathered in front of a Japanese dugout on Cape Torokina on Bougainville, Solomon Islands, which they helped to take." January 1944. National Archives, 80-G-205686.

07 06 05 04 03   5 4 3 2 1

Library of Congress Cataloging-in-Publication Data

Gailey, Harry A.
    Bougainville, 1943-1945 : the forgotten campaign / Harry A. Gailey
      p.   cm.
    Includes bibliographical references and index.
    ISBN 0-8131-9047-9 (pbk : alk. paper)
  1. World War, 1939-1945—Campaigns—Papua New Guinea—Bougainville Island. 2. Bougainville Island (Papua New Guinea)—History.
I. Title.
D767.99B68G35   1991
940.54'26—dc20   90-28496

This book is printed on acid-free recycled paper meeting
the requirements of the American National Standard
for Permanence in Paper for Printed Library Materials.

∞ ✺

Manufactured in the United States of America.

Contents

List of Maps   vii
Introduction   1
1. Japanese Advances and Retreats   7
2. Allied Planning   22
3. The Treasuries and Choiseul   39
4. Establishing the Beachhead   60
5. Naval Actions   78
6. Expanding the Perimeter   93
7. The Rear Areas   120
8. Consolidating the Perimeter   132
9. The Japanese Counterattack   149
10. The 93d Division Affair   169
11. The Final Phase   184
Glossary   212
Notes   214
Bibliography   225
Index   229

[Illustrations follow page 104]

Maps

1. Solomon Islands and Adjacent Areas   14
2. New Georgia Campaign, 30 June–4 August 1943   28
3. Bougainville Island   32
4. Treasury Islands Landings, 27 October 1943   42
5. Choiseul Operation, 28 October–3 November 1943   50
6. Cape Torokina Landings, 1 November 1943   66
7. Battle of Piva Forks, 19-25 November 1943   106
8. The Perimeter to 15 December 1943   116
9. Japanese Counterattack, 9-17 March 1944   146
10. Australian Advances in Northern Bougainville, January-June 1945   198
11. Australian Operations in Southern Bougainville, January-June 1945   200

Introduction

Historians are continually trying to impose order on the past, to simplify events that would otherwise appear chaotic. By nature and by training, they are inclined to search for first causes that would explain all subsequent events. Among military historians this desire to seek out causation is especially strong, and there is a pronounced tendency to identify the one crucial event that altered the course of a battle, a campaign, or a war. It is questionable whether this practice has any validity for conflicts that took place before the twentieth century, but certainly in the case of the two world wars, it is patently impossible to isolate a single event that irrevocably changed the course of the conflict. No event stood in isolation from its antecedents or from simultaneous actions on other fronts in these large and immensely complicated wars. Nevertheless, historians have tried to pick a turning point.

Apparently, historians of the Pacific theater of World War II are divided over two main possibilities. One group finds the key victory in the Battle of Midway, after which the Japanese never recovered the naval initiative. The other group attributes supreme importance to the land, air, and sea battles off Guadalcanal. There is some validity to both claims, but it should be obvious that however vital these conflicts were to final victory for the Allies, they were simply important links in a long chain of interconnected developments.

Japan lost the war because of a series of complex strategic and tactical defeats, among which the Solomon Islands campaigns played a significant part. It would be an exaggeration to maintain that Japan lost the war in the Solomons, but it would be equally wrong to ignore the effects on the Japanese of attempts to defend Munda, Kolombangara, and Bougainville after their defeat at Guadalcanal. The various battles on and around this long string of fetid, jungle-covered islands took a toll in ships, planes, and men that the Japanese, in attempting to meet the demands of other theaters, could never replace.

It is in this context that one must view the Bougainville campaigns. Largely forgotten today, the Bougainville assault in 1943 was considered absolutely vital to prepare for the invasion of New Britain and the negation of Rabaul, Japan's major fortress and air and sea base in the South Pacific. From mid-1942 onward the Allied commanders in the South and Southwest Pacific had concentrated on Rabaul, first as the key to defending Port Moresby and southern New Guinea and then in planning the step-by-step offensive leading to the invasion of New Britain. Under the general directives of the Joint Chiefs of Staff, General Douglas MacArthur in Brisbane and Vice-Admiral William F. Halsey in Noumea cooperated in a two-pronged series of attacks in New Guinea and the central Solomons during the spring and summer of 1943.

Both commanders, supplied with more men and materiel, had by then adopted the practice of bypassing large Japanese forces whenever possible and allowing them to "wither on the vine." They could not always do so, however. The planning for and operations against New Georgia in July and August 1943 provide a good example of the difficulty involved in a large-scale offensive directed against a clever commander with dedicated troops operating in a jungle environment. Nevertheless, despite a brilliant defense by the Japanese, New Georgia and its important airfield, Munda, were captured, and in the same month Vella Lavella was occupied without incident. Thus all the preliminaries for action against the last of the major Solomon Islands had been completed. Bougainville, with its six airfields, could not be bypassed, especially in view of its proximity to Rabaul. Fighters and medium bombers operating from airstrips on Bougainville could bring Rabaul under constant attack.

After considerable discussion and the abandonment of a number of plans, Admiral Halsey, with MacArthur's concurrence, decided to forgo attacking the main Japanese bases on Bougainville. Rather, after a feint by a marine landing party on Choiseul Island and a strike to negate the Japanese airfields in the south, Halsey would send the 3d Marine Division into Empress Augusta Bay against lightly held positions at Cape Torokina. The mission of the marines, backed up by the army's 37th Division, was at first to seize and hold a lodgment and then expand it outward to permit the construction of airfields from which Air Solomons planes could strike at Rabaul.

This first phase of the conflict on Bougainville was begun on 1 November 1943 and proceeded without great difficulty. In conjunction with land-based Allied planes, the navy struck at the Japanese air bases on Bougainville and rendered them ineffective. By mid-November work was well under way on a fighter strip at Cape Torokina, and survey teams were operating farther in the interior on what eventually would be two larger airfields. During this phase of the operation the marines and army units encountered only moderate opposition from the Japanese as the perimeter was expanded. The jungle-covered terrain, swamps, and the generally foul climate caused more problems than did combat, even during the heaviest fighting for the Piva Forks area.

The second phase of the Bougainville operation was entirely an army affair. Most of the marines had been withdrawn by the end of 1943 and the 37th Division was joined by the Americal. In both sectors in-depth defenses were established. The main goal had become protection of the airfields and supply bases within the perimeter. No American commander gave serious thought to the conquest of the entire island. This quiescent period was shattered when the Japanese, finally reacting to the invasion, shifted a large portion of their southern garrison northward and struck the American perimeter in a three-pronged attack in March 1944. Despite localized losses of part of the defense lines, the army units held and totally devastated the attackers.

Within two weeks the Japanese commanders had admitted defeat and pulled what was left of their forces back to the high ground farther to the east and south. Except for localized attacks, the Japanese would never mount another offensive on Bougainville. They had suffered battle casualties and deaths from illness; later they would endure lack of food. By the spring of 1944 the tide had turned against the Japanese everywhere. MacArthur had even given up plans for the invasion of New Britain since Rabaul was no longer a viable air or sea base. Land-based planes from New Guinea and Bougainville bases, combined with carrier forces, had all but destroyed this once-formidable base. The Japanese on Bougainville were cut off from outside aid, and a large portion of those who were still healthy were occupied simply in planting crops in large garden plots located all over southern Bougainville.

The third phase of the Bougainville operation, that of the Australians, is more difficult to understand. For over six months after the

4 Bougainville

disastrous Japanese counterattack of March 1944, the front was relatively quiet. After a slight displacement forward to better defensive positions in both the 37th and Americal sectors, continuous aggressive patrolling had become the major task of all frontline units. Behind the lines life for the service troops and even many of the combat units had become peaceful and relatively comfortable. The American commanders saw no need to expend lives unnecessarily in what by this time had become a backwater. Nothing done on Bougainville now would affect the outcome of the war one way or another. MacArthur and his staff, primarily concerned with the Philippines operation, paid little attention to Bougainville and the New Guinea enclaves, expecting that the Australians would follow the general pattern of simply containing the Japanese. This was not to be the case.

Troops of the 37th and Americal divisions were pulled out of Bougainville by December 1944, leaving only a few service personnel and artillerymen on the island. The two divisions were replaced by the Australian II Crops, whose commander, General Stanley Savige, backed by the overall Australian ground commander, General Sir Thomas Blamey, decided to adopt a strategy counter to that of the departed Americans. The unspoken truce was broken when the Australians launched a three-pronged attack on Japanese positions with the overall aim of conquering the entire island. Sustained fighting in the mountains and swamps continued throughout the spring and summer of 1945. Gradually the Japanese were pushed off the central highlands and confined to the extreme northern portion of the island. The Japanese in the south, operating without air or naval cover, defended the major fords of the many streams, at times exacting heavy casualties on the Australians. By the beginning of August 1945 General Savige was ready to mount his final offensive against a narrowing Japanese perimeter around Kahili. Before he could act, however, the war ended. After some difficulty largely occasioned by disbelief among the Japanese that they had lost the war, General Savige arranged a surrender ceremony, which brought to an end this bloody and largely unnecessary final phase of the twenty-one-month campaign on Bougainville.

A number of interesting side issues related to the Bougainville operation could each properly be the subject of a book. One such issue concerns the command structure established by the Allied leaders. At first the command was arbitrarily divided between the Southwest and South Pacific areas along longitude 159° east, but this division proved impractical and was never really followed. The invasion of Guadalcanal called for a modification of the spheres, as did the Bougainville venture. The Joint Chiefs of Staff sidestepped this difficulty because it brought into question the broader issue of a unified command for the entire Pacific war. Instead, they left MacArthur responsible for strategic decisions and gave Halsey the tactical responsibility. This solution worked for Bougainville because MacArthur and Halsey liked and respected each other. One wonders whether such an arrangement would have succeeded if their personal relationship had not been so good.

Closely linked to the question of overall command was that of cooperation among various branches of the service. In many areas of the Pacific war a casual observer might have concluded that individual commanders were more concerned with their own interests than in defeating the Japanese. Rivalry among navy, marine, and army units concerned not only supply and materiel problems but also what could be called territory. Rear Admiral Richmond Kelly Turner was notorious for protecting his "turf," General Lt General Robert Richardson in the central Pacific vociferously defended the rights of the army, and General H.M. Smith of the marines created some unnecessary conflicts because of his low opinion of the army. Yet the critical early phases of the Bougainville landing, like all the Solomons operations, was remarkable for the lack of unhealthy interservice rivalry. Part of the reason for this harmony was the desperate nature of the early operations, particularly on Guadalcanal, where it was absolutely vital to cooperate. Even later, however, when the Allies had achieved a definite superiority, cooperation continued. The best example was the rotating command of AIRSOLS, the air force that combined elements of the United States army, navy, and marines, as well as Australian and New Zealand air forces. One can speculate that a major reason for the lack of friction in the Solomons was the very clear message delivered by Admiral Halsey, subordinating all else to his desire to defeat the Japanese.

Another major issue that demands close examination is the relationship between the Australian and New Zealand commanders and MacArthur's headquarters. After the first crucial year these commanders were shunted aside, their troops used basically for mopping-up operations, for example, in the last phase of the Bougainville operation and the final campaigns on New Guinea and Borneo. Perhaps one reason for the rejection of the American containment policy on Bougainville was the need to vindicate the Australian commanders and their units. Thus when left alone by MacArthur, Blamey and Savige decided to show the Americans the true worth of the Australian fighting man. This decision obviously had its political overtones, but no other explanation for the radical change in a successful strategy seems adequate.

A larger issue that came to be focused on Bougainville was the racial problem. The American armed forces in World War II were segregated, and many senior commanders had no desire to deviate from a policy that seemed to them to be based on sound, pragmatic evidence. They simply believed that blacks made inferior soldiers. Some even questioned the intelligence and courage of black troops. Despite this generally prevalent attitude, the army decided in 1944 to commit black troops to action. General George C. Marshall chose the 25th Regiment and units of the 93d Division for this experiment and decided upon Bougainville as the place. The actions of one company of the 93d Division when confronted with the Japanese for the first time appeared to confirm what the critics of the plan had said. The poor performance of this company in a series of misadventures overshadowed the good combat performance of most of the black troops who had been adequately trained. In the rumors that flew around the Pacific, the failure of one company was soon attributed to a battalion and then to a division. The higher commanders deemed the Bougainville experiment a failure, and it was not repeated again in the Pacific. Black troops, even those who were now battle tested, were used throughout the war generally as garrison or service troops.

Bougainville in the final analysis was important in several ways. Not the least was that it showed how an efficient command structure could overcome initial difficulties and how intelligent planning could facilitate the attainment of the larger goal with minimal loss of lives. The Japanese, as they had done before, committed significant naval and air units to thwart the Cape Torokina invasion. In so doing they hastened not only their defeat on Bougainville but also the reduction of Rabaul, their main base of operations, to a cipher. Bougainville should be remembered not for the offensive operations of the last year but for the early months, in which the perimeter was established and defended, major elements of the Japanese navy were destroyed, and three airfields were built. These bases aided in removing Rabaul as a factor in future operations in the South Pacific.

1. Japanese Advances and Retreats

Few examples in the history of warfare would match the success of the Japanese during the first six months of World War II. Once Imperial General Headquarters made the decision that Japan's future could be secured only by aggressive actions against the United States and its Pacific allies, it set in motion a series of attacks that were, in retrospect, gambles of the highest order. The first of these, the strike against Pearl Harbor on 7 December 1941, was perhaps the biggest gamble of all, but the attack was absolutely necessary if Japan was to carry out its plans for further expansion in the Pacific and Southeast Asia, and it was the key to Japanese victories elsewhere in the ensuing months. Some later critics have faulted Admiral Chuichi Nagumo for not continuing his attacks against the vital docks and the supply and storage areas of Oahu, but he had succeeded in his primary mission of neutralizing the powerful United States Pacific fleet. The damage wrought during the few minutes of that raid canceled all immediate offensive plans of the United States and made defense the only possible alternative for the military planners in Washington and Pearl Harbor.[1]

The second gamblers' throw was to send an army and naval force against the British in Malaya. Operating against superior numbers of British and Australian troops, General Tomoyuki Yamashita conducted a most brilliant rapid advance in difficult terrain, which culminated in the capture of Singapore on 15 February 1942. The British fleet in the Indian Ocean was largely neutralized by the air attacks on Admiral Sir James Somerville's force, during which the battleships *Prince of Wales* and *Repulse* were sunk. Simultaneous

8 Bougainville

actions had begun against the Phillipines on 8 December 1941, and successful Japanese air attacks destroyed almost all the U.S. fighter and bomber force on Luzon. Although the Japanese timetable for conquering the main Philippine islands was set back by the heroic defense of Bataan and Corregidor, the final issue was never in doubt since there was no reasonable possibility of reinforcing General Douglas MacArthur's outnumbered force. General Masaharu Homma, although dissatisfied with the progress of his army, all but finished his task when the Bataan defenders surrendered on 8 April 1942.[2]

These early victories were complemented by others—the conquest of Wake Island, the occupation of Hong Kong, the defeat of the British in Burma. Finally, in March 1942 one of their major goals, the petroleum-rich Dutch East Indies fell to the Japanese. Everywhere the Japanese navy and army had been successful. The Pearl Harbor stroke had assured the commander of the Japanese Combined Fleet, Admiral Isoroku Yamamoto, of short-term naval dominance of the Central and South Pacific. During the early months of 1942 only token Australian forces stood in the way of Japanese occupation of New Guinea and ultimately, perhaps, even the conquest of the sparsely inhabited continent of Australia itself.

Yet the rapid and, in some cases, unexpected successes in all areas had negative overtones also. Imperial General Headquarters, enamored of the victories, did not assign clear priorities to its objectives. Instead, Japanese naval, army, and air forces were spread thin over the vast area of Southeast Asia and the Pacific. As a result, commanders in the field had insufficient forces in any one region to achieve the necessary intermediate objectives. This was certainly the situation facing the Japanese commanders in the southernmost part of the newly conquered Co-Prosperity Sphere. The lack of troops and materiel was one major factor in the failure of the Japanese to take Port Moresby and place themselves in a position to threaten northern Australia directly.

Those first months of the war proved to be a heady experience for the Japanese commanders; throughout much of 1942 they blithely advanced their plans for continued offensive operations, despite the fact that Allied strength was slowly recovering from the devastating blows delivered earlier. On 8 and 9 March a large Japanese task force stood off northern New Guinea and landed troops at Lae and Salamaua. Two days later the Japanese had secured Finschaven to the north. Within a few weeks radio stations and airfields had been established at both Lae and Salamaua.[3] Thus the Japanese before the end of March were firmly established on the north coast and were ready not only to expand their lodgments but to move southward over the Owen Stanley Mountains toward Port Moresby. The only definite resistance they met, a portent of the future, was the air strike delivered by ninety planes from the *Enterprise* and *Yorktown*. Flying over the seven-thousand-foot-high mountains, it caught the invading transports and their naval escorts by surprise on 10 March. This raid on Lae and Salamaua sank four transports and damaged thirteen others. The Japanese casualties were 130 killed and 145 wounded. It was the worst loss of ships and men to their southern forces since the war began.[4] Still, this daring U.S. air raid had little effect on the Japanese control of the Huon Peninsula and the entrance to the Bismarck Sea.

Earlier, on 23 January, an amphibious force of the Japanese 4th Fleet, supported by Admiral Nagumo's carrier striking force, had landed at Rabaul on New Britain. The small Australian garrison was overwhelmed, and soon the Japanese had extended their control over northern New Britain and neighboring New Ireland. Despite these successes, the offensive halted. The entire southern area was considered of secondary importance; the Japanese High Command was more concerned with operations in Malaya, Burma, and the Indian Ocean area, where Nagumo's carrier striking force was sent next. Also Admiral Yamamoto was planning to expand the Japanese main line of defense far to the east by occupying Midway Island. Thus, what many Japanese leaders later called the victory disease played an important role in stopping their heretofore relatively unimpeded southern offensives. The Japanese, so confident of ultimate victory and buoyed by their early successes, believed that they could continue those advances in all directions and in all theaters. One who disagreed was Admiral Shigeyoshi Inouye, commander of the 4th Fleet in charge of the offensives in the Central and South Pacific. From February on, he bombarded his superiors with requests for more ships and men in order to take Port Moresby, occupy the Solomon Islands, and thus directly threaten the long, tenuous American supply line to Australia and New Zealand. It was not until April that all was in place for a combined operation to seize crucial Port Moresby. Even then, the plan, called Operation MO, was not based on the overwhelming numerical superiority the Japanese could have brought to bear. Rather, they attempted the invasion with a much smaller task force than Inouye wanted.

The complex MO invasion plan was thwarted by the only Allied force readily available, the carrier task force of Vice Admiral Frank Jack Fletcher. The subsequent battle for the Coral Sea, fought on 7-8

May, cost the Americans two cruisers and the carrier *Lexington* from their depleted force in the South Pacific; in return they sank the small carrier *Shoho* and a few small craft at Tulagi. The action, fought completely by the air arms of both navies, was a tactical victory for the Japanese but undoubtedly a strategic victory for the United States. The eleven transports carrying the Japanese 3d Naval Landing Force and the army's South Seas Detachment, which were scheduled to take Port Moresby, were turned back.[5] For Australia, the Coral Sea engagement was one of the most significant of the entire war.

The Allies were forced to counter a further threat to the vital port on 22 July, when General Tomitaro Horii landed sixteen thousand men at Buna on the north coast. After consolidating his position there, he sent his troops south over the Kokoda Trail with the objective of capturing Port Moresby. Opposed by the Australian infantry of the 7th Division, which they outnumbered, the Japanese struggled through thick jungle, across nearly impassable streams, up over the Owen Stanley Mountains, of which some peaks rose higher than thirteen thousand feet. By mid-September 1942 they had reached the southern foothills just a few miles from Port Moresby. Here they were halted by the dogged determination of the Australians, together with exhaustion and sickness in the Japanese ranks and the demands made by the Guadalcanal operation. Meanwhile, Australian troops and American combat engineers stopped the second prong of the Japanese thrust, a landing at Milne Bay in eastern Papua.

The Japanese would never get any closer to Port Moresby. What was left of Horii's command retreated to Kokoda in September, pursued by reinforced Australian units now confident that they could beat the Japanese in any environment. Kokoda fell to them in October, and in November the American 32d Division was given the unenviable task of taking Buna, which finally fell on 2 January 1943 after some of the bloodiest fighting of the war to date. The last Japanese bastion in this vital area of the north coast, Sanananda, was captured on 22 January. The defense of eastern New Guinea had cost the Allied command eighty-five hundred casualties, including three thousand dead, but Port Moresby was secure, and the Allies had regained the offensive in New Guinea, never again to relinquish it.[6]

Shocked by the rate of Japanese conquests in all theaters during the first months of the war, the Allies confronted the enemy with a highly divided command structure. The short-lived ABDA (American, British, Dutch, Australian) command in the Dutch East Indies exemplified how disastrous such division could be. A similar set of problems handicapped the British, Americans, and Chinese who were attempting to halt the Japanese in Burma. Finally, in late March 1942 the Joint Chiefs of Staff reached an agreement on how to divide command responsibility in the Pacific theater. Accepting the reality of the areas where the war was being fought, they divided ultimate responsibility between General Douglas MacArthur in the Southwest Pacific area and Admiral Chester Nimitz in the vast Pacific Ocean areas extending from Alaska to New Zealand. Nimitz kept direct command over the most crucial portion, the Central Pacific, and allowed his subordinate commanders in the North and South Pacific considerable freedom in decision making.

The south had particular autonomy after October 1942, when Vice Admiral William F. Halsey assumed command from his predecessor at Noumea, Vice Admiral Robert Ghormley. The Southwest Pacific theater included Australia, New Guinea, the Solomon Islands, the Philippines, and all the Netherlands Indies except Sumatra. The eastern boundary of the Southwest Pacific area was arbitrarily established at longitude 159° east, but this division proved unworkable. Already, in late 1942, the Solomons presented a problem. The projected invasion of Guadalcanal should by definition have been under MacArthur's command, but logic dictated that it be directed from New Caledonia. The competing headquarters agreed to give the Commander, South Pacific Area, control of the Solomons operation, but he was to cooperate fully with MacArthur's headquarters in Brisbane.[7]

Since the major ground actions to contain the Japanese offensives were at first all in the Southwest Pacific, most of the men and material supplied to the Pacific in 1942 went to MacArthur. Troops dispatched to the South Pacific were mainly to defend the islands guarding Australia's line of communications with Hawaii and the west coast of the United States. Although MacArthur, with some justification, complained bitterly against the "Europe first" doctrine of the Joint Chiefs, the fact is that between January and March 1942 nearly eighty thousand troops were sent to the Southwest Pacific. Before the end of the year more than a quarter of a million men would be under MacArthur's command. By midyear, the 32d and 41st American divisions had arrived in Australia to beef up The Australian forces. The 37th Division was in Fiji, the Americal Division was posted to New Caledonia, and the 147th Regiment was in Tongatabu—all guarding the vital supply routes to Australia and New Zealand.

In addition there had been a slow, almost reluctant buildup of air power in Australia. When Lieutenant General George Kenney arrived to take command of the 5th Air Force, he found the organization a shambles and almost totally committed to a defensive role. This was not surprising since the Allied fighter planes, P-39s and P-40s, were distinctly inferior to their Japanese counterparts above fifteen thousand feet. In July, in the South Pacific, Admiral John McCain, commanding AirSoPac, had fewer than three hundred planes of all types scattered from Samoa to Espiritu Santo. The most important component of his force prior to the Guadalcanal landings were two marine squadrons, which had been provided by Admiral Nimitz to give air cover for that invasion.[8]

Although the Japanese still had the upper hand in the vast southern areas and could still determine where to launch an offensive, they had been halted in New Guinea and by the close of the year would stand on the defensive at Buna. The Allies in both Pacific areas were slowly building up the necessary force not only to blunt those offensives but to turn the tide of the war. The three keys to the Allied reversal of fortune were northern New Guinea, the Battle of Midway, and the contest for Guadalcanal.

Admiral Yamamoto's belated, complex plan for bringing the bulk of the United States Central Pacific fleet into one final confrontation was put into motion in late May. He had concluded correctly that Admiral Nimitz would not allow the Japanese to occupy Midway Island without a struggle. He was not aware, however, of the degree to which the Japanese naval code was understood by the Americans. The ability to decode Japanese messages, together with a gambler's intuition, enabled Admirals Raymond Spruance and Frank Jack Fletcher to ambush Yamamoto's leading elements—his carrier striking force, commanded by the Pearl Harbor admiral Nagumo. Many experts have considered the Midway engagement, begun on 3 June, to be the most crucial of the Pacific War. Like the Coral Sea battle, it was fought entirely by aircraft. The following day witnessed the practical end to Japan's attempt to dominate the vast reaches of the Central Pacific. Dive bombers from the *Enterprise* and *Yorktown* struck Nagumo's carriers with devastating force. Before the end of the next day, 4 June, all four Japanese carriers—the *Akagi, Kaga, Soryu,* and *Hiryu*—had been sunk. Almost all of Japan's most experienced pilots were also lost. The Americans sustained minimal damage to the facilities on Midway Island, and the *Yorktown* and one destroyer were sunk. Without air cover for the main elements of his battle fleet and transports, Yamamoto did not dare continue with the invasion plans and ordered a general withdrawal from the area on 6 June.[9]

The Midway defeat had ramifications far beyond a mere tactical victory. Although the Japanese fleet remained a powerful force for another two years, it would never again be so dominant. American shipyards were already busy on the construction of new fleet carriers and fast battleships, which by mid-1943 would give Admiral Nimitz his hoped-for big Blue Water Fleet. Indeed, his concentration on building up the Central Pacific naval forces helped put Admiral Halsey at a disadvantage against the Japanese later that year, during the Solomons battles. Still, Halsey did not generally have to contend with enemy aircraft carriers; most of the Japanese ships involved in South Pacific operations were cruisers and destroyers. Yamamoto and his successor, Admiral Mineichi Koga, like Nimitz, concentrated on the Central Pacific, where they expected a further decisive battle would be fought.

Japanese occupation of the Solomon Islands proceeded in an unhurried fashion during the spring of 1942 (Map 1). From the central base at Rabaul, General Hitoshi Imamura, in command of the 8th Area Army, and his naval counterpart, Vice Admiral Jinichi Kusaka, in charge of the Southeast Area Fleet, had their attention firmly fixed on Port Moresby. They were aware that no Allied force protected the many islands stretching southeast from New Ireland for over six hundred miles. Therefore, there was no reason to rush significant numbers of troops to any of these islands while the demands in New Guinea were still high. Nevertheless, key points on New Ireland were occupied in February, followed by landings adjacent to the Buka passage and on the east coast of Bougainville by the end of March. Then by the close of April a small force was sent to Tulagi in the southern Solomons, there to establish a seaplane base.

At first the Japanese paid little attention to the main southern island, Guadalcanal, located twenty miles from Tulagi across a stretch of open water that would later earn the name of "Iron Bottom Sound." Then in mid-June, Japanese lower-echelon officers made the fateful decision to build an airfield on Guadalcanal. Within a month more than two thousand workers were clearing the jungle there and doing preliminary work for the airstrip. The discovery of this construction frightened Admiral Ernest King, the American Chief of Naval Operations, since it threatened to checkmate the American military buildup eastward in the New Hebrides. Land-based bombers sited on Guadalcanal would directly threaten Allied convoys bound for New Zealand and Australia. The Joint Chiefs on 2 July hastily decided to mount the first American offensive of the war, a shoestring operation code named WATCHTOWER.[10]

The decision to capture Guadalcanal came as a shock to both General MacArthur and Admiral Ghormley in Noumea. MacArthur's forces were attempting to halt Horrii's advance on Port Moresby, and

Map 1. SOLOMON ISLANDS AND ADJACENT AREAS

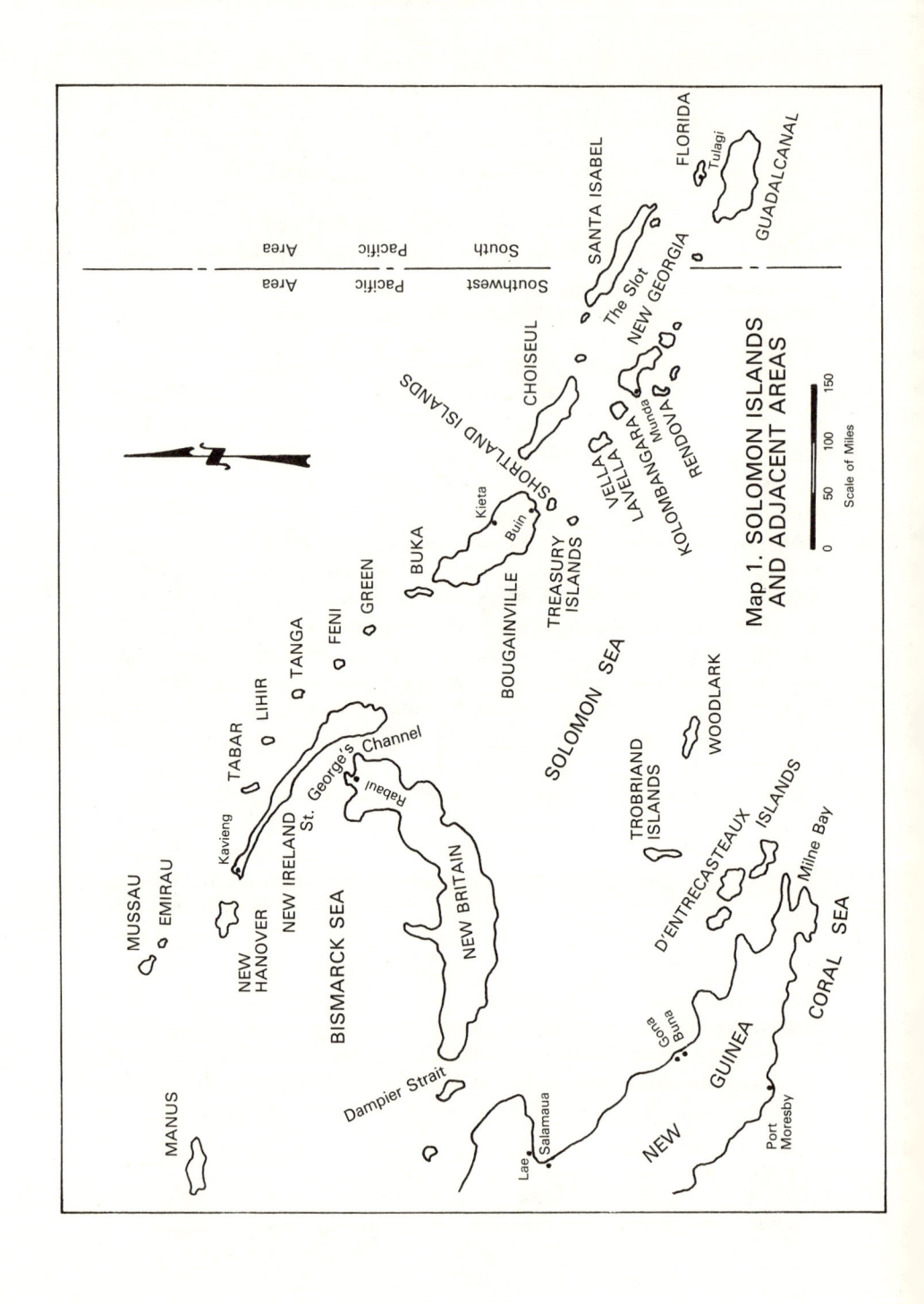

he certainly could not spare his green reserves to open a new front hundreds of miles away. The assault force Ghormley was ordered to use was the 1st Marine Division, only one of whose regiments, the 7th Marines, had arrived. The rest of the division was at sea on its way to New Zealand. Admiral King had promised the commander of the "Old Breed," Major General Alexander Vandegrift, that the unit would have time to prepare for its first combat, not projected until early in 1943. Instead, Washington issued orders to seize the airfield the Japanese were building on Guadalcanal now, shrugging off the objections of MacArthur and Ghormley, who were told to get on with the invasion. The only concession was to postpone D day until 7 August. Thus the overreaction of Admiral King and his staff began a chain of events that would culminate in the worst defeats suffered by the Japanese army and navy in the war up until that time. The battle for Guadalcanal was basically an encounter conflict; neither side had planned for a decisive meeting, but once engaged, neither would pull back.

The early stages of the battle for Guadalcanal were replete with bad planning and errors on both sides. The projected covering force for Vandegrift's marines contained three of the four carriers the United States had in the Pacific, in addition to a new battleship and a division of Australian cruisers. Admiral Fletcher, who had his misgivings about the entire operation, made it clear, however, that he would not risk his carriers to protect the amphibious force. The commander of that force, Rear Admiral Richmond Kelly Turner, argued that he would need four days to get all the marines and their equipment unloaded. The landings by the 5th Marines on Guadalcanal on 7 August were unopposed, but the Japanese on Tulagi put up a brief, stiff resistance. The airfield, named Henderson Field by the marines, was taken the next day, but true to his promise, Fletcher pulled his task force with its seventy eight planes back from protecting the beach and headed for Noumea. At that instant Japanese Admiral Gunichi Mikawa was proceeding toward Guadalcanal with five heavy cruisers and two light cruisers. This force was sighted but not reported soon enough, and Mikawa was able to slip into the Slot. There, he surprised the Allied cruiser screening force during the early morning hours of 9 August off Savo Island and delivered the Allies a stunning defeat. Before retiring, Mikawa's cruisers sank four Allied cruisers, the *Canberra, Astoria, Quincy,* and *Vincennes.* Admiral Turner continued to unload the much-needed supplies until noon that day before he too retired, leaving the untried marines on shore with a critical shortage of equipment.[11]

The Japanese, for their part, despite Mikawa's victory, were slow to press their advantage, believing that only a reconnaisance force was involved, perhaps with no more than two thousand men. Lieutenant General Harukichi Hyakutake, commanding the Japanese 17th Army at Rabaul, dispatched a thousand-man combat team, which landed east of the airfield on 18 August. This ill-conceived attack against the marine perimeter resulted in the near destruction of the Japanese unit, the first of many that would be fed into Guadalcanal over the next few months.

On 24 August the Japanese attempted to bring major reinforcements to Guadalcanal, committing three of their precious carriers to cover the landings. Admiral Fletcher's task force intercepted the flotilla, however, and in the naval engagement of the eastern Solomons on 24 August, sank the light carrier *Ryujo*. Marine dive bombers from Henderson Field sank the troop transport *Kinryu Maru*. Nevertheless, in the next two weeks the Japanese used destroyers, which the marines nicknamed the "Tokyo Express," to bring in almost six thousand men under the cover of night. The Japanese commanders were now taking the American invasion so seriously that they ordered General Horii's advance on Port Moresby stopped until the situation in the southern Solomons could be clarified, and they sent reinforcements scheduled for New Guinea to Guadalcanal instead.[12] Vandegrift's strategy, largely born of shortages of men and materiel, was to establish a defensible perimeter around the airfield and then hold it. He was aided in this objective by the impressive record of the marine aviators flying against the superior aircraft of the Japanese. Although the Japanese had far more planes at Rabaul than were available to the Americans, they never could establish command of the sky over the island.

Their attacks on the ground were no more successful. General Kiyotake Kawaguchi on the night of 13 September launched a series of banzai attacks against Colonel Merrit Edson's marines, who were holding "Bloody Ridge," only a thousand yards from the airstrip. By daybreak the marine lines were intact and Kawaguchi had lost more than half of his men.

Despite this defeat, the Japanese continued to funnel men into Guadalcanal, covered by main units of the combined fleet. On 9 October, General Hyakutake arrived on Guadalcanal to take personal charge of the destruction of the marines. Meanwhile, Vandegrift had finally received welcome reinforcements, the 7th Marines from Espiritu Santo. Perhaps even more important for ultimate success was the change of command, which replaced Ghormley with Halsey, who viewed Guadalcanal as crucial and promised to commit everything the navy had to holding the marine gains.[13] On 13 October the first army unit, the 164th Regiment of the Americal Division, landed. The scene was set for the crucial battle for Henderson Field.

General Hyakutake began his offensive from west of the field on 23 October with a frontal attack by a full regiment against well-dug-in marine positions along the Matanikau River. The Japanese frontal attack was destroyed by combined infantry and artillery fire. Then, near midnight, Hyakutake launched his main elements against a thinly held four-thousand-yard section of the perimeter defended by Lieutenant Colonel Lewis Puller's 1st Battalion of the 7th Marines and some of the newly arrived troops of the 164th. The battle raged all during the night, with Puller feeding army units into the line to reinforce his outnumbered marines. After the attack the Japanese left behind in this one sector alone more than a thousand dead. Hyakutake nevertheless continued the same type of attack the next night with the same disastrous results. It is estimated that these futile attacks cost the Japanese more than thirty-five hundred men killed.[14] Although the Japanese would continue to bring reinforcements to Guadalcanal and keep trying to break through the perimeter, this series of attacks on 23-24 October would be the high-water mark of the Japanese attempt to recapture Guadalcanal.

True to his promise, Halsey did not hesitate to commit his small naval force against the superior Japanese fleet. There would be no more disasters like the Savo Island encounter, but at best the six Guadalcanal naval battles were a tactical draw. At the Battle of Cape Esperance, fought during the night of 11 October, the cruiser squadron of Rear Admiral Norman Scott turned back one section of the "Tokyo Express," sinking one heavy cruiser and badly damaging another. The only American ship to sustain serious damage was the cruiser *Boise*. Then on 26 October, Admiral Nobutake Kondo, supporting Hyakutake's offensive with a major force including carriers and battleships, was intercepted by an American task force off Santa Cruz Island. Two of Kondo's carriers were badly mauled, but his planes sank the *Hornet* and damaged the *Enterprise*, forcing the Americans to withdraw. Threatened by land-based aircraft, Kondo broke off the engagement.[15] During early November the Japanese contented themselves with bringing their cruisers and battleships down the Slot and bombarding Henderson Field.

Japanese Combined Fleet Headquarters at Truk was planning a major effort to dislodge the Americans. The Japanese gathered an entire infantry division and three thousand naval landing troops, loaded them into eleven transports, and set out for Tassafaronga.

18 Bougainville

Escorting them was Vice Admiral Hiroaki Abe's force of two battleships, a light cruiser, and six destroyers. Turner, then in the process of unloading another regiment of the Americal Division, detached his covering cruisers and destroyers in hopes of halting Abe. This outgunned force of five cruisers and light destroyers under Rear Admiral Dan Callaghan's command fought a very confused action off Savo Island. Boring in at close range, the Americans suffered heavy damage from the big guns of the battleships. Three American destroyers were sunk and two others damaged almost immediately. The cruisers *San Francisco* and *Portland* were seriously damaged. But Abe inexplicably broke off the action leaving behind one sinking destroyer. His flagship, the battleship *Hiei*, was badly shot up and was caught early the next morning by planes from the *Enterprise* and sunk. On 14 November planes from Henderson Field sank yet another Japanese cruiser and damaged two others.[16]

Despite his previous losses, Admiral Kondo decided to bring down his last battleship, the *Kirishima*, and four cruisers in one final try to knock out Henderson Field before Rear Admiral Shimishi Tanaka's transports landed their assault troops. He was intercepted by Rear Admiral Willis Lee's squadron, which was organized around the new fast battleships, *South Dakota* and *Washington*. There ensued one of the few battleship conflicts of the war. After suffering a power failure, the *South Dakota* became an easy target for Kondo's capital ships and took over forty large-caliber hits, yet remained afloat. The *Washington*'s radar locked on to the *Kirishima* and within minutes the Japanese battleship was destroyed, whereupon Kondo broke off the engagement. Tanaka, now deprived of his main covering force, nevertheless pressed on with the transports to Tassafaronga. Four transports ran aground and were helpless against the strafing attacks of the marine planes from Henderson Field, aided by navy fighters from the *Enterprise*. This was a slaughter even worse than the fruitless banzai attacks; fewer than two thousand Japanese soldiers survived. Although fighting would continue on land and sea, this action was the major blow to Japan's attempts to wrest Guadalcanal from the Americans.[17]

By early December the once hard-pressed Americans now had over thirty-five thousand men on the island and more than two hundred planes. On 9 December, General Vandegrift turned over command on Guadalcanal to Major General Alexander Patch, commanding XIV Corps, comprising the Americal and the 2d Marine divisions, which had earlier relieved the battle-weary 1st Marine Division. His force was augmented toward the end of the month by the arrival of the

25th Infantry Division. Patch's troops cleared the high ground around Henderson Field and on 10 January launched a major offensive against the Japanese troops in the west. By then, however, the Japanese had finally decided to cut their losses and attempt to remove as many of their half-starved, sick troops as possible from the island. General Patch was fooled into believing that a new Japanese drive was being planned, and so he called off the 25th Infantry offensive in order to protect the airfield. In three nights between 1 February and 7 February 1943, the Japanese, using destroyers, managed to take off almost eleven thousand survivors of the six-month's-old action. They left behind the corpses of nearly twenty-one thousand men.[18] In the six naval battles the Japanese had fought in defense of the island, sixty-five Japanese combat ships had been sunk. Their naval air force had lost an estimated eight hundred planes and more than twenty-three hundred pilots and crewman. General Kawaguchi summed up these losses when he said that the Japanese army was not the only service "buried in the graveyard of Guadalcanal."[19]

The twin defeats of the Japanese at Guadalcanal and at Buna definitively marked the turnaround in the fortunes of the war only hinted at by the naval victory at Midway. Henceforth, the Japanese would be on the defensive everywhere, and the growing might of the United States would systematically penetrate the farflung defensive perimeter, while the Allied High Command would begin furiously to prepare offensives. Perhaps Admiral Tanaka was overstating the case when he wrote that "Japan's doom was sealed with the closing of the struggle for Guadalcanal."[20] However, from that date forward the history of the war for Japan was a litany of defeats. Guadalcanal became the major supply and training base for later South Pacific operations, and in early February marines and army units of the 43d Division captured the Russell Islands, moving an American logistical base forward. In March, during the Battle of the Bismarck Sea, the Japanese in a few hours suffered casualties equivalent to their losses in months of fighting in Guadalcanal. Eight transports escorted by eight destroyers left Rabaul with the objective of landing six thousand reinforcements of the 51st Division at Lae in New Guinea. This convoy was intercepted by planes of General Kenney's 5th Air Force on 2 March. By midday of the 3rd, the bombers had sunk or severely damaged every transport, sunk two destroyers, and damaged two others. Fewer than nine hundred Japanese were rescued and taken to Lae.[21]

Other Japanese efforts to strengthen their garrisons were not as disastrous. New Georgia and Bougainville, which until the Guadalcanal invasion had relatively small guard forces, now received a steady stream of men and equipment. Many of the survivors of Guadalcanal were relocated, particularly to Bougainville. Robbed of an air base in the southern Solomons by the Guadalcanal defeat, the Japanese in late November 1942 began constructing an airfield at Munda Point on New Georgia, and this thirty-two-hundred-foot strip was operational by mid-December. Soon naval defense units had also constructed bases on Kolombangara and Santa Isabel. Allied estimates of the ground strength of the Japanese in the central Solomons were far from accurate, but it was obvious that there were at least ten thousand men at Munda, Kolombangara, and Rekata Bay on Santa Isabel. Prior to the New Georgia invasion by the American 43d Division, significant reinforcements were sent to the key islands of the central chain. The Japanese 6th Division, participants in the rape of Nanking, were moved from Truk to Bougainville to provide the bulk of the garrison for this more strategically located island.

Its importance in the defense of Rabaul can be seen in the rapid construction of six major airfields, two adjacent to the Buka Passage in the north, one at Tenekau, one at Kieta near the east coast, and two in the Kahili area of the far south. In addition, another field was constructed at Ballale in the neighboring Shortland Islands.[22] The exact number of Japanese naval and army troops on Bougainville prior to the marine assault on Cape Torokina will never be known exactly. American estimates placed the number at anywhere between 35,000 and 45,000 men, but by Australian calculations there were 65,000 present in November 1943.[23] Whichever figure is tentatively accepted, the fact is that within a year of the marine landing on Guadalcanal the Japanese had prepared as best they could to defend the major bases still in their possession in the Solomons.

The key to all Japanese defenses in the southern Pacific was the bastion of Rabaul located on the Gazelle Peninsula of New Britain. As a naval base it was second in importance only to Truk. The Japanese, early realizing the potential of this location, had expended every effort on the construction of naval and air facilities. To the two Australian airfields built before the occupation, the Japanese added three more, making Rabaul the air hub for their activities in New Guinea and the Solomons. The five airfields, with their supporting service facilities, could handle more than four hundred aircraft and had living quarters for ten thousand men of the 11th Air Fleet.[24] Guarding the eastern approaches to Rabaul were four additional airfields, located on the 220-mile-long island of New Ireland. Simpson Harbor at Rabaul provided anchorage for more than twenty large-tonnage vessels and a host of smaller craft. The headquarters of the Southeast Area Fleet and the 8th Area Army were both at Rabaul. By the summer of 1943 the Allies were estimating 30,000 to 40,000 Japanese army and navy troops in northern New Britain, but the actual number, according to Japanese sources, was much higher: 55,000 army and 35,000 navy personnel on 30 June 1943.[25]

General MacArthur and his staff were fully aware of the vital importance of Rabaul from the beginning, and by mid-1942 they began to plan for the negation of this base. The demands of first the New Guinea campaign and later Guadalcanal stretched the thin Allied resources to the limit, however. Only after the Guadalcanal struggle appeared to be won and they could count on a continuing flow of men and materiel did Allied commanders seriously consider concrete steps to end the threat of Rabaul.

It is within this context that Bougainville ultimately became important. Until the decision was made to begin a meaningful, coordinated offensive in New Guinea and the Solomons, Bougainville and its airfields presented only minor annoyances to the Allied buildup in the southern Solomons. In the final planning Bougainville became the last objective in the expulsion of the Japanese from the Solomons. The possession of airfields on Bougainville would put Allied aircraft within 250 miles of Rabaul and would ultimately obviate the need for a massive invasion of eastern New Britain. Before the Bougainville operation could begin, however, a series of strategic plans would be drawn up for actions in the Solomons and then abandoned. Finally, the Allies decided they would have to reduce New Georgia and clear the Japanese presence from the central Solomons.

2. Allied Planning

The need to neutralize Rabaul was constantly in the minds of the planners in Australia, Hawaii, and Washington throughout 1942. Any actions in either command theater had to take into account the "Europe first" policy of the Joint Chiefs, which resulted in a relative shortage of men and materiel for the Pacific theaters. Even with this knowledge many commanders who should have known better assumed that with proper support the Allies could easily take Rabaul. In mid-1942 General MacArthur announced, perhaps only for effect, that all he would need to seize Rabaul was one full well-trained division.

The long-range plans of the Joint Chiefs enunciated in their directive of 2 July 1942 also reflected this optimistic viewpoint.[1] Soon, however, the desperate actions in New Guinea and Guadalcanal injected caution and even pessimism into the assessment of Rabaul. The changing nature of the war, combined with a new respect for the abilities of the Japanese and complicated by two different command areas, prompted many revisions of the plans for the ultimate conquest of Rabaul and produced an ambivalence that affected the planning for the invasion of the central Solomons and then Bougainville. Because the invasion of Bougainville was to be the last in a series of assaults on Japanese-held territory in the Solomons, any alteration in plans for the neutralization of Rabaul had a direct influence on how, when, and where the Bougainville assault would be mounted.

The directive of 2 July had envisioned a three-phase set of linked operations in the South and Southwest Pacific areas. The first of these was to be the seizure of Tulagi and Guadalcanal. "Task Two" projected the conquest of the other main Solomon Islands and Allied capture of

Lae and Salamaua and other key locations in northern New Guinea. "Task Three" projected the invasion of New Britain and the capture of Rabaul itself. This early strategic outline assigned the first phase to the South Pacific command and the other two to General MacArthur. The commanders of the two theaters and their staffs held meetings in Melbourne after receiving this directive and reached agreement on some of the broad outlines that would govern Allied activity for Tasks Two and Three. MacArthur and Halsey agreed to a general advance to seize naval and air bases in New Guinea, the Solomons, and ultimately New Britain.[2] These would enable the Allies to knock out Japanese bases on target islands and ultimately to bring the entire Bismarck Archipelago, particularly Rabaul, under continuous bomber and fighter attack. Little could be undertaken, however, until the successful conclusion of the struggle for Guadalcanal.

By early 1943 the Guadalcanal campaign was in its last stages, the Japanese were contained in New Guinea, and there had been a consistent buildup of men and materiel in both the Southwest and South Pacific theaters. It was therefore time to begin implementation of Task Two of the directive of the previous July. At this juncture the differences between Halsey's plans, which in general echoed King's and Nimitz's ideas, and those of MacArthur's headquarters came to the surface.

MacArthur's headquarters now had fairly accurate information on the numbers of Japanese troops, planes, and naval forces available in New Guinea and the Solomons. MacArthur wanted to make certain that sufficient troops and equipment were available before launching any of the offensive operations contemplated by the 2 July directive. Halsey, having just seized the Russell Islands, wanted to utilize the forces then available to him for controlled advances against specific targets. He was mainly concerned that Nimitz would remove much of the naval force from the South Pacific for use in the projected Central Pacific offensives. Halsey wanted to invade New Georgia and capture the vital airfield at Munda by midyear. Since that island was within General MacArthur's command area, however, any action in the central Solomons would need his approval.

This difference in approach was far from being an impasse, but it did suggest to the Joint Chiefs the necessity to clarify goals, command structure, and timetable in the Pacific theater. They were prodded in this direction by the more generalized agreements on strategy made at Casablanca by President Franklin D. Roosevelt and Prime Minister Winston Churchill. Therefore, in early March the Joint Chiefs convened the Pacific Military Conference in Washington, at which representatives of MacArthur's, Nimitz's, and Halsey's staffs met with the Joint Chiefs. The deliberations of this conference established goals and priorities in the Pacific war for the rest of the year.

General MacArthur's representative, Major General Richard Sutherland, his acerbic chief of staff, presented MacArthur's plan to the conference on 12 March. Code named ELKTON II, it called for the accomplishment of Tasks Two and Three in five stages: the seizure of air bases on the Huon Peninsula, capture of Munda, seizure of air bases on Bougainville and New Britain, capture of Kavieng, and finally the capture of Rabaul. To do all this, MacArthur, through the imperious Sutherland, asked for five additional divisions and a doubling of the size of his air force with an emphasis on heavy bombers. This request took the Joint Chiefs by surprise. With their eyes firmly fixed on Europe and the increasing demands for men and equipment in that theater, they could not imagine meeting MacArthur's request. Instead, they decided to modify the ambitious goals of the 2 July directive and concentrate on Task Two.

After receiving the input from Nimitz's and Halsey's delegates, the Joint Chiefs issued a new directive on 28 March. It called for MacArthur's forces to occupy Woodlark and Kiriwina islands and build airfields there. This occupation would bring Rabaul and the northern Solomons within range of Kenney's fighters and medium bombers and thus in part compensate for the scarcity of heavy bombers in the 5th Air Force. At an earlier meeting Sutherland had requested that any invasion of New Georgia be postponed until after the offensive in the Huon Peninsula succeeded. Halsey's representative, Lieutenant General Millard Harmon, vehemently opposed this suggestion, arguing that enough forces were available in the South Pacific to push on toward the Munda objective before the Huon Peninsula was secure. From New Georgia he proposed a very quick movement to Bougainville. Although timing of the various operations was not settled by their directive, later developments showed that the Joint Chiefs had not accepted MacArthur's argument about the need to postpone the New Georgia operations.[3]

In the background of these high-level discussions had been the question of command. The earlier division of MacArthur's and Nimitz's areas in the Pacific along longitude 159° east had already been modified for the Guadalcanal campaign. The question raised by the proposed Solomons operations went far beyond the adjustment of boundaries. Gernerals Marshall and MacArthur favored a unitary command for the entire Pacific area with MacArthur as supreme commander. This propoasl, put forth by Marshall, was vehemently rejected by Admiral King, who believed that the vast reaches of the Central Pacific logically called for a naval commander. Not only did he not want the army in total control of the Pacific operations, but he put forward Nimitz's name for the sole command even in MacArthur's bailiwick.

The 28 March directive sidestepped this crucial issue, not even readjusting the boundaries. Instead, the Joint Chiefs placed Admiral Halsey in direct command of the Solomons operations under the strategic direction of General MacArthur. Thus Halsey was required to answer, at least in theory, to two different commanders. This arrangement could have been very difficult had Nimitz not allowed Halsey wide latitude in command and had Halsey and MacArthur not found after their first meeting that they liked each other. Further, Halsey remained very circumspect, not challenging MacArthur's planning and advisory roles during the Solomons campaign.[4]

A revised ELKTON plan, the third from MacArthur's headquarters, was issued on 26 April after a conference between MacArthur and Halsey. ELKTON III simply modified the earlier plan to bring it in conformity with the 28 March directive from the Joint Chiefs. It was agreed that the occupation of Woodlark and Kiriwina would take place at the same time as the New Georgia operation. Halsey would also supply the occupation force and air squadrons for the Woodlark operation. It was understood that this phase of the two-pronged offensive, code named CARTWHEEL, would not involve significant forces.[5]

The landings on Woodlark and Kiriwina went off without problems between 30 June and 12 July. Neither was contested, and by the end of the month the engineers had completed an airstrip on each. An army fighter squadron was assigned to Woodlark, and an Australian squadron occupied Kiriwina. MacArthur also began his offensive against Salamaua on 28 June by sending an amphibious force to Nassau Bay to cooperate with Major General Stanley Savige's Australians operating in the interior. The various campaigns on New Guinea would continue throughout the year, and by December, MacArthur's forces were strong enough that he believed he could begin preliminary operations against New Britain using the 1st Marine Division to seize Cape Gloucester.[6] Meanwhile Admiral Halsey in his theater of operation was launching the first step toward the pincers movement aimed at Rabaul. This was the attack on New Georgia, whose main objective was the seizure of Munda airfield, appropriately code named TOENAILS.

The forces available to Halsey for the central Solomons campaign were considerable. Only warships of the New Zealand navy were ever permanently assigned to him, but Admiral Nimitz detached whatever warships he could spare from the Central Pacific, depending on his analysis of Halsey's requests for support. Moreover, the South Pacific Amphibious Force (Task Force 32), commanded by Admiral Turner, was permanently assigned to Halsey and requisite land forces could be added according to the needs of a particular operation. Task Force 33, at this time commanded by Vice Admiral Aubrey Fitch, comprised all land-based air forces, including General Nathan Twining's 13th Air Force and the two marine air wings as well as Australian and New Zealand squadrons. Rear Admiral Marc Mitscher, commander of Air Solomons, exercised tactical control under Fitch. By mid-1943 Halsey had available more than eighteen hundred aircraft of all types, though they were scattered throughout the vast area of his command. Directly available for the TOENAILS operation Fitch had 213 fighters, 170 light bombers, and 72 heavy bombers.[7]

Halsey's army commander for the remainder of the Solomons campaign was Air Force Lieutenant General Millard Harmon, who, in addition to the air units and base personnel, also controlled four army infantry divisions: the Americal, 25th, 37th, and 43d. Halsey's commander of marine ground elements was Major General Clayton Vogel, who had the 1st and 3d marine divisions, one raider regiment, six defense battalions, one paratroop regiment, and service troops.[8] Altogether, approximately 275,000 men were under Halsey's command at midyear.

The main objective in the New Georgia operation was the airfield at Munda. Protective reefs around the island limited the possible invasion routes, however, and Munda Point itself could not be approached by large vessels. Therefore Halsey's planners created a complicated scheme that called for the step-by-step occupation of protected anchorages at Segei Point, Wickham Anchorage, and Viru Harbor on the south coast. At the same time Rendova Island would be siezed to act as the staging ground for the attack on Munda itself (Map 2).

The unit selected for the New Georgia invasion was the reinforced 43d Division, commanded by Major General John Hester. The 37th Division was to act as the reserve, but few in command believed that it would be needed, though the 43d was a National Guard division, as yet untested in combat. Admiral Turner, in command of the landing operations, had decided that Hester should not only handle his division but retain overall command of the entire land operation as well. From the very beginning, this arrangement placed a heavy burden on Hester, for he had to maintain two separate staffs and attempt to coordinate movements while directing the main battle. Much of the difficulty caused by this double duty came later, however, when the army and marine units began the attack.

The first part of the plan worked without any problems. There was no Japanese ground resistance in the occupation of the harbors on New Georgia, although the Japanese mounted heavy air attacks against the task forces. Then on 30 June, the 172d Regiment landed on Rendova, and by 5 July most of the New Georgia occupation force was on either New Georgia or Rendova.[9]

Admiral Turner and General Hester had decided against landing the main assault force on Laiana Beach, located slightly over two miles from Munda, because their intelligence sources indicated that it was heavily defended. Instead, on 2 July they landed at Zanana Beach on the south coast, approximately three miles farther away, intending to approach Munda along a few trails cut through the hilly, jungle-covered terrain. The Japanese force of approximately five thousand men was concentrated near Munda, from which the commander, General Noburu Sasaki, could quickly move various units to wherever the main landing occurred. His men had built the major defense line on the hills east of Munda and had constructed a series of pillboxes and roadblocks between that line and the invasion beach. Thus when Hester's main force, the 169th and 172d Infantry regiments, had consolidated the positions at Zanana and begun the push toward Munda, they ran into unexpectedly heavy opposition. So well did the Japanese defend their key positions that an entire battalion of the 169th was held up for two days by a platoon of Japanese infantry dug in along the main trail. Men of the 43d Division, many of them in their first fire fight, shied away from aggressive action, imagining that the Japanese were all around them. They were stopped cold in front of Sasaki's main defenses and pinned down by artillery and mortar fire. Hester, worried about his dwindling supplies, shifted the 172d southward, where they captured Laiana Beach on 13 July.

At the same time that Hester's main force was slogging toward Munda, twenty-six hundred marines and soldiers of the Northern Landing Group, which had been landed near Rice Anchorage between 21 June and 1 July under Colonel Harry Liversedge of the marines were attempting to move south in order to block reinforcements from reaching Sasaki. Marine raiders, after a sharp fight with the defenders, secured Enogai Point by 11 July, five days behind schedule. Units of 3/148 established a roadblock on the main trail between Kula Gulf and Munda. The Japanese, however, continued to bring in reinforcements through Bairoko Harbor and shift them southward.

Rear Admiral Walden Ainsworth, commanding the covering force

Map 2. NEW GEORGIA CAMPAIGN
30 June–4 August 1943

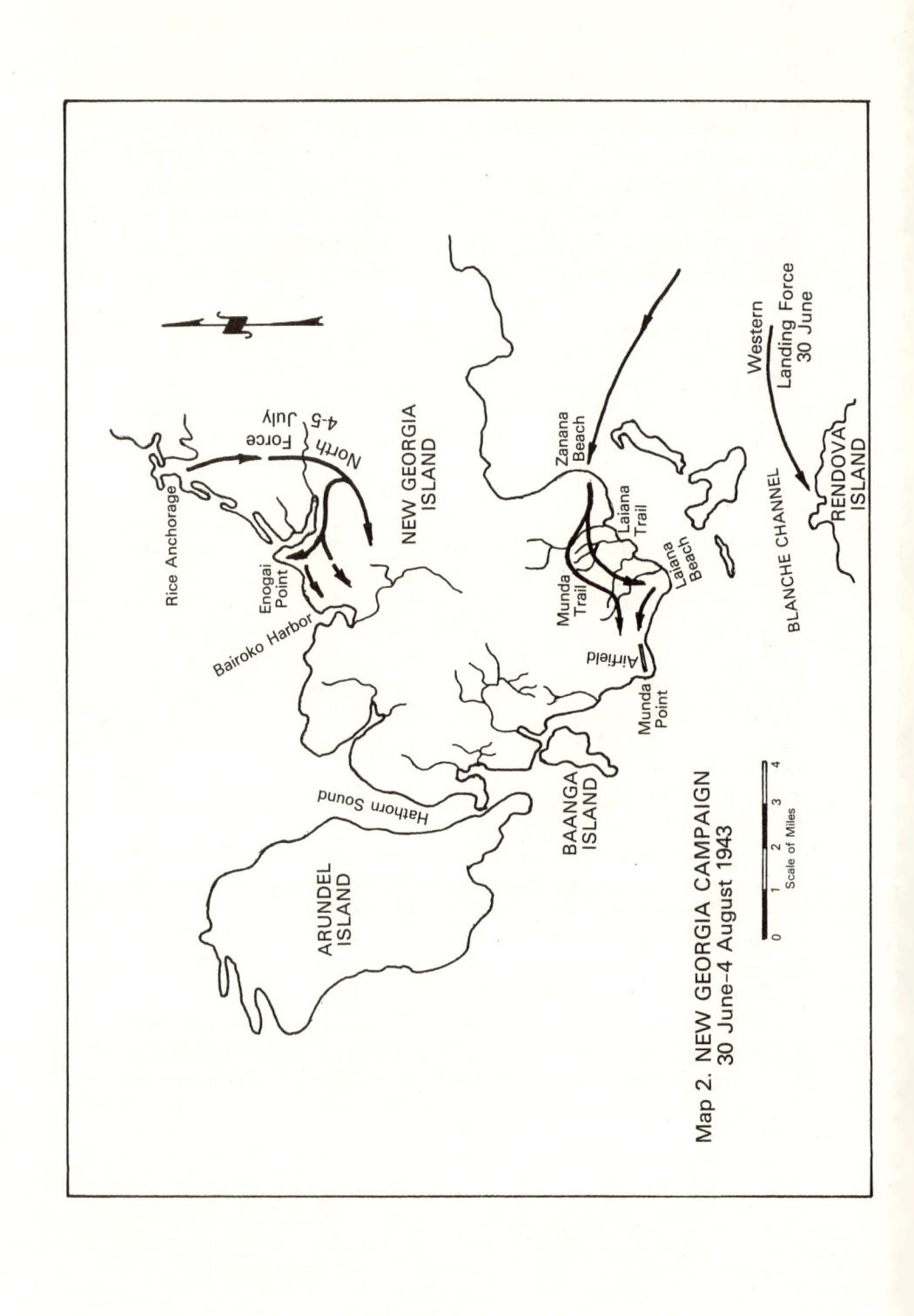

of cruisers and destroyers, fought three engagements off the west coast of New Georgia with the Japanese, who were bringing men to reinforce Munda. In the first of these, Ainsworth's ships, after supporting the landings of Liversedge's men at Rice Anchorage, encountered a Japanese squadron and lost a destroyer to the Japanese long-lance torpedoes. On 6 July, Ainsworth's ships once again confronted the deadly Japanese torpedo in Kula Gulf, where he lost the light cruiser *Helena*. Worse, Ainsworth failed to prevent the landing of sixteen hundred Japanese troops. In a further contest, the Battle of Kolombangara, the Japanese lost the destroyer *Jintsu*, but their torpedoes once again did terrible damage, sinking the destroyer *Givin* and seriously damaging the cruisers *Honolulu* and *St. Louis*.[10] Thus, although the American naval units here were superior in numbers and fire power, they were not successful in keeping the new version of the Tokyo Express from delivering troops and supplies to Munda.

The slowness of the advance brought Major General Oscar Griswold, commander of XIV Corps and Hester's immediate superior, to New Georgia on 11 July. He found the situation far from satisfactory. He was particularly critical of the dual role assigned to Hester and was disheartened by the condition of the 43d Division: the men were exhausted, morale was low, and psychoneurotic stress symptoms were common. In his report Griswold made it clear that fresh reinforcements were absolutely necessary if the 43d Division was not to fold up.

Halsey acted immediately. He put General Harmon in charge of the operation with orders to do whatever was necessary to take Munda. Harmon dismantled Hester's dual command role: he ordered Griswold to take over the operation and left Hester in command of only the 43d Division. General Robert Beightler, commander of the 37th Division, which already had some units on Rendova and New Georgia, was ordered to move two full regiments, the 145th and 148th, to the island. Major General J. Lawton Collins, commanding the 25th Division on Guadalcanal, was also ordered to provide one regiment, the 161st, to aid the Munda offensive.[11]

After the arrival of the needed reinforcements, Griswold moved the 37th Division in line north of the 43d and planned for a two-division frontal assault on the strong Japanese defenses. He hoped that the units of the 37th would be able to envelop Sasaki's line and surround Munda. The attack began on 25 July in the 43d's zone. Soon after a heavy air, artillery, and naval bombardment, the 37th attacked the heavily fortified ridges. The Americans made few gains during the first days, but by the end of July the Japanese began to weaken.

Continuous air and artillery bombardment had knocked out many of the fixed defenses, and some Japanese infantry units had suffered over 75 percent casualties. Eighth Fleet headquarters then ordered Sasaki to withdraw his forces to a narrow perimeter around Munda Point and give up the airfield. He reluctantly obeyed, and by 5 August, Griswold's forces had captured the prize. He radioed Halsey, "Our ground forces today wrested Munda from the Japs and present it to you . . . as the sole owner." To which Halsey replied with "a custody receipt for Munda. . . . Keep 'em dying."[12]

The 27th Infantry of the 25th Division along with the 161st Regiment was given the major task of driving northward to cut off Sasaki's escape route. Lack of trails and the continuing rains that turned the few existing ones into morasses slowed these movements. By 9 August 1/27 had made contact with Liversedge's men, but it was not until 25 August that army troops were in possession of Bairoko Harbor. Throughout that time the Japanese were busy evacuating troops by barge at night. General Sasaki had decided soon after he lost Munda that he could hold out no longer, and he began to withdraw most of his troops to Kolombangara (Map 1) and a few to Baanga, a long narrow island across the Diamond Narrows, from which some of his big guns intermittently bombarded Munda. This nuisance was ended when units of the 169th and 172d Infantry captured Baanga on 21 August after a hard fight. The long, costly struggle for New Georgia was finally finished with the occupation of Arundel Island in September. It had cost the American forces 1,094 dead and 3,873 wounded, almost half the casualties from the 43d Division. Sickness and combat fatigue had multiplied these losses, particularly in the 43d division. Exact Japanese losses are unknown. Corps headquarters reported counting 2,483 dead, but the final casualty count was obviously much higher.[13]

Having managed a masterly evacuation to Baanga and Kolombangara, General Sasaki had expected reinforcements that, with his twelve thousand troops, would enable him to take the offensive and reinvade New Georgia. All his plans came to nothing on the night of 6 August when Commander Frederick Moosbrugger with six destroyers surprised a reinforcing convoy of four destroyers, three of which were packed with troops. Very quickly the American ships launched twenty-four torpedoes and sank the three Japanese troop-carrying destoyers. In addition this Battle of Vella Gulf cost the Japanese more than nine hundred soldiers and persuaded higher commanders at Rabaul to cut their losses and abandon all plans for further offensive action on New Georgia. Sasaki had been ordered to evacuate Baanga and move all trops to Kolombangara to await the expected American assault directed at securing Vila airfield on this well-fortified island.

Admiral Halsey had earlier decided to bypass Kolombangara and had managed to persuade MacArthur to modify the original TOENAILS plan to avoid another slugging match like Munda. So on 15 August, Rear Admiral Theodore Wilkinson, who had replaced Turner in command of Task Force 32, began landing six thousand troops, mostly from the 25th Division, on the southern tip Vella Lavella. There was no regular garrison there, only an estimated 250 stragglers, who were soon overcome. Halsey then had possession of a forward base less than a hundred miles from southern Bougainville and the Shortland Islands.[14]

This bypassing operation rendered the Japanese position on Kolombangara untenable, and Imperial Headquarters ordered the island evacuated. Under cover of air units from Rabaul and protected in part by submarines and destroyers, Sasaki's men were taken off the island in three nights on thirty-eight large landing craft and eighty army barges (*daihatsus*). The Japanese lost twenty-nine of the landing craft and one destroyer to American action, but almost all of Sasaki's troops were safely transported to southern Bougainville. When the advance elements of the 27th Infantry landed on Kolombangara on 6 October, they found only some abandoned Japanese equipment and a few stragglers.

The important Vila airstrip was now under Allied control, another forward base for future action directed at Rabaul. Altogether General Twining, who had assumed command of AIRSOLS, now had four excellent functioning airfields in the central Solomons.[15] With the capture of Kolombangara the fight for the central Solomons was finished and the way to Bougainville and beyond had been brought within range of Allied land-based aircraft.

The ELKTON III and CARTWHEEL plans had all indicated that at some date after the capture of New Georgia Bougainville would be invaded. No specific time or strategy had been decided. Both MacArthur's and Halsey's headquarters recognized the necessity of an invasion. Japanese air power, which operated from six air bases on the island, had to be neutralized. Moreover, the capture of these airfields would provide the Allies with bases closer to the ultimate target, Rabaul. In March, MacArthur warned Halsey to be prepared to invade Bougainville in the very near future. So in July, while the New Georgia campaign was just getting under way, Halsey and his staff began to deal with the practical problems of a Bougainville invasion.

Map 3. BOUGAINVILLE ISLAND

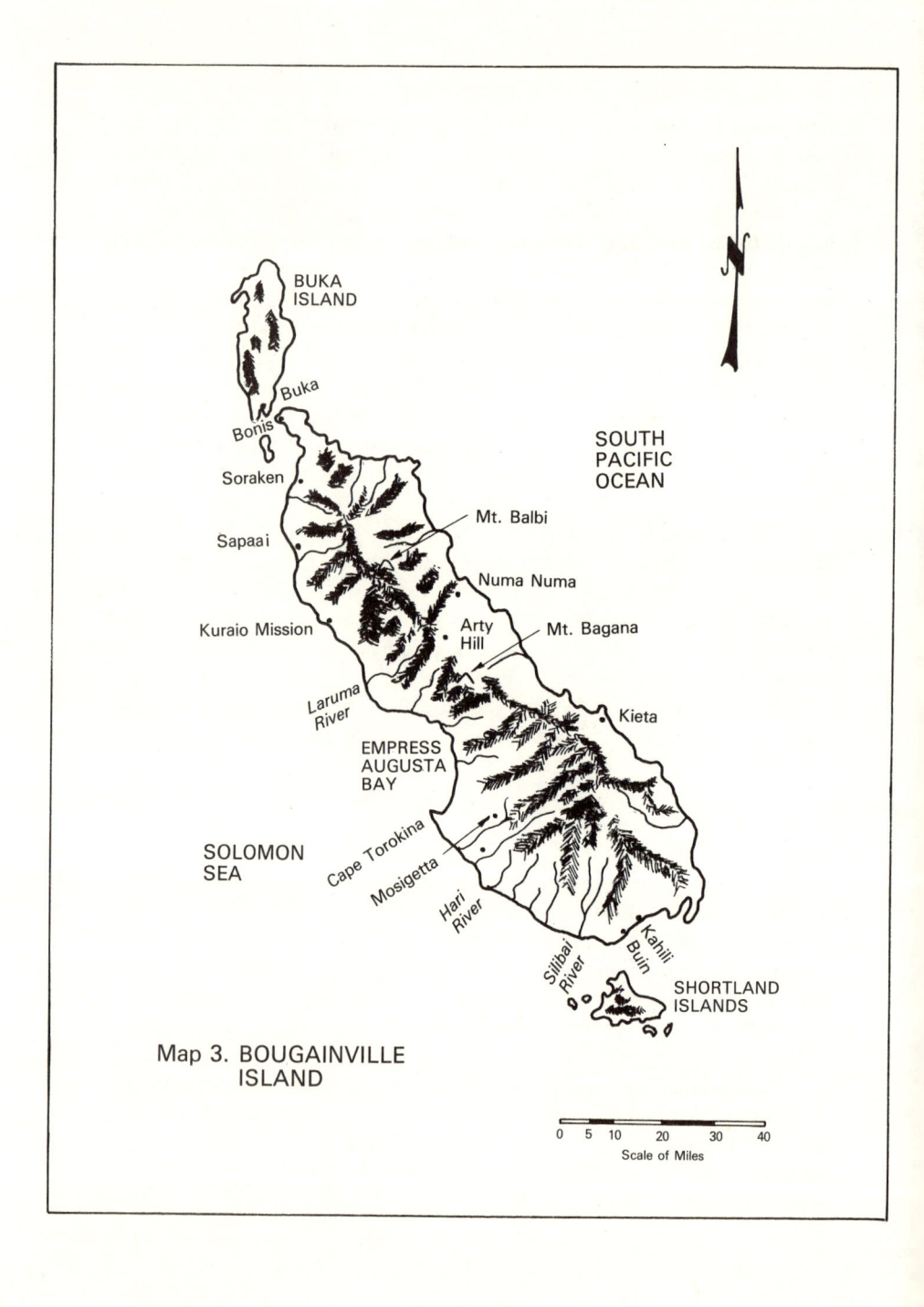

The obvious target was the Buin-Kahili area of southern Bougainville (Map 3). Here were the two largest airfields and Tonolei Harbor, which provided an excellent anchorage for Japanese ships. With this in mind Halsey alerted General Vandegrift commanding the I Marine Amphibious corps to prepare detailed plans for the seizure of Buin, Kahili, Tonolei Harbor, and Faisi and Ballale islands in the neighboring Shortlands.[16]

The 43d and 37th Divisions were involved in the New Georgia campaign at this time. Of the five divisions remaining to him, Halsey planned to use the fresh and as yet untried 3d Marine Division and the army's 25th Division for the invasion, keeping the 2d Marine Division and the 3d New Zealand Division in training for the conquest of Rabaul. Factors beyond his control radically changed this initial plan, however. Because of the intense Japanese resistance on New Georgia, the 25th Division had to be committed. Casualties there, both combat and medical, added to those the division had suffered on Guadalcanal, mandated rest and reorganization. Then the decision to strike at the Japanese at Makin and Tarawa in the Gilbert Islands removed the 2d Marine Division from the South Pacific. These changes ultimately dictated the substitution of the 37th Division, which, although it had suffered more than eleven hundred battle casualties on New Georgia, was nevertheless in better condition than the 25th. The initial plan to use the 3d Marine Division as the spearhead remained unchanged.

By the end of July, Halsey's staff had been reconsidering other aspects of the tentative invasion plans. Intelligence reports indicated that half of an estimated thirty-five thousand Japanese on Bougainville were located in the south.[17] Thus any invasion there would obviously encounter very strong resistance. By then the New Georgia campaign had bogged down, and Halsey was not eager to plan for a similar slugging match. He had been impressed by the success of artillery fire from offshore islands against Munda and so proposed seizing the Shortlands and Ballale. He could then place heavy artillery on the Shortlands to negate Kahili airfield. He could also construct airfields on these islands and use the harbors as anchorages for his fleet. MacArthur's headquarters found nothing to object to in this change of plans.

Once again, however, events dictated a different scenario. Halsey had come to believe that the Japanese were reinforcing the Shortlands, and further intelligence work had indicated that the landing beaches were unsuitable for unloading heavy equipment. Nor were there good sites for airfields. In addition, estimates placed the requirements for a Shortlands operation at two divisions, more than Halsey could afford to commit if he planned to invade Bougainville later on. Instead, noting the ease with which Vella Lavella had been taken, Halsey proposed a similar bypassing maneuver. Within two months, he said in September, he could capture the Treasury Islands and Choiseul Island, each only lightly held by the Japanese. He would use these islands as air-base sites in conjunction with increased bombing of southern Bougainville from the recently captured fields in the central Solomons. Thus he would strangle the Japanese on the main island. On 10 September his representatives, Rear Admiral Robert Carney and Colonel William Riley, U.S. Marine Corps, presented this plan to MacArthur's staff.

They were surprised by MacArthur's opposition to it. He was planning an invasion of the Cape Gloucester area of New Britain, to begin by 1 January 1944, and wanted all available aircraft to strike at Rabaul in order to neutralize Japanese air power before the invasion. Halsey's plan would not put maximum South Pacific air support over Rabaul until much later. MacArthur's staff proposed continuing heavy air strikes against all Japanese airfields on Bougainville throughout the month of October. Then sometime after 20 October, Halsey's forces would occupy the Treasuries and possibly northern Choiseul to provide radar coverage and P.T. boat bases. On 1 November, Halsey's attack forces could land at Empress Augusta Bay on the west coast, seize a beachhead, later expand it, and then construct airfields that would bring AIRSOLS planes within striking distance of Rabaul in time to help take pressure off MacArthur's troops advancing in New Guinea and New Britain. This suggestion of a Bougainville landing location was only tentative; MacArthur later left it to Halsey to decide whether to land on the east or west coast of Bougainville.[18]

This main target island, 125 miles long and 30 miles wide, is the largest of all the Solomon Islands. Eastern and western coastal plains of varying width are separated by two extensive mountain ranges that run almost the entire length of the island. The highest of these, the Emperor Range in the northern part of the island, is anchored by the 10,171-foot Mount Balbi, and just inland from Empress Augusta Bay is Mount Bagana, a still-active volcano. The southern Crown Prince Range is lower and less rugged. The southwestern part of the island, a broad plain with many rivers, has the best harbors, and before the war most of the plantations were located there. To the east the mountain ranges slope down to moderately broad plains, which widen to over ten miles near the village of Numa Numa. Many of the beaches on the east would provide good, flat landing sites, in contrast to the western side, where only a few anchorages and beaches could accommodate a large landing force. Western Bougainville is characterized by many mountain streams, which carry much silt downstream. The silt gradually blocks the flow of water, creating wide swampy areas adjacent to the coast, which extend inland over a mile in places. These swamps are covered by thick growth of marsh grass, bamboo, and other plants that thrive in that kind of environment. This geography was one major reason that the Japanese discounted the possibility of invasion from the west and concentrated their troop strength in the south.

The interior of Bougainville is covered by dense rain forest and matted jungle growth, which, combined with the mountainous terrain, made east-west movement very difficult. The bulk of the estimated forty thousand islanders lived in small villages on the eastern plains or in the extreme northern and southern parts of the island. Few villages were located in the inhospitable interior. Most of the trails traversed the southern part of the island, but the Numa Numa Trail spanned the center, connecting Empress Augusta Bay to Numa Numa village on the east coast. One of the southern trails would prove especially useful to the Allied invaders. The East-West Trail, which joined the villages of Mawareka and Mosigetta to Buin in the south, skirted much of the swampy area and was usable most of the year. It would be the main artery for the Japanese as well when they attempted to reinforce their small garrisons near Empress Augusta Bay.[19]

The Japanese established themselves in the north adjacent to the Buka Passage, in the east around Kieta, and in the south at Buin early in March 1942. As in most of their newly conquered empire, they did very little to improve the defenses of Bougainville until the fortunes of war began to turn against them. For the first year of their occupation they concentrated mainly on constructing airfields at either end of the island. They paid little attention to the interior, supplying coastal garrisons by barge. Since there was little overland travel, the few roads and trails were never improved. The native population throughout much of the island had little to do with the Japanese until well into 1943. Most of those in the southern and northern areas in direct contact with the occupiers accommodated themselves to their conquerors and worked on the various building projects needed by the Japanese army and naval units.

Many of the natives cooperated fully with the few Australian coast watchers who were active on Bougainville. These men did valuable service for the Allies, particularly during the early stages of the Guadalcanal campaign. Unfortunately, when the Japanese began seriously to build up all their defenses in the Solomons during the spring of 1943, it became too dangerous for the coast watchers to continue to operate along the coasts. At first they abandoned their radio equipment and withdrew into the interior. Those who survived were later taken off the island by submarine. Thus they were silenced during the critical planning stages for the Bougainville invasion, when their services on the island would have been most helpful. They and a few missionaries and planters did give Halsey and his staff some vital information, but in the main the planners had little knowledge of most of the interior areas of the island.

The maps available to corps planners in October 1943 were a four-sheet photomap of the Solomons and Bougainville, five maps at 1:20,000 scale, and air force charts with a scale of 1:250,000 and 1:600,000.[20] The inadequacy of these maps would become very clear as soon as marine and army units began to move out of the initial lodgment. As early as D + 1 they would discover that much of the detail on even the best maps was incorrect.

More information had been obtained from two separate patrols landed by submarine in September. One marine-navy patrol using native guides scouted possible landing sites in the Kieta area along the east coast. Another patrol landed near the Laruma River on the west coast. They carefully scouted that region, took pictures of the Cape Torokina area, and checked the beach and conditions in the immediate interior. They discovered a narrow beach strip extending approximately five miles along the bay and immediately bordered by swamps. The tides in the bay were found to be moderate, only about three and one-half feet. Soil samples taken from the interior indicated that it would support an airstrip, at least in the vicinity of Cape Torokina. In their four-day reconnaissance they saw only one Japanese soldier.[21]

Admiral Halsey, who did not want a repitition of the Munda campaign, was in early September already inclined toward the Empress Augusta Bay site. He was obviously influenced by intelligence reports that the Torokina area was held by no more than a thousand Japanese. The jungle-covered hills and mountains surrounding the swampy plain would make movement of Japanese reinforcements from southern Bougainville very difficult. The probability of heavy air attacks from Rabaul, even if the Bougainville airfields were neutralized, would be the same as for any other invasion site. Halsey hoped this location would encourage the Japanese to commit more of their capital ships to halt the invasion. Thus the reports of the two reconnaissance patrols only confirmed the decision issued to his subordinate commanders on 22 September to land the 3d Marine Division at Empress Augusta Bay.

Five days later General Charles Barrett, who had replaced Vandegrift in command of the operation, alerted the 3d Marine Division that its mission was "to land in the vicinity of Cape Torokina, seize and occupy and defend a beachhead including Torata Island and adjacent island—3750 yards west of Cape Torokina—allowing approximately 2250 yards inland from the beach and 3600 yards east of Cape Torokina. To prepare and continue the attack in coordination with the 37th Infantry on its arrival."[22] The following day a letter of instruction was sent to the New Zealand 8th Brigade Group outlining its mission to seize and hold the Treasury Islands and to establish long-range radar stations and landing-craft staging there.[23]

Admiral Halsey issued his operations plan on 12 October. He organized five task forces that would be involved either directly or indirectly in the landings. The attack force, Task Force 31, commanded by Admiral Wilkinson, included the transports, covering ships, and the assault unit, the 3d Marine Division, commanded by Major General Allen Turnage and the 1st Brigade of the 3d New Zealand Division, which would invade the Treasury Islands. This phase of the offensive would be handled by the southern section of TF 31, commanded by Rear Admiral George Fort. Wilkinson retained control of the northern part of TF 31, which would be responsible for the Torokina landings. Other troops available were the 3d Marine Defense Battalion, the 198th Coast Artillery, the 2d Provisional Marine Raider Regiment, and the 1st Marine Parachute Regiment. In reserve was the Americal Division, located in Fiji, and other heavy artillery units on Espiritu Santo. Major General Ralph Mitchell, commanding Task Force 33 (AIRSOLS), had almost five hundred land-based fighters, dive bombers, and torpedo bombers in the Russell Islands and New Georgia. Available also for air cover were the planes of Task Force 38, under Rear Admiral Frederick C. Sherman, which was built around the carrier *Saratoga*, later joined by the *Princeton*. Task Force 39, commanded by Rear Admiral Aaron Merrill, comprised Cruiser Division 12 and Destroyer Division 23. Submarines in the area were organized under Task Force 72.[24] D day for the Empress Augusta Bay action, code named CHERRYBLOSSOM, was set for 1 November and the invasion of the Treasury Islands at D - 5.

Meanwhile, Halsey was faced with the necessity to find another commander for the operation. On 8 October Major General Barrett had fallen, struck his head, and suffered a cerebral hemorrhage; he died soon afterward. Lieutenant General Alexander Vandegrift, the previous commander of the I Marine Amphibious Corps, had been appointed commandant of the Marine Corps and was on his way to Washington to assume this position. Halsey's appeal to Vandegrift reached him at Pearl Harbor, and he agreed to reassume command of the Amphibious Corps until the beachhead was secured. At that time Major General Roy Geiger, who was then in Washington as director of Marine Corps aviation, would take over the land operations.[25]

A final change in the overall plan was made when Halsey's staff decided not to attempt to seize northern Choiseul but instead to send a marine raiding party there in hopes of persuading the Japanese to divert troops to Choiseul from southern Bougainville. The other secondary action, the seizure of the Treasury Islands by the New Zealanders, was retained. The southern section of TF 31 loaded supplies and the New Zealand brigade at Guadalcanal, Rendova, and Vella Lavella and departed for its destination on 26 October. The final phase of the long, bloody struggle for control of the Solomons, the seizure of a perimeter on Bougainville, was about to begin. Before it was concluded the campaign ultimately would involve one marine and two army divisions and a reinforced Australian division, and fighting on the island would continue until the Japanese surrendered in August 1945.

3. The Treasuries and Choiseul

Admiral Halsey's final decision, relayed to General MacArthur on 1 October, making Empress Augusta Bay the prime target on Bougainville confirmed the importance of the Treasury Islands. As early as mid-September these two small islands, Mono and Stirling, lying only seventy-five miles southeast of Cape Torokina, had been targeted for occupation by COMSOPAC. The rationale for their seizure was to provide a staging area and an advance naval base at Blanche Harbor in addition to establishing a radar station on the north coast of Mono Island. Allied possession of these small islands would ultimately aid in the supply of the combat troops on Bougainville. Part of the flat scrubland of Stirling Island afforded a promising site for a small airstrip. The timing for the Treasuries operation, set for D Day − 5, was also designed to confuse the Japanese as to the location of the major effort in the northern Solomons and to keep them from shifting any significant number of troops away from the Buin area of southern Bougainville.[1]

Mono, the larger of the two main Treasury Islands, is nevertheless quite small, measuring approximately four miles north to south and slightly over six miles east to west. It is heavily forested, and highlands dominate the southern portion. These hill masses, many of which were more than a thousand feet high, gradually give way to a plateau in the center and north of the island. Reconaissance patrols had determined that the only beaches where LSTs could land were in the south, to the east of the Savake River and Falami Point. Stirling Island, lying slightly over a mile south of Mono, is only about four miles long and varies from a quarter of a mile to a mile in width. It is covered with scrub forest and tall grass. Aside from a few very small lakes inland, it has no significant features that would aid in its defense or seriously impede the advance of an attacking force. Between the two islands is a very good deep-water anchorage called Blanche Harbor. Among the many tiny islands in the harbor is Watson Island, a few yards offshore from Falamai Point. It would prove valuable as a site for mortars that would be used to pound the interior of Mono.[2]

The unit designated for the assault on the Treasuries, code named GOODTIME, was the 8th Brigade (reinforced) of the New Zealand 3d Division. The first elements of this division had been formed in late 1940 and soon afterward were sent to Fiji, where they had remained with the bulk of the troops on Suva Island until the Allied victories removed the possible threat of a Japanese attack on vital New Caledonia, New Hebrides, and Fiji islands. No longer needed in Fiji, the two brigades of the division were transported to Guadalcanal. The 14th landed on 29 August 1943, and the 8th arrived two weeks later. They were assigned campsites on the north side of the island near Mantanikan River and were attached to I Marine Amphibious Corps. On 28 September, Brigadier General R.A. Row, commanding the 8th Brigade, learned that his command, supplemented by support troops from marine units, had been chosen to seize the Treasuries. He and the landing force commander, Rear Admiral George Fort, immediately began to plan for the attack.

Allied knowledge of the numbers of Japanese and their disposition in the Treasuries was unusually good, compared to that for other operations in the Pacific. In August a patrol had spent six days on the islands, and friendly natives had helped them spot most of the possible strongpoints and survey the best landing beaches. Some further information had been received from air crewmen who had been forced down and later rescued from Mono after raids against Buin. All this information was supplemented by aerial photographs. It was estimated that 150 Japanese occupied the large island, but none were on Stirling.

General Row's plans called for a full-scale invasion by as many troops of the 8th Brigade as could be accommodated in the limited shipping available. Ultimately thirty-one ships were involved in transporting the New Zealanders and their supplies, including eight APDs, eight LCIs, two LSTs, eight LCMs, three LCTs, and two APCs. In addition, Admiral Fort from his flagship the USS *Raton* controlled the destroyers *Pringle* and *Philip*, which would provide preliminary bombardment and heavier-caliber support once the troops were ashore.

General Row had available for the operation more than 7,500 men, of which 3,795, belonging to three battalions—the 29th, 34th, and 36th—would be used in the assault. Also available were approximately 1,900 support troops from the I Marine Amphibious Corps.[3]

At a time when assault forces were in such short supply throughout the Pacific and the Bougainville invasion was only days away, it is difficult to understand why an entire brigade was to be used to subdue a tiny enemy garrison on one small island. One possible explanation is that Halsey and Vandegrift were reluctant to use untried New Zealand troops in a more ambitious undertaking but were under pressure to allay the criticism then current in Australasia that American commanders did not want to use British Empire troops. For whatever reason the Treasury operation was one of the few examples of Allied overkill during this midstage of the Pacific War.

Despite the probability of little Japanese resistance, the New Zealanders prepared as if they were to make a full-scale landing under intense fire. In addition to ongoing company-level training on Guadalcanal, there were landing exercises. On 14 October the troops were taken across Sealande Channel, where they clambered down into assault boats for landings on beaches on the east coast of Florida Island. Returning to Guadalcanal, the commanders discovered that because of shortages of landing craft only six hundred men per company could go in the first wave. The companies were reduced in strength accordingly, and the overage from the assault companies was distributed in subsequent waves.

The plan issued to subordinate units on 21 October called for the 34th Battalion to land on beaches code named Purple, on the north side of Stirling, while the 29th and 36th battalions would land abreast near Falami Point on southern Mono. It had been belatedly discovered that for radar to be effective the installation would have to be sited on the north coast of Mono, directly across the island from the site of the landings. Therefore Company D of the 34th, accompanied by twenty seabees with heavy equipment and sixty American technicians, was to be landed at the mouth of the Soanotalu River (Map 4). The Soanotalu landing group was called Logan Force, named for its commander, Major G.W. Logan.[4] The major landings in the south would be covered by direct fire from two destroyers and from the new LCI gunboats. Although Japanese air strength in the northern Solomons was waning, the Allies felt it necessary to provide air cover by planes from Vella Lavella. These would also fire on any targets of opportunity on the two islands.

Despite heavy rain, the landings went as planned. Just prior to

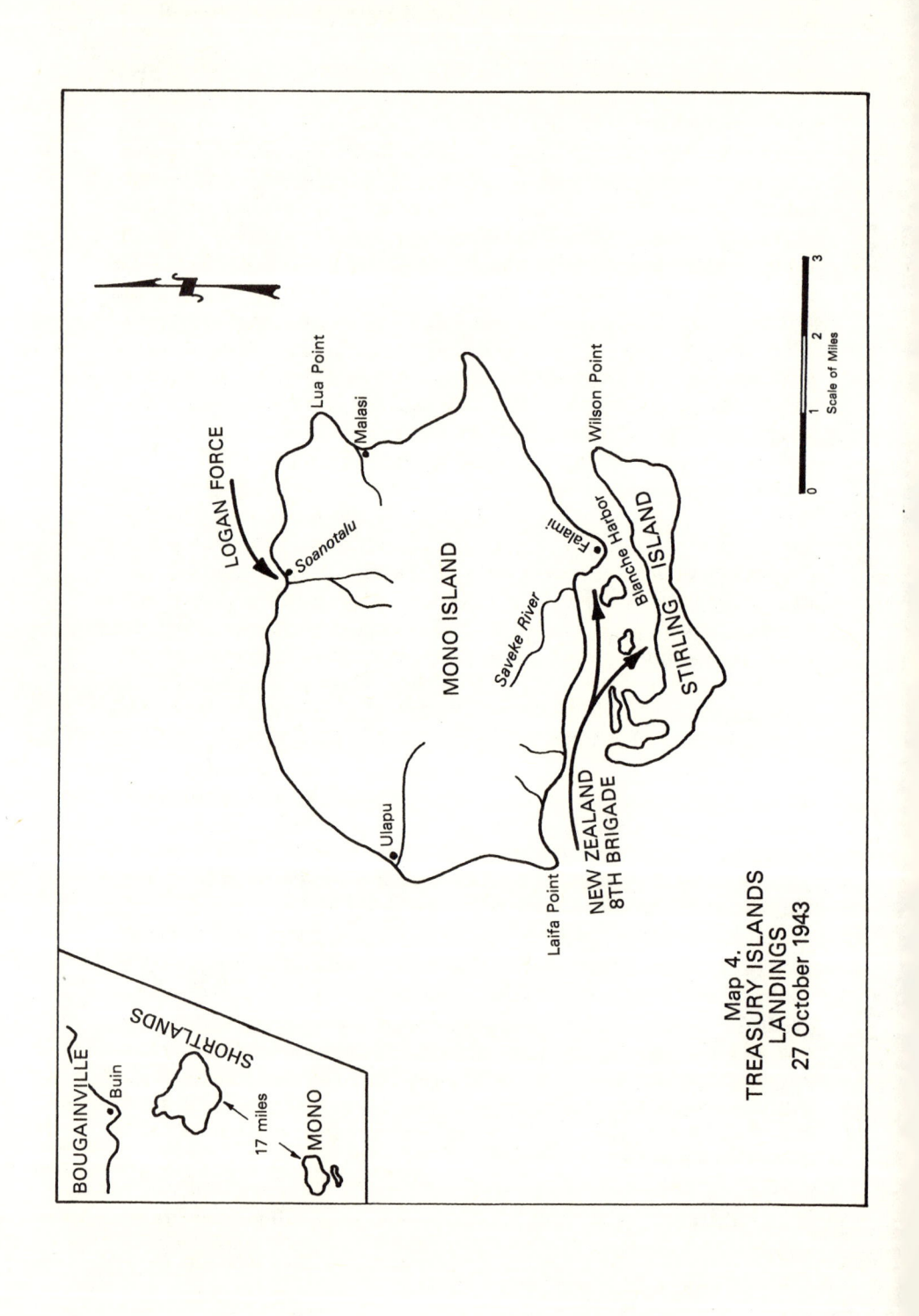

Map 4.
TREASURY ISLANDS
LANDINGS
27 October 1943

0600 on 27 October the destroyers moved into Blanche Harbor and began their bombardment. Although the accuracy of their fire was later criticized, it was obviously reassuring to the New Zealand troops undertaking their first engagement against the Japanese. Thirty-two COMSOL fighters appeared on schedule and began to harass the beaches on both islands. Just after the supporting fire was lifted, the assault waves raced through the harbor in two columns to the assigned beaches. The advance LCTs touched down at a few minutes before 0630. As expected, there was no opposition on Stirling. Patrols were sent out immediately to ascertain if there were any Japanese on the island; mortars were set up on Watson Island to assist, if needed, those troops landing on Mono. By midafternoon it was obvious that the intelligence reports concerning the Japanese on Stirling had been correct, and a portion of one company was sent to Mono to help defend the perimeter that had been established there.

The landings on Mono were barely contested by the Japanese, who in all probability had not expected the attack. There was only sporadic machine gun and rifle fire to greet the first wave, and only six invaders were wounded. The second wave had no casualties. Moving rapidly inland the New Zealanders had established a significant perimeter before the Japanese mortars began to zero in on the beach areas. Before being silenced by fire from the destroyers, this mortar fire struck two LSTs, killing two and wounding thirty men. The expected Japanese air attack materialized in midafternoon, when an estimated twenty-five bombers struck the beachhead and the support ships. The USS Cony took two hits; eight crewmen were killed and ten wounded. Although twelve of the bombers were shot down in this attack, there were two more raids that evening, which killed two New Zealanders.[5] Nevertheless, by the close of D day all but one LST had been unloaded and had cleared the harbor on the return journey to Guadalcanal. The Falami beachhead was secure.

Small groups of Japanese made a number of attacks during the night of D day, particularly against the 36th Battalion on the left flank near the Saveke River, but all were beaten off. A reinforced company left the perimeter on 28 October for an overland march to occupy the town of Malasi on the northeast coast. Ground action on that day had tapered off as the Japanese survivors in the southern part of Mono began to retreat northward in the hope of escaping to Bougainville. With the arrival of the rest of the brigade on 1 November systematic searches and occupation of central and northern Mono began. There was continual danger from snipers and stragglers hidden in the underbrush, but it was the weather and the dense vegetation that caused the

New Zealanders the most trouble. As elsewhere in the South Pacific, continual rains made the trails into miniswamps and the defensive positions into mudholes, and the heat was oppressive.

Logan Force had no difficulty in landing at the mouth of the Soanotalu River at 0630 on D day, despite cliffs and densely wooded sheer ridges on all sides of the small beach. There was no opposition, and a 150-yard perimeter was quickly established. Patrols determined that there were no Japanese within a quarter mile of the beach. The seabees brought in a bulldozer and before noon had begun to build a road up the steep ridge leading inland. The equipment for the radar stations arrived the next day. By 1 November it was operating, and despite the fighting, work had begun on a second installation. The first significant contact with the Japanese occurred in the late afternoon of 29 October, when about twenty enemy soldiers attacked the western part of the perimeter. They were beaten off by a combination of rifle and mortar fire, leaving five dead behind. All remained relatively quiet the next day with only intermittent firing against the concealed Japanese force. Patrols confirmed the presence of a significant number of Japanese to the west of the perimeter but the area between Soanotalu and Malasi was clear of the enemy. The seabees constructed a small blockhouse near the landing barge, which became the main objective of the Japanese, since it represented their only hope of escaping the island. The New Zealanders set out booby traps each night in front of the perimeter and the blockhouse. Two platoons of the 34th, not needed on Stirling, had also been sent to reinforce Major Logan in response to the continuing Japanese attacks.

The main attempt to breech the New Zealanders' lines occurred on 1 November. By early evening there were reports of Japanese activity in front of the eastern part of the perimeter as well as in the west. By midnight a significant number of Japanese had infiltrated the lines and cut the telephone wires from the blockhouse to company headquarters. Soon after, they began a concerted attack against the blockhouse, which was defended by six New Zealanders and three Americans commanded by Captain L.J. Kirk. Their automatic weapons, one 50- and one 30-caliber machine gun, were soon put out of action by the attackers, estimated to number between seventy and a hundred men. The fight for the blockhouse continued until dawn, with the surviving defenders beating off a number of attacks, mainly by using grenades. Captain Kirk was killed, as was his sergeant, D.O. Hannafin, and command of the blockhouse was taken by the cook of Company D, Private J.E. Smith. By daybreak, when the Japanese were finally beaten off, only three of the defenders were unwounded.

Twenty-six Japanese had been killed trying to overrun the blockhouse and seize the landing craft. Elsewhere the troops on the perimeter had also repulsed a number of attacks, killing fifteen Japanese in the western section and nine in the east.

This had been the best hope of the Japanese for escaping the island. Their attacks in the next two days were not as strong and by 4 November the New Zealanders' forward patrols fanning out from the perimeter were killing or capturing the stragglers from the attack on Logan Force. The last significant action on Mono was on 6 November when about a dozen Japanese were routed from a cave in a two-hour fire fight half a mile east of Soanotalu.[6]

By then the Treasuries operation had receded even farther in importance because of the marine landings at Cape Torokina. The New Zealanders continued to fear a counterinvasion from the Shortlands, but given Allied air and naval superiority, there was little possibility of this. The GOODTIME operation had destroyed the entire Japanese garrison of approximately two hundred men, but not without some cost; 40 New Zealanders and 12 Americans had been killed, and 174 men had been wounded.[7] In return the Allies had secured important intermediate supply bases and a radar station. The bulk of the 8th Brigade remained in the Treasuries after its relegation to important yet quiescent functions. Mono and Stirling, despite the large permanent garrison of New Zealanders, soon became a backwater as the more important actions then occurring in the Solomons centered on Bougainville.

At the same time that the New Zealanders were attacking the Treasury Islands, a far more adventuresome and potentially more dangerous diversionary attack was occurring on the large island of Choiseul located less than fifty miles from the southeastern end of Bougainville. At one time the planners at Halsey's headquarters had seriously considered a full-scale assault on the western part of the island as a necessary preliminary to any attack on Bougainville. The plans for this were in the advanced stages when COMSOPAC decided against a landing on the southern end of Bougainville. The plans were then discarded until Major James Murray, IMAC staff secretary, raised the possibility of a smaller-scale landing on Choiseul, which could serve to further confuse the Japanese as to Allied intentions.[8] In mid-October General Vandegrift and Admiral Wilkinson decided that a raid on Choiseul near the point originally scheduled for the larger-scale attack was worth attempting. Risking only a small number of men could possibly gain measurable results in convincing the Japanese commander on Bougainville that even if Choiseul was secondary, the main objective would be the Buin area of southern Bougainville.

Choiseul, an island approximately seventy-five miles long and twenty miles across at the widest point, lies midway between Bougainville to the north and Santa Isabel to the south, on the eastern side of "the Slot." Like many Pacific islands, it is protected by reefs, particularly in the south. Only a few beaches are suitable for a large-scale landing, one of the best being near Voza village in the northwest section of the island. Most of the beaches are narrow with the dense jungle foliage growing close to the water's edge. The interior is dominated by a spine of hills and moderate-sized mountains. Spurs from this highland extend toward the sea on both sides of the island making it difficult to move quickly from one point to another, even along the coasts. East-west movement was particularly difficult, a fact that was important in the decision to use only a small force for the diversionary attack. Except for a few places along the coasts, the entire island was covered by dense and in many areas nearly impenetrable rain forests. General Victor Krulak, then a lieutenant colonel chosen to command the Choiseul raid, recalled: "The island is the most rugged of all the Solomons. It's the home of the giant banyan whose roots cover an acre. It's different. It's never daylight in most of the island. The jungle cover makes it like late afternoon."[9] As in all the Solomon Islands, rain and heat were debilitating factors. Average daytime temperatures during this time of year were in the mid-90s with comparable humidity.

Before the war, the island had been governed by Australia. The Melanesian population had numbered almost five thousand persons, living in small villages mostly near the coasts. Missionaries of different faiths had brought Christianity to the islanders, along with rudimentary educational and health systems. Most of the Melanesians on Choiseul during the Japanese occupation remained loyal to the Australian government. Coast watchers were therefore able to function with considerable effectiveness during the crucial battles for Guadalcanal, providing COMSOPAC with valuable information about ship movements down the Slot. In September 1943, two coast watchers on Choiseul, Charles J. Waddell and Sublieutenant C.W. Seton of the Australian navy, were in regular radio contact with Guadalcanal. Seton had even organized a few of the natives into a military force, which had ambushed a landing barge on 2 October, killing seven Japanese.[10]

Information concerning Choiseul came from a variety of sources, but the most important, aside from direct discussions with the coast watchers, were the patrols sent in to investigate when the island was being considered for a major assault. On 6 September one patrol was landed by PT boat on the southwest part of the island. With the assistance of natives, it proceeded up the coast and then crossed the island to the vicinity of Kasaba before being evacuated by air. Two other patrols operated in the northern end of the island for eight days before being withdrawn. They reported on the best landing sites, the terrain and ground cover, and the difficulty of moving from place to place. According to them, about a thousand Japanese were concentrated near Kasaka, and another three hundred near Choiseul Bay.

These estimates of Japanese strength later changed radically because of the reports of coast watcher Seton, who was monitoring the movement of Japanese troops northward following the evacuation of the New Georgia group. Choiseul was an important link in the relocation of the surviving Japanese to Bougainville. Japanese *daihatsus* would bring troops to the southern end of the island. They would then move overland or by barge to Choiseul Bay in the north, where temporary camps were established, and eventually other barges, operating at night, would transport them to Bougainville. Seton estimated that perhaps as many as four thousand Japanese troops had passed his observation station on their way north and that there were approximately three thousand men at Choiseul Bay and at Sangigai farther south. He also indicated that these troops were in fairly bad condition, short of rations, and trying to live off the natives.[11]

Seton and two of his native soldiers were brought off Choiseul by submarine to meet with Lieutenant Colonel Krulak on Vella Lavella on the 24 October so the latest information on conditions on the island could be communicated directly to the colonel and his staff. Seton then accompanied the marines back to Choiseul.

The final decision on the Choiseul raid was made by General Vandegrift on 19 October, and on the following day the commanders of the two units that would make the assault, Lieutenant Colonel Robert Williams of the 1st Parachute Regiment and Colonel Krulak, in charge of its 2d Battalion, were ordered from Vella Lavella to Guadalcanal to confer with the IMAC staff and to plan the action given the optimistic code name BLISSFUL. Krulak recalled:

> I went to Guadalcanal and they said "we've changed our plan—instead of landing first at Choiseul and then Bougainville we're going to land at Bougainville and bypass Choiseul. We want to make a credible demonstration that we are going to land there. We want to make it about a week ahead of the Bougainville landing. You get together with the staff and plan it." So their G-2 had such

intelligence data as there was. It was not too bad because they had coast-watcher contacts on the island. Their G-3 was prepared to do anything I wanted. G-4 gave me what I wanted. They took me to the navy. I had asked to have some boats attached to my battalion—got the boats and the planning was a piece of cake.[12]

Krulak said that he "didn't believe anybody went into an operation knowing as much as they needed to know as I did about Choiseul."[13]

Despite the obvious cooperation from higher headquarters and information from coast watchers and friendly natives on the island, there is considerable evidence that the raiding party had few details concerning the physical features. Gerald Averill, then a lieutenant commanding a platoon of Company E, commented:

> The maps issued for BLISSFUL were unbelievable, next to useless. A gridded overprint of aerial photographs of our area of operations, which supplemented these maps, left much to be desired. The jungle growth was so dense that the camera's eye had no more success in penetrating it than did the eye of a human. Trails were inked in and overprinted, pure guesswork, for beneath the umbrella of the rainforest no trails actually could be observed. Native villages and known Japanese installations were overprinted, their locations the most accurate of any on the map. The larger streams and rivers were portrayed with some accuracy also. What were *not* shown, perhaps not known about at all by the planners of BLISSFUL, were the rocky spurs that extended from the central mountain mass, east and west, projecting into the sea in places. In following the northwest trail along the beach, there was no way to circumvent these spurs except to seaward, so it was up and over— the slow tedious, exhausting method of making headway.[14]

The IMAC operations order for BLISSFUL issued on 22 October designated the landing area as the beach near the village of Voza approximately twenty miles down the southern coast from Choiseul Bay. The decision to land there was Krulak's. He had been given great latitude in the selection. He recalled that "the Navy did not have any interest in selecting it; they were just going to haul us over there."[15] His choice was based largely upon the reports from Seton. There were villages in the vicinity of the good beaches, and the natives could be expected to assist the marines in every way. The latest reports also indicated that there were no Japanese troops nearby. The task organization for the operation was to be the 2d Parachute Battalion reinforced with a machine gun platoon from regimental weapons, a boat detachment (four LCP (R)s) and an experimental rocket detachment—a total of 656 officers and enlisted men.[16]

Krulak's troops were among the elite of the Marine Corps. In 1940 responding to the successful use of paratroops by the Germans, both the army and the marines decided to experiment in a small way with airborne companies. In the following year the marine version was expanded into the 1st Battalion. Training facilities were provided at Camp Lejeune in the east and at Camp Gillespie in San Diego. In 1942 this battalion was sent to the South Pacific undoubtedly in the mistaken belief that its unique talents could in some way be used in the conquest of some of the Japanese-held areas. The 2d Battalion was formed later that year and, with the 1st, composed the 1st Parachute Regiment. Later two more battalions would be created.

These marine paratroops never jumped into combat.[17] Instead, they were used on missions similar to those undertaken by raider units. Prior to Choiseul the 2d Battalion had not had combat experience; the 1st had taken Gavutu and Tanambogo Islands and helped defend Guadalcanal during the later stages of that struggle. Although these paratroops would never use their chutes, they were uniquely prepared for a mission like BLISSFUL. The battalion's three companies had more automatic and semiautomatic weapons than a regular company because the previous year the Marine Corps had decided to purchase limited quantities of two products from the Johnson Arms Company. One was a light machine gun and the other was the semiautomatic rifle which had, in tests, beaten the Garand M-1 for rate of fire and accuracy. Each Paramarine platoon had three of the light machine guns and six of the Johnson rifles, as well as 60-mm mortars.[18] Although Krulak's force for BLISSFUL was small, it thus had considerable fire power.

Krulak had written his operations order for his battalion at Henderson Field on Guadalcanal while waiting for a plane to take him back to Vella Lavella. Once back with the battalion he prepared quickly but carefully. His men would have only four days to be briefed, gather all needed supplies, and get in some dry-land boat practice. There were intelligence briefings twice a day, inspections of weapons and equipment, and the troops were drilled continuously in the coconut groves to aid in debarkation from the LCP(R)s at the beachhead.

On the afternoon of 27 October the troops and necessary equipment for the operation were loaded on eight LCMs and later, after dark, the paratroops were transferred to four APDs that had been used by the

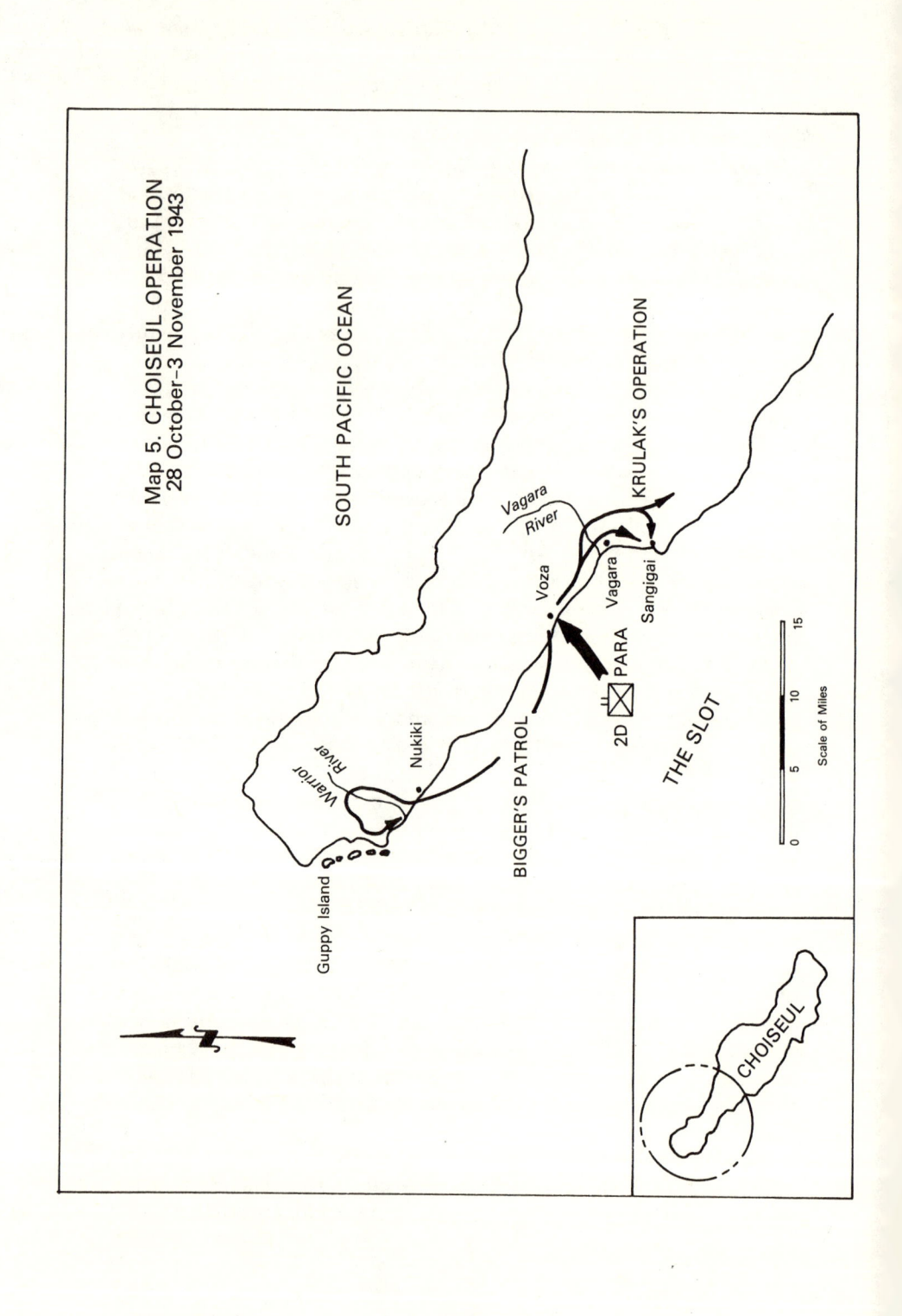

Map 5. CHOISEUL OPERATION
28 October–3 November 1943

New Zealanders in the Treasury operation. Escorted by destroyers, the APDs moved out in column a few minutes after 1900. Approximately four hours later, the convoy was sighted by a Japanese plane, which dropped one bomb that fortunately missed the APDs. Just at midnight, approximately a mile off Choiseul, the invasion force halted and a reconnaisance party was sent in to ascertain if any Japanese were present near Voza (Map 5). They were to flash a signal if no enemy was present. After waiting and seeing no light, Krulak decided to send the troops in anyway. Then, a few minutes after the orders to go in were given, the signal light was spotted from the beach. The landing, led by Company F, was unoposed. The last hostile action by the Japanese during the landings was another attack by an enemy plane on the escort destroyer *Conway*.

The early morning hours of 28 October were spent unloading the supplies from the landing craft, which had been concealed on a small island just offshore, and carrying them up the narrow trail leading from the beach to the place selected as the base camp. It was located about a mile northwest of Voza on high ground, near a clear stream, and well concealed from air attack by heavy forest growth. Nearly a hundred natives, alerted by men in Seton's constabulary, helped the marines carry the considerable amount of equipment up from the beach. This was just the first instance of assistance; the natives also proved invaluable as guides and trackers.

It was obvious from the two plane attacks during the night that the Japanese knew some kind of landing had been made on Choiseul. Just to make certain that the landing had not escaped them, Allied radio broadcast the news. It was essential that the Japanese command know the Americans were ashore but equally important that the marines conceal their exact numbers, location, and intentions.[19] So as soon as the marines left the beach, a large number of natives did their best to obliterate any signs of the landing.

The marines devoted the remainder of the day on 28 October to setting up a defensive perimeter and dispersing the troops around the base camp. It is fortunate that they did so, for they were attacked in the morning by a flight of enemy planes, which straffed the area blindly without effect. Native guides told Krulak that approximately eight miles south of the camp was a barge-staging base at Sangigai, defended by approximately 150 Japanese. Krulak decided to attack Sangigai.

The following day the colonel sent out reconnaisance patrols north and south of his base. Lieutenant Averill, assisted by a native guide, took one group north to scout the possibility of using Moli

Point as a base for the landing craft. This patrol ran into unexpected difficulty not from the Japanese but from the terrain. Averill's maps had shown six miles of good trail from Voza to the point. Instead it was an eight-hour up-and-down march through nearly impassable forest and swamp. Skirting the beach areas for fear of detection, the patrol reached Moli before nightfall and determined that it was not suitable for the boats. They had discovered considerable evidence of the Japanese presence in the form of discarded equipment and ration and ammunition cases, but encountered no enemy soldiers. After reaching a small, deserted village, the patrol settled down for the night, only to be disturbed by a Japanese barge with a load of troops heading into shore nearby. Fortunately, the coxswain of the barge decided to turn north presumably to find a better landing place. The patrol's luck held on 30 October when the guide warned them of many Japanese who had landed on either side of their cover in the night. Thus the patrol was forced to take an even more tortuous mountain trail back to intersect their old route just north of Voza, where they met a large marine patrol sent out to search for them.[20]

In the meantime two strong patrols went south to scout the Japanese base near Sangigai. One patrol covered the higher ground to the rear of the village; the other, led by Krulak, took the more direct beach route toward the Vagara River. This patrol surprised some Japanese unloading a barge and opened fire, killing seven of the enemy and then sinking the barge. After both patrols had returned to the base camp, the colonel sent a squad back to the scene of the recent engagement to block any pursuers and try to maintain a landing point for the boats. This patrol ran into a Japanese patrol of platoon size. The marines drove the enemy patrol off in a brief fire fight, killing another seven Japanese soldiers.[21]

Early in the morning of 30 October Companies E and F moved from the base camp toward Voza, where they planned to take to the boats for an attack on Sangigai. The preliminary air strike Krulak had requested arrived at a few minutes past 0600, when twelve TBFs, accompanied by twenty-six fighters, struck Sangigai. Unfortunately, some of the planes mistook the marines at Voza for the enemy and made a number of strafing passes. No marines were killed, but one of the boats Krulak hoped to use was sunk.[22] He was therefore forced to move overland, and so he decided to put his plan into effect from the Vagara River.

Company E, commanded by Captain Robert Manchester, moved along the coastline to attack the Japanese directly from the north, while Krulak, Seton and his scouts, and Company F moved inland in order to take the village from the rear. Evidently, the Japanese at Sangigai were alerted, for one of their outposts opened fire on the marines at about 1100. The coordinated attack was planned to begin at 1400. Company E, finding the beach route easy to traverse, was in position shortly after that time and began firing rockets and dropping mortar shells into the town. The riflemen then moved into the village, only to find it abandoned; the Japanese had moved to the higher ground in the interior. Manchester's men then began a systematic destruction of the village. The marines blew up everything that could conceivably ever be used by the enemy, including administrative buildings, a field hospital, bunkers, and all types of supplies. They even found a relatively new barge, which was immediately scuttled. Sergeant Vernon Hammons, searching through the administrative buildings, stumbled upon a veritable treasure trove of documents and charts.

Colonel Krulak and Company F were late in beginning their phase of the attack because the terrain was much worse than expected. Fortunately, when they heard the firing from the beach area, they were almost in position. Had Company F been a few minutes later in arriving, all the Japanese might have escaped. As it was, their withdrawal to the high ground exactly complemented Krulak's envelopment plans, and they blundered directly into the fire of Company F. The engagement lasted for almost an hour, and although the marines had more fire power, they were outnumbered. "The outcome appeared to be in question," Krulak later wrote, "until the Japs destroyed their chances by an uncoordinated banzai charge which was badly cut up by our machine guns. Seventy-two Japs were killed an an undetermined number wounded. Marine losses were 6 killed, 1 missing and 12 wounded."[23] Among the wounded were Krulak and Company F commander, Spencer Pratt. This was not the first time, nor would it be the last, that the Japanese would do as much to destroy their own units as their enemy by futile banzai charges.

After destroying Sangigai, Company E retired to the Vagara River and was evacuated by boat to the Voza area. Company F was delayed by the engagement and then stayed to bury its dead. The company eventually reached the river and established a tight perimeter since there was no way of ascertaining how many Japanese might be on its trail. Krulak's radio was broken, and he could not communicate with his executive officer, Major Warren Bigger, who was in charge of evacuating the marines by boat. Bigger had decided not to attempt a pickup after dark for fear of running aground. Thus it wasn't until early the next morning that Krulak and Company F were evacuated from their perimeter along the Vagara River.[24]

Among the papers discovered at Sangigai were a number of possible importance, but one was unquestionably crucial. "The one that fascinated me," Krulak later recalled,

> was a chart that portrayed the minefields around southern Bougainville. When I reported this, the night after the Sangigai attack, I saw my first flash message. I had never seen one before. It came back and said, "Transmit at once the coordinates of the limits of the minefields and all channels as shown going through it." So we laboriously encoded the critical locations and sent them off. To an armada going into that area this is not incidental information. This is necessary information. Halsey in true Halsey fashion was not satisfied to know where the minefields were; he, before the Torokina landings, sent in a minelayer there and dropped mines in the entrance ways to those channels and they got two Japanese ships.[25]

All the captured documents were sent on to higher headquarters on a PBY that landed offshore from Voza on 1 November to take off the wounded and leave behind supplies for the marines and the natives.

Krulak had already tentatively planned his next move. He sent a strong patrol by boat northward to reconnoiter a reported Japanese concentration near the Warrior River just south of Choiseul Bay. No opposition was encountered, the Japanese all being north of the river. On the next day Krulak despatched eighty-seven marines of Company G by boat under the command of Major Bigger back to Nukiki. Their objectives were to "destroy the southern outposts of CHOISEUL BAY, and if possible to shell the Jap supply depot on GUPPY ISLAND."[26] Bigger's patrol was supplied with 60-mm mortars in order to bring the major Japanese base at Choiseul Bay and the installations on Guppy Island under fire.

At the same time Krulak sent a thirty-six-man patrol from Company E south toward Sangigai to ascertain the Japanese reaction to the raid. The patrol encountered Japanese near the village of Vagara at midday. After a brief fire fight the Japanese broke off the engagement, and the patrol returned to base camp by 1400. Two hours later the 3d Platoon of Company E was sent back to Vagara in hopes of springing an ambush on any of the enemy moving north. Lieutenant John Richards, commanding the platoon, set up his ambush on both sides of the trail and shortly after 1700 about twenty Japanese imperial marines were caught on the trail. The Americans lost one man but killed eight Japanese and drove off the rest.

Other patrols included Lieutenant Averill's group, sent to establish a northwest outpost on the east bank of the Baragosonga River to block any Japanese use of the good trail leading north of the river. On 2 November Krulak sent still another patrol south to the Sangigai area to observe and block any Japanese movements northward. If necessary the patrol was to repeat the performance of the previous day, and it was to return by midafternoon. When it did not and radio contact could not be made, Krulak feared it had encountered a large force of Japanese and had been lost. He was also worried about Bigger's group, which had not returned either. Not until well after dark was his anxiety eased when the southern patrol made its way into Voza, and the men of the northwest patrol also began returning to base.[27]

Major Bigger's northwest patrol had achieved considerable success, although the operation became highly confused at times. At first all went well; the patrol was taken by boat past Nukiki to the Warrior River. The boats ran aground a number of times, however, and Bigger, fearing that the sounds of the engines would betray them, ordered his marines ashore and sent the boats downriver. The patrol, led by native guides, then began an overland march along the eastern bank of the river. By midafternoon they were in a swamp and the natives admitted they were from another part of Choiseul and knew nothing about this area. Bigger sent back a small patrol under the command of Lieutenant Rea Duncan to the outpost he had established farther downriver to contact Krulak at Voza and to order the boats back. Upon hearing of Bigger's problems, Seton sent a native who knew the area well to get Bigger's men out of the swamp. Meanwhile, the small patrol at the outpost discovered on the morning of 2 November that the Japanese had been alerted to their presence and had almost surrounded them. They managed to elude the Japanese, made their way to Nukiki, caught the boats, and returned to Voza. Krulak ordered the boats back to Nukiki with orders to evacuate Bigger's men. Bigger sent out another small patrol, led by Lieutenant Duncan to Nukiki to arrange for the pickup of his men on the afternoon of 2 November. This patrol ran into a larger Japanese force and had to fight its way through to the village. There, the men waited for the boats. Krulak at base camp had radioed IMAC asking for fighters and also for PT boats to help cover the withdrawal of Bigger and his men.

Meanwhile, Bigger's main force, with the new guide who knew the territory, was attempting to complete the mission. Proceeding north along the beach, the marines surprised a small enemy outpost of four men. Although they shot three of the Japanese, one escaped, and Bigger then concluded that he had lost the element of surprise. He could no long hope to attack his main objective with any hope of success. Instead, he decided to shell Guppy Island. The trees and vines at the selected point for the attack grew down to the edge of the beach; so the mortar platoon of Company G had to set the base plates of the 60-mm mortars in the water. The rounds that the riflemen had so laboriously carried were passed down to the mortars. They bombarded Guppy Island with 143 rounds, setting two large fires; one obviously in a fuel dump. Taken by surprise, the Japanese were able to reply only with a few poorly directed machine gun bursts. Bigger and his men then began their retreat back to the Warrior River without knowing that the Japanese had landed troops between them and the river. They beat off four separate attacks before reaching the river, where they established a strong defensive perimeter and waited to be picked up.[28]

Had the Japanese commander at Choiseul Bay known the position of the marines, backed up to the river, he could easily have surrounded them and wiped them out. Fortunately, only small Japanese units were in the vicinity, probably searching for the marines. One such unit caught a number of the marines washing themselves in the river and began firing. The marines immediately returned the fire, and the Japanese fire stopped. Bigger then sent three men to swim across the river to determine whether there were Japanese there or only on the flank where the firing had come from. Perhaps he believed that Lieutenant Duncan's patrol was on the other side of the river. The Japanese opened fire again, killing one of the swimmers and wounding another. Lieutenant Sam Johnson of the intelligence detachment reached the other side but was never seen again.[29] By this time it was almost sundown and Bigger's position was increasingly desperate. Darkness was coming, and Bigger was certain that he was surrounded. Fortunately, the LCP(R)s were soon sighted. The ensign commanding the lead boat was reluctant to land in the face of enemy fire but a marine sergeant on board persuaded him to take his boat into the river and beach it on the west shore.[30] The second boat followed, and as soon as all the marines had scrambled aboard, the boats backed off the beach and headed toward Voza. For those on the second boat, however, the drama was not yet over.

Colonel Krulak's message requesting help to evacuate Bigger's command reached the PT base at Vella Lavella in midafternoon on 2 November. Lieutenant Arthur Berndtson at that time had five boats under his command, of which two were already assigned to other missions and one was laid up for repairs. Even worse, PT 59, one of the two available boats had its tanks only one-third full of fuel. The commander of PT 59, Lieutenant John F. Kennedy, agreed with Berndtson that the boat should go anyway. It had enough fuel to get to Choiseul, and the other boat could tow it back to base.

Berndtson and Kennedy knew little more than that they were to rescue marines somewhere on the northeast Choiseul coast. They had been given a compass bearing and assurances that a guide boat would be standing offshore to guide them. The compasses on board the PT boats were questionable, and the boats would have to go at full speed to locate the guide boat before dark. On the first pass, they missed the guide boat, but after turning back they spotted it. The boat had been late getting on station because of engine difficulty. Berndtson and Kennedy, after being briefed on the situation by another PT officer on board the disabled guide boat, left immediately, trailing the two boats that Duncan had managed to round up at Nukiki. The LCP(R)s made it to the pickup point without further incident, and as already related, Bigger's patrol scrambled aboard the boats. In the darkness and under increasing Japanese fire they were on their way to Voza before the PT boats arrived.

The sea had been rising because of an approaching storm. Then the second LCP(R), loaded down with exhausted marines, sprang a leak before it even cleared the reef. The boat began to sink, and the engine stalled. Almost as if following a Hollywood script, the two PT boats emerged out of the darkness. While the other PT boat stood by to provide cover, Kennedy put PT 59 between the sinking boat and the shore and began boarding the soaked and grateful marines. More than fifty-five men crowded the decks of the small PT boat as it struggled with the overload to make way against the squall. Despite the overheated engines, sometime after 2130 that evening the convoy reached Voza, and Bigger's men were off-loaded. As expected, Kennedy's PT 59 did run out of fuel on its return down the Slot and was taken under tow back to the base at Lambu Lambu Cove on Vella Lavella.[31]

Even before Bigger's patrol had been safely evacuated, IMAC had solicited Krulak's opinion on withdrawal of the entire battalion. By this time, landings had been made at Cape Torokina on Bougainville, and headquarters had relayed General Vandegrift's opinion that the main objectives of the decoy mission to Choiseul had been achieved. Krulak had come to the same conclusion. Averill later analyzed their situation accurately:

58 Bougainville

By now the Japanese had doped it out, not off-balance anymore. We had hit hard, torn things up, laid down a lot of fire, but we had never remained on position, had never occupied a tactical locality once we had seized it. We were tapping at the Japanese, not hammering as a strong force would. The native scouts went north and south, into the mountains and along the rivers. The Japanese were patrolling in strength, down from Choiseul Bay toward Moli, up from Kakasa toward Sangigai, reinforcement already in place at that destroyed base.[32]

Krulak was worried that the Japanese might cut off the route to the beach and began considering the possibility of moving across the island to another pickup point. It was time for the marines to leave.

The departure came not a moment too soon. Within hours the Japanese moved in on the base camp from all directions. By then the marines had moved to the departure point just north of Voza. The marines had rigged booby traps and sent out blocking patrols to protect the evacuation site. During the night of 3 November three LCIs from Vella Lavella arrived. All supplies were loaded except the rations, which were left behind for the natives who had been so helpful during the operation. The blocking patrols were called in, and the LCIs pulled away from the beach. They were safely back on Vella Lavella just before dawn of 4 November.

There they were incongruously met by a marine band and a welcoming committee of officers from the regiment and the other parachute battalions. Nine marines had been killed, twelve were wounded, and five were missing in action. Of the four MIAs who were later declared dead, one had been executed by the Japanese near the Warrior River.[33] The immediate results of the raid are indisputable. The Paramarines, outnumbered by six to one, had killed an estimated 143 Japanese, destroyed a major staging base at Sangigai, sunk two hard-to-replace barges, and destroyed a considerable amount of the enemy's fuel and supplies when Bigger's patrol shelled Guppy Island.

It is very difficult to assess how successful the Choiseul raid was as a diversion. Henry I. Shaw and Douglas T. Kane declare that "the effect of the diversionary attack upon the success of the Cape Torokina operation was slight." Yet they later assert that the Japanese were convinced by the Choiseul action that "the Allies would now move to cut Japanese lines and then land on the southern part of Bougainville in an attempt to seize the island's airfields. . . . The enemy had no hint that such an unlikely area as Empress Augusta Bay would be attacked."[34] Colonel Krulak, not surprisingly, was convinced that the

Choiseul operation did exactly what it was supposed to do—help confuse the Japanese about Allied intentions. The captured documents at Sangigai, moreover, were quite important for later navigation of the waters off southern Bougainville. In his after action report, Krulak mentioned evidence that the Japanese had sent reinforcements from the Shortland Islands to counter the Choiseul operation. On 1 November, the day of the Cape Torokina landings, the Japanese sent a large bomber force south to Choiseul in search of a reported task force. They found nothing, but by the time they were diverted back to Empress Augusta Bay, the lodgment had already been made, and American fighter planes were prepared to deal with them. The Japanese also revealed their confusion in increased communications from Bougainville and in the content of those messages intercepted.[35]

The ultimate effect of the raid remains debatable, but the planning and execution were unquestionably superb. Despite the confusion when Bigger's patrol was lost in the swamp, all tactical goals were achieved. Krulak's leadership won him a Navy Cross and the recognition by his superiors that he could be trusted with even more complex operations. Undoubtedly the colonel was correct in claiming "that the strategic effect for the commitment of 750 men in an undertaking where they were bringing in 38,000 men was significant.[36]

4. Establishing the Beachhead

The Japanese were fully aware of how Allied activity in the Solomons endangered Rabaul, their main naval and air base in the southern Pacific, but they were in a difficult position. The loss of New Georgia and the occupation of Kolombangara had left only the two islands of Choiseul and Vella Lavella in the central Solomons with any Japanese troops present. Then, during the first days of October, the Japanese command at Rabaul decided, against all logic, to rescue the six hundred men isolated in northern Vella Lavella. Although successful after a drawn naval engagement on the night of 6-7 October off Horaniu, Vella Lavella, the withdrawal left Admiral Halsey's forces in total control of the central Solomons. Admiral Koga and his subordinates recognized the probability of an early assault on Bougainville, which, if successful, would bring Rabaul within less than two hundred miles of Allied air power. The Japanese were convinced that any such invasion had to be countered with all the planes and ships available in the southern theater. Yet they could not concentrate their entire naval and air force against the Solomons because of the American and Australian forces on New Guinea and the fear that a land invasion of New Britain was imminent. Admiral Koga also expected the United States to attempt a landing in the Gilbert or Marshall islands. The two-pronged Allied strategy had served to freeze the Japanese army units in their locations in New Guinea and the Solomons. Later U.S. naval and air superiority would effectively isolate these troops and make it nearly impossible to shift reinforcements to a threatened area.

It was obvious to the planners at General MacArthur's and Admi-

Establishing the Beachhead 61

ral Halsey's headquarters that Japanese air power sited at Rabaul and at the Bougainville fields of Kahili, Buin, Kieta, and Buka must be neutralized before the Empress Augusta Bay operation could take place. The task of keeping the Japanese air power at Rabaul busy fell to General Kenney's 5th Air Force, while the more direct attacks on the Solomons' fields would be left to AIRSOLS. Photographs of the four airfields at Rabaul taken on 11 October showed 128 bombers and 145 fighters. The next day Kenney hit Rabaul with the largest air strike yet in the Pacific war, sending 213 heavy and medium bombers escorted by 125 P-38s over the target. They sank three large merchant vessels and scores of smaller ships, blew up ammunition dumps, and destroyed over a hundred planes on the ground. Bad weather over New Britain kept the 5th from repeating this action there, but Kenney's fighters had a field day intercepting Japanese dive bombers and fighters on 15 and 16 October. On 18 October, fifty-four B-25s, operating with a ceiling of only two hundred feet, hit and almost totally destroyed Rabaul's Tobera airfield. As soon as the weather improved the large-scale raids on the Rabaul airfields continued. Sixty-two B-25s escorted by fifty-four P-38s struck once more at Vunakanau, Rapapo, and Tobera fields and destroyed many more planes on the ground. In addition, the fighters and bombers shot down forty-three of the Japanese fighters sent up to intercept. The constant raids against Rabaul and Wewak in New Guinea had reduced Kenney's force so that by 29 October, on the eve of the Bougainville landings, he was able to send only fifty-three P-38s and thirty-seven B-24s over Rabaul, once again with good results. Kenney planned a further strike for 31 October, but bad weather postponed this until 2 November.[1]

In the meantime other air groups were hitting targets in the Solomons. The eclectic AIRSOLS, comprising units of the Royal New Zealand Air Force, General Twining's heavy bombers of the 13th Air Force, and 1st and 2d Marine Air Wings, by mid-October had 314 fighters and 317 bombers attacking various targets in the Bougainville area. Most of the bombers continued to operate out of Guadalcanal, but the bulk of the fighter strength had been moved forward to the new airfields on New Georgia and Vella Lavella. Although the Japanese from the Rabaul airfields were a nuisance during and immediately after the landings at Cape Torokina, they had on 1 November only an estimated 154 planes in the northern Solomons, one-third the number of Allied land-based planes. AIRSOLS increased its level of activity over Bougainville as D day drew nearer. Its planes were active twenty-one days during October in raids as diverse as low-level strafing runs and medium- and high-level attacks from B-24s and B-25s. Kahilia and Kara were hit most often, but Balalele, Buka, Choiseul, Kieta, and the Treasuries were also struck. Balalele airfield was so pockmarked with bomb craters that it could not be used, and by 22 October, Kahili was also nonoperational. AIRSOLS planes had done such efficient work that the airfields on Bougainville were virtually useless to the Japanese on D day.[2]

Admiral Halsey did not have the naval forces he believed he needed prior to the Bougainville operation. He was certain that the Japanese would do as they had at Guadalcanal and use all available air and naval units in attempting to maintain their control of the northern Solomons. With the departure of the British carrier *Victorious*, he had only the large older carrier *Saratoga* available to counter any hostile air activity if Admiral Koga chose to commit any of his remaining carriers. Halsey expected that Nimitz would let him have at least one of the fast new carriers that had recently arrived at Pearl Harbor. Nimitz, however, was building the 5th Fleet around these new arrivals and besides was planning to invade the Gilberts on 20 November. He believed that Halsey could make do with what naval units he had. After ordering the assault on Cape Torokina, Halsey flew to Hawaii and persuaded Nimitz to release the light carrier *Princeton* to him immediately. Nimitz also promised to consider allowing Halsey to have an additional carrier group. The *Princeton* joined Rear Admiral Frederick Sherman's Task Force 38 based at Espiritu Santo, which then comprised two carriers, two light cruisers, and ten destroyers. In addition Halsey had Task Force 39, commanded by Rear Admiral Aaron Merrill located that last week in October at Purvis Bay on Florida Island. The heart of TF 39 was four new light cruisers—the *Montpelier, Cleveland, Denver,* and *Columbia*—and eight destroyers. Task Force 38 left its base on 28 October, and Merrill's force departed Florida Island three days later. They intended to rendezvous near Buka Passage in order to attack the Buka and Bonis airfields to make certain that the Japanese would not be able to direct any significant number of planes against Admiral Wilkinson's invasion force.[3]

Task Force 39 arrived on station first, early in the morning of 1 November, and immediately began firing at Buka and Bonis airfields. After pumping twenty-seven hundred rounds of five- and six-inch shells onto the airfields and surrounding areas, TF 39 retired to the Shortlands to put Poporang, Ballalo, and Faisi under fire.

Task Force 38 arrived off Buka Passage shortly after 0400 that morning, the first time that Halsey had sent any of his carriers within fighter range of Rabaul. In a dead calm, two separate air strikes were launched against the airfields. The first, made up of eighteen fighters, fifteen dive bombers, and eleven torpedo bombers, struck Buka just after daylight. The second, comprising fourteen fighters, twenty-one dive bombers, and eleven torpedo bombers hit Buka again at midmorning and shot up a number of small ships in the harbor area. The next day Sherman mounted two further attacks against the fields before heading south toward Guadalcanal. In two days TF 39 had destroyed an estimated thirty planes and several small ships at a cost of eleven planes lost to enemy action and other causes. Most important, the attacks by the two task forces had rendered the two Japanese airfields nearest Empress Augusta Bay unusable during the crucial days following the landings.[4]

The Japanese plane and pilot losses at Rabaul and Bougainville during October had been severe. Without reinforcements, Rabaul would have been almost negated, even without the proposed airstrip that was to be built as soon as possible at Cape Torokina. From his Truk headquarters, Admiral Koga, commander in chief of the Combined Fleet, had planned his own air and naval offensive to begin in mid-October. For this operation, code named RO, he had stripped his mainline carriers, *Zukaku*, *Shokaku*, and *Zuhio*, of most of their planes. Eighty-two fighters, forty-five dive bombers, forty torpedo bombers, and six reconnaisance planes were sent south to reinforce Admiral Kusaka's dwindling air fleet at Rabaul. Operation RO's objectives were to cut Allied supply lines to Australia and New Guinea and prevent the buildup for future offensives aimed at Rabaul. This RO offensive, aimed primarily at the New Guinea area, was postponed by Koga's fears of a U.S. attack on the Marshall Islands. Hoping for the classic naval showdown against the Americans, Koga sent his main fleet units to Eniwetok. When, after a week's wait, the American fleet did not appear, he ordered his forces back to Truk and then sent the carrier air groups to Rabaul. Admiral Takeo Kurita was preparing to carry out plan RO when the Treasury landings caused him to shift his attention to the Solomons. Despite the heavy air attacks against Rabaul, toward the end of the month it appeared that no further Allied activity could be expected immediately in that area. The Japanese believed that the Americans would wait for the symbolic date of 8 December to invade southern or eastern Bougainville. So once again Kurita's fleet and air units were primed to attack New Guinea. The fleet was in position just north of the Bismarck Archipelago on 1 November and out of position to disrupt the landings at Cape Torokina.[5]

During the last week of October, while air action continued and the marines and New Zealanders were involved in the Treasuries and Choiseul operations, Task Force 31 on Guadalcanal was making final preparations for the invasion of Bougainville. The latest intelligence reports showed that the Japanese had fewer than three hundred men in the vicinity of Cape Torokina and Puruata Island. The massive preparations for the commitment of the reinforced 3d Marine Division, with the army's 37th Division in reserve, was designed not merely to overcome these few enemy troops but to make certain that once a defensive perimeter had been established, the Japanese commander on Bougainville could not dislodge the marines, even if he utilized all his available forces. The long beach area west of Cape Torokina varied in depth from thirty to fifty yards. With steel mats the Allies believed it could support the landing of heavy equipment. The physical factors at Empress Augusta Bay, combined with the desire to get as many men ashore quickly as possible, had persuaded Admiral Wilkinson and General Vandegrift to land two full regiments and the 2d Raider Battalion abreast on eleven designated beaches covering a distance of eight thousand yards. The 3d Raider Battalion would land simultaneously on Puruata Island to overcome the estimated seventy Japanese troops there.

The assault troops after their final practice at Efate and Espiritu Santo in the New Hebrides were loaded onto the transports of Divisions A and B, commanded by Commodore L.F. Reifsnider, on 28 October. Two days later they joined with Division C, which had those support troops, and the 3d Marine Defense Battalion, which had remained on Guadalcanal. The four transports of Division A carried 6,421 men of the 3d Marines, reinforced, while Division B took on 6,103 men of the 9th Marines, reinforced. The marines in the assault went aboard the transports with light combat packs, and each man had only one canteen of water. The riflemen carried one unit of fire, approximately eighty rounds, for the M-1, and each BAR man was supplied with ten 20-round clips. Although the use of light packs allowed the marines more comfort and maneuverability, it also made the quick unloading of the ships imperative. By the end of the second day the marine units would begin to feel the need for water, food, and possibly ammunition.[6]

The three transport divisions rendezvoused with eleven destroyers, eight minesweepers, and small craft on the morning of 31 October.[7] From there the approach toward Bougainville was south and west of Rendova, Vella Lavella, and the Treasuries under cover of navy PBYs and Liberators. Early in the morning of 1 November the minesweepers, led by the destroyer *Wadsworth*, were sent ahead to clear any mines in the approach area and to determine any dangerous shoals. The *Wadsworth* had a number of tasks. In addition to direct-fire support from as close in as three thousand yards, it was to use its radar to confirm the actual location of Cape Torokina, Puruata Island, and the landing beaches. Earlier, the submarine *Guardfish* had reported that the air force and naval charts had mislocated Cape Torokina by approximately seven miles. This discrepancy was confirmed by the *Wadsworth*'s radar. Its safe passage into Empress Augusta Bay did not change Admiral Wilkinson's decision not to land the marines until after daylight, when it would be possible to detect the offshore shoals only imperfectly shown on the charts.[8]

The minesweepers and destroyers began a slow, steady bombardment of the targeted landing areas and Puruata Island shortly before sunrise. The *Sigourney* and *Wadsworth* began firing at ranges up to thirteen thousand yards and continued the long-range bombardment while the destroyer *Terry* worked closer to the shore of Cape Torokina. As each transport passed the cape, it fired its three-inch antiaircraft guns with the hope of hitting Japanese positions or at least minimizing any return artillery fire. By 0645 the transports were anchored three thousand yards from shore; the cargo ships were positioned approximately five hundred yards seaward of the transports. Admiral Wilkinson had tentatively set 0715 as H hour but changed to 0730 on arrival off the beaches. When the assault waves had been off-loaded into the landing craft and were on the way in to the beaches, all the destroyers began a systematic sustained fire along the perimeter of the beaches. At 0721, thirty-one torpedo bombers from New Georgia bombed and strafed the landing areas and adjacent jungle for five minutes. By then the first marines had scrambled ashore and within a few minutes between seven and eight thousand troops, more than half the total force, had been landed.[9]

Shortly after the landing craft had cleared the ships, the Japanese launched the first of two air attacks, and for the next two hours the transports and supply ships maneuvered to evade the dive bombers and fighters sent from Rabaul. General Twining had arranged for continuous fighter cover of thirty planes to be over the beachhead all day. These P-38s, P-40s, and F4Us, controlled by a director team on the destroyer *Conway*, shot down four planes during the initial attack, but a number of dive bombers broke through the screen. The attacks did no damage to the transports, and the strafing of the beach resulted in only a few casualties.[10]

The 9th Marines, landing on the five northern beaches (Map 6), were fortunate in meeting no resistance from the Japanese. Nevertheless, ignorance of the hydrographic conditions played havoc with the landing. These beaches were quite narrow and steep, backed by a

Map 6.
CAPE TOROKINA LANDINGS
1 November 1943

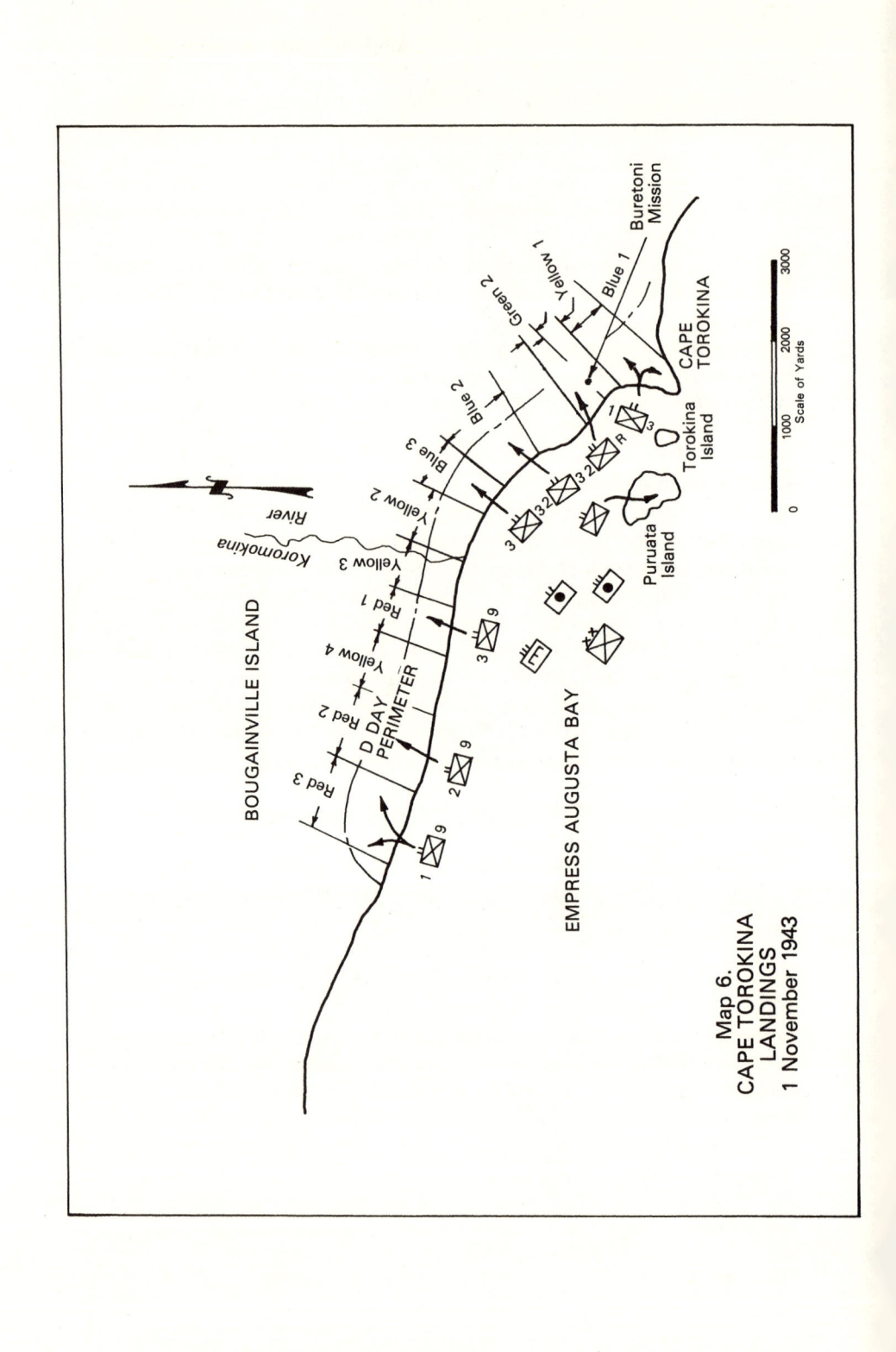

high embankment. The surf, whipped by a stiff breeze, was much higher and rougher than the planners had expected. A marine platoon sergeant recalled his experiences in landing:

> Each of the landing craft carried thirty to fifty men, and on the back of the landing craft was a flat deck and on the deck was mounted a .50-caliber machine gun we used against the enemy aircraft. As we approached the beach we could see that the surf was quite high. We were in those LCVPs, and the closer we got to the beach the swells became greater and finally we were in kind of a canyon. If you were between swells you could look up and see water on one side and also water on the other side of you. It just pitched our landing craft right up on the beach.[11]

The surf conditions played no favorites. After General Turnage and his staff had gone ashore, General Vandegrift debarked from the *George Clymer* and went ashore to inspect the beachhead. All went well in landing the general and the men accompanying him, but when he decided to leave he discovered as had the earlier landing parties just how treacherous was the surf. "He darn near got swamped right on the beach there," his chief of staff recalled; "the surf began to break heavily, the boat broached and everything suddenly looked bleak. I was standing on the beach, helpless, and I could see the Commandant of the Marine Corps about to be upended right underneath the broached boat. I was very much worried for him, but he got away neatly after a while."[12]

Many of the marines in the initial assault were not so fortunate. The high surf combined with the inexperience of some of the boat crews caused a number of problems. Some of the LCVPs broached; others smashed into them; and some of the later-arriving boats could not get in to shore and had to discharge their marines in deep water. Others, damaged by collision, could not lower their ramps, and the marines had to clamber over the sides into waist-deep water. More than thirty landing craft were wrecked during the initial phase of the operation. Despite the wrecked boats littering the inadequate sites, more landing craft were sent in. As a result, before these beaches were closed, sixty-four LCVPs and twenty-two LCMs were beached, some of them damaged beyond repair.[13] Such a loss could hardly have been duplicated by severe enemy resistance, and the shortage of boats hampered the unloading of supplies and reserves.

Japanese planes attacked the beachhead three times during D day. The first attack, delivered almost immediately after the landings, did little damage, and seven of the attackers were shot down by New Zealand P-40s flying close cover. Ten minutes later AIRSOLS beat off another, similar attack, destroying eight planes, and the antiaircraft crews on the destroyers claimed four. The next attack, by an estimated seventy planes, occurred just before 1300. The transports, were warned by radar, and all but the *American Legion*, which was grounded on a shoal, moved away from the beach area and took evasive action. The *American Legion* had run aground after being ordered to shift its unloading to the southern beaches. A destroyer remained on guard during the air attack while two tugs pulled the grounded transport off the shoal. The Japanese in the three attacks used 120 planes and lost 26, inflicting no serious damage to either the American ships or marines on shore. The major effect of all the raids was to delay the unloading of supplies and equipment for more than four hours.[14]

The 9th Marines, once ashore, sorted themselves out and moved inland, only to discover that the terrain immediately to the rear of the beaches presented unimagined difficulties. In most places the beaches rose sharply for about ten yards and then fell off into an almost impassable swamp. One observer related that it "was like running across thirty feet of the Sahara and suddenly dropping off into the Everglades."[15] Nevertheless, the marines waded into the swamp using fallen logs and debris to help as they searched for solid ground. By midmorning they had established a narrow perimeter around the beaches and immediately began aggressive patrolling into the interior nearby. They established a strong outpost on the Laruma River and by 1300 had reached the 0-1 line in all areas assigned to them. The three battalions had maintained contact with each other, and despite the heavy jungle, the regiment had tied in to units of the 3d Marines on their right. Without any Japanese opposition, the regimental commander, Colonel Edward Craig, could allow a large number of the riflemen to remain on the beaches to help speed up the unloading. However, with the midmorning diversion of boats to the southern beaches, a great amount of the operational equipment of the 9th Marines was dumped far down the coast, and some was never recovered.

The 3d Raider Battalion had been assigned the task of seizing Puruata Island with one reinforced company in the assault and two in reserve. Lieutenant Colonel Fred Beans, its commander, later recalled the landing:

> One of the platoons of the Japanese company was on Puruata Island. They had three or four deep, well-sandbagged emplace-

ments on the seaward side. And we—this was the plan and I had nothing to do with it—landed back of this island and swept across. In landing all the boats were shot at, but it was small machine gun caliber and other than the boat I was in—I took an LCR which was unarmored because it was the only one left, and there were two Marines killed and one wounded. But other than that we had no casualties getting to the beach and that was only going around the point where they opened up with machine guns.[16]

Two hours after landing, the raiders had a secure beachhead 125 yards inland. Beans committed his reserves early in the afternoon and, supported by 75-mm guns borrowed from the 9th Marines, moved halfway across the island, encountering only sporadic sniper fire

When the marines did meet resistance, the Japanese, although greatly outnumbered, resisted in the same fanatical manner as they had on Guadalcanal and as they would in all future conquests. The marines responded with the a ferocity that would make their very name anathema to the Japanese. One marine and his Japanese counterpart fought a long-drawn-out cops-and-robbers-type shootout that took them across the island. Each used every trick to kill the other until finally they reached the seaward beach, where the Japanese threw down his weapon and jumped in the water. The raider recalled,

I don't know where in the hell he thought he was going. I was too God-damn mad to shoot him. I threw down my gun and helmet, took a good run and dove in after him. The little bastard was scared to death. I grabbed him by the neck and pulled him toward the beach. That was the hardest part—getting him back on solid ground. I couldn't get him up on the beach but went to work on him in shallow water. Then I dragged him up on the sand and kicked his head apart. The slimy bastard. I'd been chasing him for over an hour.[17]

Early in the morning of 2 November, Beans sent the raiders out in a two-pronged attack against the hopelessly outnumbered Japanese. By 1530 all Japanese resistance had ended. The marines had casualties of five killed and thirty-two wounded; twenty-nine Japanese dead were found. The remainder of the estimated seventy enemy soldiers probably escaped to Bougainville.[18]

The 3d Marines, landing south of the Koromokina River, did not have problems with shoals, nor was the surf as high as that to the

70 Bougainville

north, but they were landing directly in front of the main Japanese defenses. The Japanese, estimated at fewer than three hundred men, had no permanent defense line along Yellow 2, Blue 2, and Blue 3, beach sectors. Therefore, the resistance to 2/3 and 3/3, although disturbing to the green troops, was not significant, and within a few minutes after the landing, the few Japanese defenders had been either killed or driven into the jungle. Patrols were then organized and began a cautious move inland, making linkage with the 2d Raider Battalion on the right of 2/3. The Raiders had encountered somewhat more resistance by an estimated reinforced platoon operating from two bunkers and trenches thirty yards inland. Once the bunkers had been blasted away, the remaining Japanese retreated into the dense undergrowth. The swampy terrain behind Yellow 1 made movement into the interior difficult, but by midmorning the raiders had reached the Buretoni Mission Trail and one company had been sent ahead to establish a trail block considerably in advance of the perimeter.[19]

The main Japanese resistance was against 1/3, which landed at Blue 1 beach, immediately adjacent to Cape Torokina. The Japanese had constructed twenty-five large and small log and earthen pillboxes around the perimeter of the cape. Those on the south of the cape were all connected by trenches. Those on the northern shore were not as elaborately interconnected, but one large pillbox measuring six feet by six feet by five feet contained a 75-mm field piece and was supported by two smaller pillboxes, a trench system, and a series of rifle pits. Each of the pillboxes was covered by earth and camouflaged by jungle plants. At best they presented only six feet of vertical rise to an observer, and from a distance they appeared to be nothing but small hillocks.[20] The machine guns in the pillboxes were positioned to give the Japanese interlocking fields of fire.

Only three of the pillboxes had been knocked out by the naval and air strikes prior to the landings. Few amphibious operations had been undertaken prior to Bougainville, and those who planned the operation, both naval and marine, were slow to understand how ineffectual short-term naval bombardment really was in destroying the Japanese capability to resist a landing. During the planning phase for Bougainville one midlevel marine officer, Frederick Henderson, proposed sending the destroyers and available cruisers up to three thousand yards off the beaches to fire point-blank into the areas suspected of being fortified. He bitterly recalled his experience at IMAC headquarters trying to sell his plan to take the beach defenses apart:

There was a Marine lieutenant colonel, and I don't remember the guy's name, fortunately, anymore, he jumped on this. Oh, he jumped all over this—"who the hell ever heard of running ships three or four thousand yards off to the beach? Lie to and shoot . . ." on and on. "Who ever heard of having four cruisers . . . ?" I said, "Well colonel, just wait a minute and I can explain this." Well, maybe he was stupid. It was very clear to me that the guy didn't know what he was talking about. He was stupid. He started talking about 75-mm equivalents, and all that, and he didn't know the faintest goddamned thing about what the hell was going on in naval gunfire.[21]

In the end, as Henderson reported, the staff lieutenant colonel "refused to take our plans and drew up his own and it was an absolute disaster. That's why so many boats were lost going into the beach, even Morison in his history said it was a disaster, the gunfire plan. I am convinced that if they had taken our plan it would have been a cakewalk to have gone in and taken those beaches."[22]

Henderson's comments on the failure of the naval gunfire support plan as adopted are largely correct. The destroyers' gunfire must have seemed awe-inspiring to the marines watching from their LCVPs, but it did little good. Admiral Wilkinson was one who later recognized as much:

> The gunnery performance of our destroyers left much to be desired, when firing on shore targets. Some ships fired short for almost five minutes with all salvos landing in the water. Two or three salvos should have been sufficient to get the point of impact in the target area. Although a short bombardment practice had been fired at EFATE it was not sufficient. Poor antiaircraft gunnery also characterizes most of our new ships on first arrival in the South Pacific. Some training should be conducted at home before sending a ship into a combat area. It is hoped that the gunfire ships for the next operation can be stabilized sufficiently in advance for a thorough course of instruction in bombardment and fire support.[23]

Wilkinson's hopes were not to be achieved until near the end of the war, and lack of long-term sustained naval gun support would force assault troops in the Carolines, Marshalls, and Marianas to waste time and men taking objectives the high command considered already neutralized. On Bougainville this lack would have claimed many more lives than it did had there been more Japanese to man more fixed positions. Even with fewer men than a battalion and only one small-caliber gun, the Japanese on Cape Torokina gave a portent of things to come.

The landing craft bearing 1/3 had immediately come under fire from Puruata Island and the pillboxes on Cape Torokina as they neared the beach. The most devastating came from the 75-mm field-piece, which opened fire when the boats were five hundred yards offshore. It was fortunate for the marines that the Japanese had only one such gun. If there had been more concealed in the bunkers most of the boats carrying the battalion might have been destroyed. Even this single gun could have been more effective, but its emplacement allowed for only a few degrees of lateral movement. Even so, its fire was quite accurate. One of its first shots was a direct hit on the LCP carrying the boat group commander. This fact and the need for other boats to take evasive action resulted in a mixup of the assault waves. The Japanese had correctly surmised that the unarmed LCPs carried more important personnel and concentrated their fire on these. Most of the six boats hit were LCPs and the loss of the boat commanders later added to the confusion on the beach. One of the LCVPs hit only 30 yards from shore was Boat 62, carrying two squads of Company C, a demolition squad and a detachment from Company C, 19th Engineers. The first shell hit the upper part of the ramp, killing the coxswain; then two more struck the boat. One of the squad leaders, Sergeant McAllister, recalled,

> After the first shell hit, the men in the forward part of the boat fell back toward the center as if a big wave had pushed them over. A shell fragment from the second hit me in the left thigh. The boat grounded and I started over the side. It was an awful mess. Bloody men pulled themselves off the deck and forced themselves over the side. One man had part of his back blown off. Everyone kept hold of his rifle. Some of them only had a half a rifle. The water was up to my chin. As I looked back I saw that Smith wasn't going to make it; he had a wound in his head. He was one of my boys. I went back, pulled him in and dragged him behind a coconut log.[24]

One of the casualties was Lieutenant Colonel Leonard Mason, the battalion commander, who was wounded but nevertheless continued to supervise operations on the beach. Almost all units that landed under heavy machine gun and mortar fire were out of position, in a reverse order to that planned. Only B Company landed at the proper location on the left of the battalion's line. Company A was immediately to the right in the position planned for Company C, and Company C found itself to the extreme right near the point of the cape. Elements of Headquarters Company and the reserve company upon landing found that instead of being behind the front line, they were a part of the assault units directly engaged with the Japanese. Despite the mixup and the concentrated fire from the Japanese machine guns and mortars, the battalion's losses were relatively light—fourteen men killed on the boats and twelve more on the beach.[25]

Even during the worst of the confusion the discipline and previous training paid dividends. Junior and noncommissioned officers took charge on the beach and in the scrub bush and began to attack the line of entrenchments. The 3d Marine Division historian noted:

> Some of the bitterest hand-to-hand fighting of the campaign took place here, in the narrow trenches outside the pillboxes. Men fought with clubbed weapons, knives and fists. Early in the struggle, Major Mason was wounded by enemy machine-gun fire. Scorning advice to await reinforcements, the wounded battalion commander told his second in command, "Get the hell in there and fight!" It was one of the first occasions in the Pacific where the amphibious assault troops encountered an occupied and organized immediate beach defense practically untouched by preliminary bombardment and was termed by some correspondents at the time as "the bloodiest beach in the entire Solomons campaign."[26]

One of the lessons learned from the actions on Guadalcanal and New Georgia was that taking one bunker in a complex weakened the entire defensive system. Ultimately the marines organized fire teams built around the BARs, which placed a high volume of fire into the embrasures while others flanked the bunkers and knocked them out by dropping grenades down the ventilators or attacking the rear with rifle fire. One by one, the bunkers were taken.

The most troublesome of the pillboxes and the one that had caused the most casualties was the one with the 75-mm fieldpiece. Sergeant Robert Owens of Company A, noting that grenades and rifle fire were having little effect on the pillbox, led three other riflemen and a BAR man in a direct assault on the gun emplacements. It is certain that Owens was not thinking of being gallant; nevertheless his actions won him the first of the ten Congressional Medals of Honor won by the 3d Division. His citation describes the action succinctly. Owens placed his men so their support would minimize the covering fire from adjacent bunkers. He moved ahead to within ten yards. Then, "choosing a moment that provided a fair opportunity for passing these bunkers he charged into the mouth of the steady firing cannon and entered the emplacement through the fire port, driving the gun crew out of the rear door insuring their destruction before he himself was killed." Silencing the main Japanese bunker undoubtedly, as Owens's citation noted, "contributed immeasurably to the success of the vital landing operations."[27] But there were equally heroic actions by other marine fire teams, which by early afternoon had eliminated the last bunker. Later 1/3 counted 153 Japanese bodies in the Cape Torokina area.[28]

By early afternoon the guns of the 12th Marines had been landed, and as planned, one battery was assigned to each landing team. Men of Battery B, attached to the 9th Marines, had a particularly difficult time because of the swamp immediately to the rear of most of the area assigned. It was necessary to use amphibian tractors to move the guns through the water to suitable high points, set them up, and then off-load the ammunition and supplies onto rubber boats. The operation was further hampered by personnel shortages: many of the crews had been detached to help unload cargo on the crowded beach.

The other batteries faced equal difficulties but all were in place and registered and ready for firing by dusk. Some of the 90-mm antiaircraft guns were brought ashore immediately after the assault waves along with the big guns of the seacoast battery. Men of the 3d Defense Battalion had landed by noon, and within a few hours, the smaller-caliber guns were brought up to support the defense of the perimeter during the first night.

The unsung heroes of D day were the men of the 3d Service Battalion and other marines drawn from various combat and support units, who worked without pause to unload the five APAs and three AKAs. Admiral Wilkinson planned to have all the ships unloaded by nightfall. To achieve this objective the assault units had been stripped to provide men for moving cargo ashore. During the unloading phase 6 officers and 120 men remained onboard a ship to work the cargo onto the boats, and 60 more became riders to direct the cargo-laden boats to appropriate landing spots. Another 200 marines were selected to stay on each beach to help unload. Later, when it became apparent that Japanese resistance was slight, even more troops were detached to handle cargo. It is estimated that approximatley 40 percent of the landing force was involved in shore-party work.[29] Some of the alligator tractors (LVTs) of the 3d Amphibious Tractor Battalion had plowed onto the beach following the first waves. Despite certain limitations, these proved a godsend not only on D day but in the subsequent phases of moving into the interior. They could operate in the swamps and jungle where it would have been impossible for any other vehicles to move.[30]

Small detachments of the 71st, 25th, 53d, and 75th Construction battalions (seabees) also landed immediately after the assault troops and began to unload what equipment they had brought with them. Because of the shallow water, the LSTs could not get any closer than seventy-five feet off the beach. So portable ramps of sufficient size and strength to support the heavy equipment had to be constructed. The first large pieces of equipment off-loaded were the bulldozers, which by D + 1 had already begun to make roads and help move supplies. The seabees, though undersupplied, nevertheless improvised sledges and attached these to tractors to pull their equipment to what high ground could be found in front of the beach. Then they established temporary workshops and fitting stations.[31]

Meanwhile marines in the communications sections were slipping and crawling with their heavy drums through the swamp and undergrowth, at first under sniper fire, laying wire that would tie together the forward units. These, in turn, were connected to the rear-area command posts. In some cases the wire crews had to use a compass to navigate through the swampy terrain. Despite all such difficulties the communications teams had laid more than a hundred miles of wire and all units were tied together before dark. This communications network enabled the 12th Marines to call in harassing fire against suspected Japanese positions during the night.[32]

One commentator on the Bougainville landing was able to capture something of the problems of the shore parties:

> Even under the best conditions, the unloading phase of a landing operation is a hot, rugged chore. With a high surf pounding against a narrow strip of sand backed by a swamp of dense jungle undergrowth, with a set deadline of daylight hours, and under the scorching heat of a South Sea November sun, the job was an exhausting nightmare. Working parties were punching with every last ounce of blood to get ammunition, oil, supplies, vehicles, rations, and water out of the boats and above the high-water line. Shoreparty commanders were frantically trying to find a few square feet of dump space and discovering nothing but swamp all along the beach. Seabees and Engineers were racking their brains

and bodies in a desperate effort to construct any kind of a road to high ground where vehicles could be parked, oil stored, and ammunition stacked. But there *wasn't* any high ground for thousands of yards—only a few scattered small islands of semi-inundated land surrounded by a sticky stinking mire. And hour after hour boats roared in to the beach jammed with supplies.[33]

Although it would be days before the near chaotic supply situation on the beaches was sorted out, the eight transports were unloaded and left Empress Augusta Bay before nightfall, headed back to Guadalcanal. The four cargo ships containing much of the division's heavy equipment were still being unloaded when Admiral Wilkinson, fearing a Japanese naval night attack, ordered them to leave by 1700 with the transports. He had definite reports of a Japanese cruiser force, which might reach the Bougainville area by early morning of 2 November. In the worst case, the cargo ships would be easy prey for the heavy-gun cruisers. However, at 2300 the cargo ships and their destroyer escorts were ordered to reverse course and head back to Cape Torokina to be unloaded on D + 1.

By the close of the first day the marines even in the contested 1/3 sector had reached their initial objectives and had dug in for an uncomfortable night of continuous rain. The perimeter of the division had been established by directing the landing teams to push forward a certain number of yards since there was nothing on the available maps to indicate outstanding terrain features to aim for. The initial objective varied in depth from approximately six hundred yards on the left to a thousand yards in front of the cape. The extreme left flank, held by a platoon of Company G of the 9th Marines, was considerably short of the Laruma River and would have been extremely vulnerable if the Japanese had had any significant number of troops in that area; luckily, most of the disorganized remnants of the Japanese units were located southeast of Cape Torokina. At dusk there was only sporadic sniper fire directed at 1/3 in the vicinity of the cape plantation and later there was an attack against a company of the 2d Raiders at the road block on the Mission Trail. Otherwise, the perimeter line was generally quiet. Of course, the marines on line had no way of knowing if this situation would continue. One marine has described his feelings:

> By six o'clock that night it was dark and every officer and man on the line and in the many C.P.s was in his foxhole. For these were trained men and they knew the law of the jungle: each man must be in his foxhole at dark and there he must stay until dawn.

Anyone *out* of a foxhole during the hours of darkness was a Jap. Sudden death for the careless. From seven o'clock in the evening till dawn, with only centipedes and lizards and scorpions and mosquitoes begging to get acquainted—wet, cold, exhausted, but unable to sleep—you lay there and shivered and thought and hated and prayed. But you stayed there. You didn't cough, you didn't snore, you changed your position with the least amount of noise. For it was still great to be alive.[34]

Despite all the problems encountered on D day and the discomfort of the heat and rain, the marines held a secure lodgment on Bougainville. Phase one of the operation was complete.

5. Naval Actions

The major threat to the beachhead established by the marines on Bougainville would not come from the Japanese army units there. General Hyakutaki was very slow to react to the lodgment at Cape Torokina, and even had he been more concerned, the terrain, weather, and lack of roads on the island would have prevented an immediate counterattack in force. Any significant Japanese counterthrust would come from the sea. As Admiral Wilkinson had surmised the Japanese, once alerted to the invasion, would muster all their available naval and air forces and attempt to isolate the invaders by destroying the transports, cargo vessels, and the covering naval force. This conclusion had led to his decision to land the two marine regiments abreast as quickly as possible and to have the transports unloaded and out of the bay by nightfall of D day.

Admiral Koga, commander of the Combined Fleet, the bulk of which was at Truk, was in many ways a prisoner of his and his predecessor's obsession with a great final battle with the main U.S. fleet units. He believed he should husband the bulk of his naval force in a central locale to be able to respond to such a challenge, which he believed would come in the Central Pacific, not the South Pacific area. Aside from his preconceptions, he had very real problems. It was apparent by the fall of 1943 that the United States fleet had recovered from the devastating Pearl Harbor strike and that Admiral Nimitz was preparing to carry out offensive operations, probably in the Marshall Islands. Another inescapable fact was the severe damage done to the Japanese fleet at the Coral Sea, Midway, and the Guadalcanal naval engagements. By the close of 1942 Japan had lost six carriers and seventeen destroyers. Action by U.S. surface and air units and particularly submarines in the three months prior to the Kolombangara action had destroyed over a quarter of a million tons of shipping.[1] There was no possibility that Japanese shipyards could replace those ships, and the portents for future actions were even more devastating for Japan. All these conditions supported Koga's decision to husband his air and surface power in the Central Pacific.

Admiral Kusaka from his vantage point at Rabaul saw the situation differently from the planners at Imperial Headquarters in Tokyo and at Combined Fleet Headquarters at Truk. Vice Admiral Shigeru Fukudome, Koga's chief of staff, later recalled that Admiral Koga, conforming to the defensive posture earlier agreed upon, had refused repeated requests from Rabaul for reinforcements. He insisted that Kusaka make do with what force he had in hand. Yet the air actions with Kenney's 5th Air Force and those related to the Allied occupation of the central Solomons had so reduced the air strength at Rabaul that something had to be done to try and wrest air control over New Britain from the Americans. Koga decided to send a total of approximately 250 planes from the five carriers of Admiral Jisaburo Ozawa's Air Fleet. Koga specifically stated that the bulk of these were on only a ten-day loan, and presumably after the situation had been stabilized they were to return to the main fleet. The invasion of Bougainville upset these plans, occurring just before the planes were scheduled to return. As Admiral Fukudome noted, although the planes were not originally to be used in such offensive operations, Kusaka "just couldn't stand by and not employ them."[2]

Similar confusion in strategy and tactics could be seen in the Japanese utilization of surface units. Koga had no intention of committing his carriers and heavy units to the defense of Rabaul. Failing major reinforcements prior to the Bougainville landings, Admiral Kusaka, who had commanded all 8th Fleet units in the South Pacific since February, had to counter the actions of the American naval forces supporting General MacArthur and at the same time those of Admiral Halsey operating in the Solomons area, and he simply did not have the ships available for both. Furthermore, there had been few opportunities for the crews of the various ships at Rabaul to train together, especially for night maneuvers.

At Bougainville, however, the key factor in the Japanese responses was the lack of good intelligence reports that would have given the planners at Rabaul the necessary information to intercept the Empress Augusta Bay task force.

The first reaction to the impending invasion came at 1000 on 31

October, when the naval command at Rabaul ordered Vice Admiral Sentaro Omori to take his Rabaul assault force and intercept the American task force, which, the Japanese had discovered, had left Guadalcanal. However inadequate their overall intelligence, the Japanese were aware of Halsey's weakness in major ships and surmised that Omori's force would be sufficient to block any landing. Omori got under way at 1500 on 31 October and set course for the Treasury Islands, believing that the American task force was heading toward the Shortlands. He had two heavy cruisers, the *Myoko* and *Haguro*; two light cruisers, the *Sendai* and *Nagara*; and two destroyers. A combination of bad weather and poor positioning of his force prevented Omori from locating Wilkinson's invasion fleet. Although he received a report early on the morning of 1 November that the American ships were near Buka, Omori conducted further futile searches by observation planes and then decided to return to Rabaul. He anchored there at 0900 on 1 November, only to learn that the Americans were already ashore at Cape Torokina.[3]

Admiral Omori was underway again within six hours, this time with a much larger force. There had been no time to formulate a battle plan. In all probability Omori had little time to discuss the situation with his immediate superior, Vice Admiral Tomoshige Samejima, and with the men who would command the flanks of his attack force, Rear Admirals Matsuji Ijuin, who had fought the Americans to a draw off northern Vella Lavella in August, and Morikazi Osugi. Omori's main force—consisting of two heavy cruisers, the *Myoko* and *Haguro*; two light cruisers, the *Agano* and *Sendai*; and six destroyers—headed out to rendezvous with five old destroyers in St. George's Channel. These ships were to serve as personnel transports, each one carrying two hundred troops who would stage a counterinvasion of Bougainville at Mutupino Point near the village of Toroko, just south of the marine beachhead. Sailing into George's channel, Omori's larger ships were to rendezvous with the transports and proceed immediately southward toward their objective. However, loading the troops took longer than planned, and it was not until 1830 that Omori was able to proceed from the rendezvous. Shortly thereafter a U.S. submarine was sighted, and Omori altered course to avoid possible detection. This evasion cost precious time too, and because the old destroyer transports were slow, Omori could not make up the lost time.[4]

At approximately 1920 a lone American plane sighted the flotilla and dropped a single bomb, which exploded next to the *Sendai*. Omori was already apprehensive about American submarines and the possibility of a night engagement and concluded that landing the troops on Bougainville was too dangerous. He recommended to his superiors that this part of the operation be canceled. Omori believed that the American transports were still in Empress Augusta Bay and that he could destroy them all, thus isolating the marines on Bougainville. Three hours after he had requested that the counterlandings be aborted, he received permission from Rabaul, and the five destroyer transports headed back. Omori increased speed to thirty-two knots, heading for a point south of Sand Island.[5]

Admiral Merrill's Task Force 39 after its bombardment missions on 1 November had retired to the vicinity of Vella Lavella for cleanup and to allow the crews a short period of relaxation. One part of the task force, Destroyer Division 45, commanded by Captain Arleigh Burke, had been sent farther away, to Kula Gulf to take on fuel from a barge. Completing this assignment by late afternoon, he took his ships at full speed north to join Merrill, who had already been alerted about Omori's force. Admiral Halsey, fully aware of the condition of TF 39, nevertheless had no choice but to order Merrill to intercept the Japanese. The main body of TF 39 consisted of the four new light cruisers *Montpelier, Cleveland, Columbia,* and *Denver.* There were also eight destroyers divided equally between Destroyer Divisions 45 and 46.[6]

Admiral Merrill was kept informed of the size, direction, and speed of the Japanese force by two army reconnaissance planes. He knew that Omori outgunned him, and although the specific details were not then known, he had to be aware that the Japanese "long-lance" torpedoes gave their destroyers a tremendous advantage. These carried over half a ton of high explosives, twice as much as American torpedos, and were effective at ranges between sixteen thousand and twenty thousand yards. Given these facts, Merrill decided his main function was to protect the beachhead, and he selected a meeting point for the two fleets approximately twenty miles west of Cape Torokina. He arranged his force along a north-south axis with the cruisers in the center and the leading destroyer of Burke's Division three miles ahead. The first destroyer of Commander B.L. Austin's Division 46 was approximately a thousand yards behind the last cruiser, the *Denver.* Merrill did not intend to tie the destroyers tightly to the cruisers; instead, they were to go on the offensive, firing their torpedoes even before the cruisers got within range of Omori's fleet. He hoped that the destroyers could get within range before the Japanese launched their own more deadly torpedoes.

Admiral Omori, although he outgunned Task Force 39, was handicapped in two ways. First he lacked specific information concerning the position of the American ships and the size of the flotilla. Even after the battle, when he ordered a retreat to Rabaul, he still did not know how many American ships had taken part.[7] Despite his ignorance of the units he was to engage, he had set his course directly toward Empress Augusta Bay because he had received reports that the transports were still unloading there. In fact they were almost forty miles to the south. His second problem was poor radar. As he said later, "We had some modified aircraft radar sets in action but they were unreliable. I do not know whether the sets or operators were poor, but I did not have confidence in them."[8] He therefore had to depend on visual sightings either from his ships or from spotter aircraft. Thus, fifteen minutes after the engagement opened he recorded in his time log, "The U.S. Forces still not in fixed position."[9]

Merrill, on the other hand, had trustworthy radar. Just before 0230 on 2 November, the radar on the *Montpelier* had picked up the Japanese ships at a range of 35,900 yards, and Merrill then ordered the destroyer divisions to proceed with the agreed upon plan. Ten minutes later he reversed the course of his cruisers to due south and ordered Austin's destroyers to attack the southern flank of the Japanese force. Burke was to take an intercept course that would place his ships in position to launch their torpedoes at the left flank of the Japanese ships. Merrill's cruisers were in the favorable position to cross the T if Omori continued his course.

The battle, once joined, broke down into three interconnected engagements. The major ship of Omori's left flank, the *Sendai*, began one engagement at 0250 by launching eight torpedoes toward Merrill's cruisers. these missed the main targets but one struck the destroyer *Foote*, which was out of position, and blew off a large part of the stern. Two other destroyers were slightly damaged when they struck each other while maneuvering to avoid the damaged *Foote*. Commander Austin, who had misunderstood Merrill's orders, was not in position to launch his torpedoes until after the cruisers had opened fire. Burke's Destroyer Division 45, as planned, closed on Omori's left flank and fired twenty-five torpedoes shortly after *Sendai* had launched its own. All missed because Omori just at that time had ordered his ships to make a hard right turn. After launching their torpedoes Burke's ships separated, and it was over an hour before they could be gathered together to turn full circle and return to their firing positions.

In the meanwhile Merrill's cruisers opened up at 0250 with their six-inch guns. The full weight of metal struck the *Sendai*, jamming its rudder. Then a series of explosions rocked the ship, and it began to sink. Two destroyers of the left-flank group, the *Shiratsuyu* and the *Samidare*, while maneuvering at high speed to avoid the incoming six-inch shells, collided and were thus removed from the battle. The initial success of American gunnery combined with this collision made the contest more equal, but Omori's heavy cruisers, with their eight-inch guns had not yet been engaged.

Omori still could not locate his enemy and so began a 360° loop followed by the right-flank column. The third ship in that column, the destroyer *Hatsukaze*, was struck by the flagship *Myoko* when the destroyer, trying to dodge the American salvos, cut across the *Myoko*'s bow. Soon after, the *Myoko* was hit by six 6-inch shells. Fortunately for Omori, four of them were duds and the other two did not cause enough damage to slow down the flagship. At about 0320 Omori finally opened fire with his heavy armament, but not with the effect one might imagine, given the relatively close range of the two fleets. The *Denver* received three hits forward, which did not detonate but let in enough water to slow the ship down, forcing the other three cruisers to match its slower speed. Soon after, Japanese planes dropped flares to light up Merrill's ships, and the eight-inch guns of the *Myoko* and *Haguro* increased their fire, but still without effect. According to Omori's time chart, the *Myoko* had launched four long-lance torpedoes and the *Haguro* six soon after the main American force had been sighted. Seven minutes later he received the report that "1 torpedo hit leading U.S. cruiser, 2 torpedo hits on second U.S. cruiser, 2 torpedo hits on third U.S. cruiser. Shell fire also reported on U.S. Force."[10] Soon after the U.S. cruisers disappeared from view, probably in their own smoke, and Omari believed that they were sinking or retreating.

Admiral Omori, who had fought the entire engagement with faulty information, now concluded that he had at the very least seriously crippled the Americans. His force had also been hurt. The *Sendai* was sinking, and three of his six destroyers were out of action. He therefore altered his course 180° and began retiring toward Rabaul. The engagement, however, was not yet over. Burke's destroyers were in hot pursuit of the damaged *Shiratsuyu* and *Samidare* and as they passed the sinking *Sendai*, they pumped a few more rounds into the ill-fated cruiser. A stroke of luck saved the two damaged Japanese destroyers when Commander Austin confused Burke into believing that the ship he saw turning northward was Austin's ship, the *Spence*, which had been struck by a shell. Actually, the *Spence* was losing speed, had dropped out of the column, and was on the other side of the Japanese destroyer Burke was pursuing. Burke gave up pursuit, turned 180°, and joined the *Spence* in battering the damaged *Hatsukaze*, which sank shortly after 0540 with no survivors. Omori with the remains of his Rabual assault force arrived safely back at Rabaul in the early afternoon of 2 November, only to suffer a raid by planes from the 5th Air Force.

Admiral Merrill at 0500 had refused Burke's request to pursue the Japanese and ordered him to gather in the destroyers, take the damaged *Foote* in tow, and rendezvous with the cruisers. He expected a heavy air attack as soon as it was light, and he had not long to wait. A Japanese scout plane had spotted the cruisers and reported the position to Rabaul. Ninety-eight of the recently arrived naval planes, most of them Zeros, took off immediately to attack TF 39. Merrill requested that all available fighters in the central Solomons be vectored to his position to protect his ships. Bad weather delayed most of the AIR-SOLS planes, but eight Hellcats, one marine Corsair, three P-38s, and four New Zealand P-40s did manage to take off. These shot down eight Japanese planes before they reached the cruisers. Later, Allied fighter cover claimed an additional eight planes.[11]

Because of this scant air cover, Merrill's ships were basically on their own. The air attack began a few minutes before 0800 and lasted for approximately twenty minutes. The eighteen Val divebombers attacked in well-spaced groups of three giving the gunners on board the ships a chance to concentrate on each wave. The ships of Task Force 39 were in the standard circular antiaircraft formation, and every gun fired continuously from the time that the five- and six-inch guns opened up at fourteen thousand yards. The maneuvering of the ships, the cordons of fire, and the inexperience of the Japanese pilots made the Japanese sortie a costly one. Admiral Merrill reported that his guns had claimed seventeen Japanese planes. In return the Japanese pilots made only two hits on the entire force, both on the *Montpelier*, causing minor damage and killing one sailor, before breaking off the attack at 0812.[12]

One noted naval historian was ambivalent in his analysis of the actions of Merrill's force, particularly the accuracy of fire from the cruisers. While in the main approving of Merrill's strategy and tactics, his statistics indicate that 4,591 rounds of six-inch and 705 rounds of five-inch shells were used with the net result of perhaps twenty hits on the Japanese ships. Clearly, the gunners' accuracy, even at the lower range, left much to be desired.[13] Nevertheless, Merrill did what he had planned. He blocked the entrance to Empress Augusta Bay, fought a night action against heavier ships, sank one light cruiser and one destroyer, and in the course of the battle forced a collision that damaged two other Japanese destroyers. All this was accomplished while incurring torpedo damage to only one of his own ships. Merrill then successfully beat off a heavy air attack without loss or even serious damage to the ships. Although no one suspected as much at the time, this was to be the last major surface engagement in the Solomons area. Never again would a powerful Japanese fleet challenge American superiority in the region.

At the outset of the naval action Commodore Reifsnider had moved his four cargo ships southwest to a position approximately forty miles from the battle. Informed at 0438 the Omori's ships had retired, he was ordered to return to Cape Torokina to complete the unloading.[14] Merrill, whose ships were retiring to Purvis Bay, was ordered at midday to cover the unloading of the transports. The unloading of the cargo was completed at 1500, before Merrill's ships could arrive at the cape, but he rendezvoued with the transports on their way back to Guadalcanal and escorted them through the night before releasing them near Rendova to a smaller force sent out from Guadalcanal.

Although cheered by the reports of Merrill's victory, Admiral Halsey was soon confronted with a problem of potentially greater magnitude. As Admiral Fukudome recalled, Admiral Koga at Truk had finally decided to commit "the crack units" of the yet undamaged 2d Fleet "to cooperate with the carrier-based planes which had been sent from Admiral Ozawa's Fleet in order to check the BOUGAINVILLE operations."[15] It is clear from Admiral Fukudome's statement that Koga, urged on by Admirals Kusaka and Samejima at Rabaul, had become convinced that with adequate force he could still destroy the American naval units in the Solomons preparatory to wiping out the beachhead at Torokina. He saw no reason to send his carriers south since their planes were already at Rabaul, and he did not want to chance his battleships that close to land-based air power. He concluded that his heavy cruisers could do the job.

This formidable portion of the 2d Fleet, under the command of Admiral Takeo Kurita, departed Truk on 3 November. It consisted of seven heavy cruisers, the *Tako*, *Maya*, *Atago*, *Suzuya*, *Mogami*, *Chikuma*, and *Chokai*; a light cruiser, the *Noshiro*; four destroyers; and a number of service ships. Kurita's fleet was sighted at approximately 1200 on 4 November. Halsey's intelligence officers concluded that it would pause only long enough to refuel and then proceed to Bougainville. As Halsey later put it, "This was the most desperate emergency that confronted me in my entire term as Com So Pac,"[16] for eight APDs and eight LSTs carrying 3,548 men of the 21st Marines along with over five thousand tons of supplies and equipment had left Guadalcanal on 4 November for Cape Torokina. If Admiral Kurita's force were not stopped, the six destroyers screening the transports would prove no match for the heavy-gun cruisers.[17] In addition, the third echelon, which would bear the army's 148th Regimental Combat Team of the 37th Division, was slated to leave Guadalcanal on 7 November. If the Japanese broke through Halsey's defenses, this movement of troops and supplies would have to be halted.

Because attention at Nimitz's headquarters at Pearl Harbor was focused on the upcoming operation in the Gilberts, Halsey's earlier requests for more ships had been refused. Halsey did not have even one heavy cruiser to oppose Kurita. Aside from Merrill's group and a few unattached destroyers, the only force available to counter the new Japanese threat was Task Force 38, commanded by Rear Admiral Frederick C. Sherman, which fortunately had just finished refueling south of Guadalcanal. The heart of this force was the old carrier *Saratoga* and the new light carrier *Princeton*, screened by two light cruisers, the *San Diego* and *San Juan*, and nine destroyers. Conventional wisdom on the use of aircraft carriers at that time dictated that they should remain as far as possible away from land-based air, and Halsey knew that the Japanese had at least two hundred planes at Rabaul. Therefore, it was possible that if he used TF 38 to strike at Kurita's cruisers, all its air groups could be destroyed.

Halsey, however, was a risk taker, as he had shown earlier at Guadalcanal. His operations officers prepared a plan to send Sherman's task force to attack Rabaul, stating the priority of smashing the cruisers. Admiral Carney, his chief of staff, recalled that Halsey fully expected Sherman's force to be either heavily damaged or sunk, an especially fearful prospect considering that his own son was on board one of the carriers. Before making the decision Halsey "suddenly looked 150 years old." Despite his trepidations, he said, "Let 'er go."[18] At 1638 a dispatch was sent to Sherman ordering him to proceed with his task force at maximum speed to launch an attack on Rabaul. General Twining's composite air force would provide whatever support it could. Halsey also asked General MacArthur to send his 5th Air Force for a joint attack on all shipping in Rabaul harbor. Such a strike by General Kenny's planes should hit their targets at approximately 1200 on 5 November. Sherman's planes, if all went according to plan, would have arrived over target approximately an hour earlier.

The Japanese command at Rabaul must have known that Kurita's fleet would soon draw increased air attacks. The Allies had shown that they would challenge Japanese air and surface forces anywhere in the vicinity of New Britain. For example, on 4 November B-24s from AIRSOLS had bombed the tankers *Nichiei Maru* and *Nissho Maru*, a part of Kurita's rear echelon, damaging them so severely that they had to be towed back to Truk. On the same day, north of Kavieng, Liberators caught three troop-laden transports escorted by a cruiser and two destroyers and protected by fighters. Nevertheless, the B-24s scored hits on two of the transports damaging one so severely that it had to be towed to Rabaul.[19]

Admiral Sherman on receipt of Halsey's order initiated a desperate race to bring Task Force 38 to a launching point off Cape Torokina approximately 230 miles from Rabaul. Weather was kind to Sherman, and calm seas allowed the ships to travel at full speed. As soon as they arrived at a suitable location, the two carriers turned into the five-knot wind and at 0900 on 5 November began launching planes. The *Saratoga* launched sixteen Avenger torpedo planes and twenty-two Dauntless dive bombers. The smaller *Princeton* could put only seven Avengers in the air. The bombing echelons were covered by fifty-two Hellcat fighters. In all, ninety-seven planes were committed, and the task force was denuded of all available planes, covered only by combat air patrols from Vella Lavella.[20]

The hastily developed plans called for the attacking planes to make their initial run at fairly low level with the dive bombers gaining altitude just before arriving over St. George's Channel. The fighters, both low-level and those protecting the dive bombers, maintained position only eight hundred to a thousand feet higher than the bombers. Rabaul harbor was ringed with antiaircraft guns, and as the American planes approached at approximately 1020, they put up a dense ring of flak. Seventy Japanese fighters had scrambled to intercept, but these made a serious tactical blunder in waiting for the incoming planes to break up into smaller groups. Instead, the Americans kept their tight formation, proceeding directly through the flak. The Japanese pilots, unwilling to fly through their own antiaircraft fire, were prevented from engaging the bombers until they had finished inside the harbor. By then the Zeros would have to deal with the Hellcats as well. The action inside Rabaul's defenses was largely dictated by *Saratoga*'s air group commander, Henry Caldwell, who flew above the bombers in an Avenger to select targets and take photos.[21]

The dive bombers aimed for Blanche Bay, the outer harbor of Rabaul, and peeled off at 14,500 feet. They selected their targets, approached them on a line parallel to the ship's movements, and dived through the intense flak, releasing their bombs at approximately two thousand feet. The Hellcat fighters stayed with the bombers until they began their dives and then remained higher up but as close as possible to them on their run away from the harbor.[22] The Avengers timed their approach to drop their torpedoes, which were set to run at a depth of six feet, just after the dive bombers had released their loads. They, too, paralleled the targets at first but then turned 90° before delivering the torpedoes at approximately two hundred feet above the water. Unlike the dive bombers, they had little flak to worry about. The raid lasted less than thirty minutes, ending at about 1044.[23]

The attack devastated Japanese plans although no ships were sunk. The *Maya* had begun to leave the harbor at the time of the attack but was struck in the catapult area by a bomb, which set off a series of explosions, gutting all the engine rooms, causing heavy casualties, and making navigation impossible. The *Mogami* managed to clear the harbor but only after being hit by a torpedo, which flooded number 1 and 2 turrets. *Mogami's* captain stopped the ship in order to put out the fires. Later that evening it was able to make for Truk. The *Atago* suffered three very near misses, which damaged its hull, armament, and machinery. The *Tako* took a bomb on the starboard side, which damaged its hull and machinery. The *Chikuma* received only slight damage and was able to depart for Truk at 2038. The *Suzuya*, which was just preparing for refueling, took evasive action, was only slightly damaged, and provided a part of the escort that evening for the badly wounded *Mogami*. The three light cruisers *Agano*, *Noshiro*, and *Yubari* were not hit, and only three destroyers suffered any damage at all.[24] The Rabaul command ordered all the ships that could move out of the harbor and later all the damaged ships of the 2d Fleet back to Truk. The more heavily damaged ones were eventually brought back to Japan for major repairs.

Despite the heavy flak over the target and the presence of seventy Japanese fighters, the navy lost only five bombers and five fighters while destroying at least eleven Zeros and probably fourteen more.[25] At approximately 1300 the *Saratoga* and *Princeton* had taken on the last of their planes, and Sherman, expecting a Japanese counterstrike, hastily moved his task force southeastward. Nevertheless, a Japanese scout plane discovered it at midafternoon and Kusaka immediately dispatched eighteen torpedo bombers after the Americans. Just at dusk the Japanese discovered what they believed to be the task force and attacked. Although they later claimed a great air victory, in reality they struck at an LCI and a PT boat escorting an LCT back from Cape Torokina. A torpedo lodged in the engine room of the LCI and killed one man.[26] That was the extent of the damage to the "task force." In return, the Japanese lost one plane. It was hardly an even exchange, and no compensation at all for the havoc wreaked earlier upon the 2d Fleet.

General Kenney discussed Halsey's request with General MacArthur, who approved Kenney's plan to support Sherman's raid. He intended not to try to duplicate what the navy had done but to take advantage of the presumption that most of the Japanese planes would be airborne searching for navy planes and the carriers. Kenney therefore decided to bomb the warehouse area on the west side of the harbor and thus destroy as much of the valuable supplies as possible. As planned, twenty-seven B-24s and sixty-seven P-38s hit Rabaul a few minutes after noon on 5 November, causing considerable damage. They were challenged by only fifteen fighters, whose pilots did not seem eager to engage the P-38s. Kenney's planes destroyed only two Zeros while losing one P-38.[27] Those unfamiliar with the results of medium-high-level bombing early in the war might fault Kenney for not going directly after the damaged cruisers. In fact, however, ships were difficult for heavy bombers to hit; they were a much more practical target for low-level dive bombing. Kenney simply went after assured targets that could not take evasive action.

Admiral Halsey was overjoyed with the results of Sherman's air strike. "It is real music to me," he radioed Sherman, "and opens the stops for a funeral dirge for Tojo's Rabaul."[28] Nevertheless, Halsey's operations in the Solomons were still hampered by Nimitz's overpreparation for the Tarawa and Makin operations scheduled for 20 November. Nimitz and his staff, believing that the main elements of the Japanese fleet at Truk would attempt to prevent any breach in the outward Central Pacific defenses, did not wish to weaken their awesome covering force. That force was originally planned to have eleven carriers and twelve battleships, together with supporting cruisers and destroyers lying close off Makin and Tarawa to counter any serious Japanese threat.[29] Nimitz eventually reconsidered Halsey's weakened position, however, and detached a carrier group consisting of the new carriers *Essex* and *Bunker Hill* and the light carrier *Independence* from his main force and sent them south. This new force under the command of Rear Admiral Alfred Montgomery, designated Task Group 50.3, would give Halsey an additional 45 torpedo bombers, 69 dive bombers, and 120 fighters.[30] Unfortunately, the carriers arrived too late to be used in the air strike, anchoring in the harbor of Espiritu Santo on 5 November, the same day that Sherman's planes were hitting Rabaul. As soon as Halsey could gather the necessary destroyers for a screen, he planned to use the new force.

Halsey's headquarters decided to hit Rabaul on 11 November with a three-pronged attack: Sherman's Task Force 38 and Montgomery's Task Group 50.3 from the southeast and Kenney's bombers from New

Guinea. In the end, fog and rain enveloped New Guinea on 11 November, preventing Kenney's planes from participating, but the other two strikes went off as planned. Sherman launched his planes at 0830 on 11 November from a point near Green Island approximately 225 miles from Rabaul. The bombers and fighters had to fly through heavy cloud cover and rain squalls. Over the harbor they were attacked by sixty-eight Zeros from Lakunai, Vunakanau, and Tobera airfields. The bomber pilots attacked almost blindly. They missed the heavy cruisers *Maya* and *Chokai*, hidden by the squall in the inner harbor, but a torpedo struck the new light cruiser *Agano* in the outer harbor, blowing off a large portion of its stern and flooding its engine room.[31]

Montgomery's task group after an all-night high-speed approach launched its planes 160 miles southeast of Rabaul. The two big carriers put up eighty planes each, while the *Independence* sent up twenty-five more. Protection for the group was provided by navy Corsairs and Hellcats from New Georgia, which landed and refueled on the carriers. The attacking planes included thirty-three SB2C Helldivers, which its pilots called the "Beast," the new dive bomber that would soon replace the sturdy SBD Dauntless throughout the fleet.

This massive attack achieved less success than Sherman's attack on 5 November simply because most of the Japanese ships present then had been sent back to Truk. Nevertheless, pilots did manage to find some targets. The destroyer *Naganami* was severely damaged by a torpedo and had to be towed into harbor. Another destroyer, the *Suzunami*, was not as fortunate. It was dive-bombed and sunk near the entrance to the harbor. Strafing from fighters and bombers also inflicted minor damage on a number of ships.[32]

The bad weather in the vicinity of Sherman's TF 38 forced him to call off his planned second strike, but it proved a good cover, allowing his ships to retire from the launch area without being detected by the Japanese. Montgomery's group was not so fortunate. Admiral Kusaka learned the location of the carriers and launched one of the largest anticarrier strikes of the war, a total of 119 planes, of which 27 were dive bombers and fourteen were torpedo bombers. Despite these incoming planes, Montgomery decided to get his planes aloft and perhaps carry out the planned second strike. He was confident that his air cover, the new carrier formation, and new antiaircraft fuses would be enough to counter the attack. His decision proved sound, but largely because of another factor then unknown to the Americans: the Japanese pilots were not of the same caliber as those available at the start of the war. The action lasted three-quarters of an hour; the covering American fighters engaged the Zeros first, creating an opening for the Japanese bombers to get to the carriers. The *Bunker Hill* suffered five near misses, a near miss punctured the hull of the *Essex* in a number of places, and the *Independence* incurred four near misses. Considering the number of attackers, the slight damage to the carriers represented a near miracle. The Japanese for their part, lost all their torpedo bombers and all but three of their dive bombers.[33]

Although Kenney's planes had been unable to participate in this second run against Rabaul, they were an ever-present factor throughout the month whenever weather permitted. The Japanese at Rabaul were never able to relax, and their air force was constantly on the alert. When they responded to either army or navy attacks, their inexperienced pilots were no match for the Americans in Hellcats and P-38s, and the New Zealanders, even though they were flying nearly obsolete Warhawks, consistently outfought the superior Zeros.[34]

It was apparent to few, if any, in the higher echelons of command, but the week-long naval and air offensive against Rabaul would turn out to be far more important than the more heralded and better supported attack on the Gilberts. In that engagement Admiral Koga would be forced into relative quiescence, largely because of the losses sustained in Halsey's actions. Much later, Koga's chief of staff lamented that an insufficiency of aircraft had prevented Koga from forcing the long-awaited decisive battle on the American naval force in the Gilberts.[35] Admiral Kusaka at Rabaul was buoyed by the false reports of his pilots, who claimed to have sunk a cruiser and damaged two carriers in the afternoon attack on Montgomery's task group.[36] He was not a stupid man, however. He could add up his losses, as could his superior at Truk. In addition to the heavy damage to the surface vessels in the American attacks, the Japanese had lost heavily in planes and their irreplaceable pilots. The *Maga* and *Chokai* with three destroyers were ordered back to Truk on 12 November, and on the same day Admiral Koga officially called off his Operation RO. In addition to the losses in aircraft normally assigned to Rabaul, the air groups from his three carriers at Truk had lost 43 of 82 Zeros, 38 of 45 dive bombers, 34 of 40 torpedo planes, all 6 of his Judy reconnaisance planes, and 86 of 192 trained air crews.[37] Japan never recovered from the beating meted out by Admiral Halsey's forces in defense of the marine perimeter at Cape Torokina.

One last night engagement took place before the Japanese finally abandoned all naval action in the northern Solomons. This relatively small action on 25 November showed clearly how dominant American naval power had become in the waters between New Britain and

Bougainville. It was precipitated by the fears of the Japanese army command that the enclave at Torokina was but a stepping stone for a real invasion aimed at Buka. The generals at Rabaul persuaded their naval counterparts to take a convoy of three destroyer transports, the *Amagiri, Yugiri,* and *Uzuki,* with approximately nine hundred soldiers on board, to Buka. These were screened by the almost new destroyers *Onami* and *Makinami.* The run to Buka was uneventful; the soldiers were off-loaded and seven hundred aviation personnel, no longer needed at the all but destroyed Buka airfields, were taken aboard. Admiral Halsey's headquarters had been alerted to this operation, and even before the Japanese troops had been transferred, three destroyers from Destroyer Division 45 and two from Destroyer Division 46 were closing in on the Japanese ships. Captain Arleigh Burke planned to launch the torpedoes of Division 45 and then have the two destroyers of Division 46 fire theirs. The Japanese commander of the screening destroyers was taken by surprise, and before he could maneuver away from Burke's destroyers, which had fired fifteen torpedoes, both of his ships were hit. The *Onami* blew up in a giant fireball, and the *Makinami* almost broke in two. It was later sunk by gunfire. The three destroyer transports fled north for the haven of Rabaul with Burke's ships in close pursuit. There ensued a running gun battle between the two opposing destroyer units with the Japanese getting the worst of it. Approximately sixty miles off Cape St. George, New Ireland, Burke's three destroyers concentrated their fire on *Yuguri,* which blew up at about 0305. The other two Japanese ships fled westward, and Burke, needing to put distance between himself and Rabaul, reluctantly gave up the chase.[38]

This last of fifteen naval battles fought in the Solomons, twelve of which had been surface engagements, depicted the overall condition of the Japanese navy in miniature. Not only would Japanese ships no longer threaten the perimeter on Bougainville, but the entire fleet went into a static defensive posture. First Admiral Koga and then his successor, Admiral Ozawa, husbanded what was left of the once-dominant fleet, hoping for a last decisive victory that was never to come. Rabaul, the object of the Allied actions, had been all but neutralized, although it would be many months before the American high command realized it. There would be no need for a costly land invasion of New Britain. For the marines and later army troops on Bougainville, the actions over Rabaul and the Bougainville airfields had reduced the Japanese air strikes to nuisance raids on the beachhead.

6. Expanding the Perimeter

The marines on the narrow beachhead adjacent to Cape Torokina were totally unaware of the crucial naval and air battles that did so much to secure their operations. They were, almost to a man, tired and wet and still apprehensive that the Japanese were ready to launch a counterattack in great force against the shallow perimeter. Such fears as the ordinary marine might have had were not shared by the higher command. General Vandegrift was so certain of the ultimate success of the operation that he relinquished command of the troops ashore to General Turnage and returned with Admiral Wilkinson to Guadalcanal. Until 9 November, when General Geiger assumed command of IMAC, Turnage was for all practical purposes in charge of operations on Bougainville.

He had two main interconnected problems. The first was the need to expand the beachhead inland to give the marines enough depth to check any major Japanese attack. The second problem concerned the need to sort out the supplies landed haphazardly on the beach. This would be no easy task, given the nature of the terrain and the lack of any usable roads leading into the interior.

General Turnage decided to realign his two combat regiments, shifting the 3d Marines, whose units had suffered the most casualties, to the left sector of the beachhead and moving the relatively fresh 9th Marines to the right, where he believed the Japanese would not mount any serious counterthrust. The beachhead was so crowded that he had to make these changes piecemeal. Some of the troops had to be transported to their new locations by amphibian tractors. After two days, most of the elements of the two regiments had been moved and

94 Bougainville

the 3d and 9th Marines had changed places. Despite the many logistical difficulties, the marines were able to move swiftly largely because of the lack of any Japanese opposition. Some small-arms fire had been directed at the beach from Torokina Island. On 3 November the small-caliber guns of the 3d Defense Battalion and one 105-mm battery of the 12th Marines fired directly at the island for approximately fifteen minutes. Marines of the 3d Raider Battalion followed up the barrage but discovered that all the Japanese who had been there were either dead or had fled the island.[1]

While some of the units were shifting positions, others were slowly advancing the boundaries of the perimeter, particularly in the center. There was also constant patrolling ahead of the main bodies and roadblocks established at key positions along the Piva and Mission trails. Other patrols searched vainly for a trail that could be used for lateral movement from the west to the east flank. An outpost far to the left of the main perimeter line guarded against a surprise attack by any Japanese who might cross the Laruma River. Further patrols on 4 November scouted as far north as the Laruma and south to the Torokina River. These patrols met not even small-scale organized resistance. Only occasional sniper fire disturbed the marines. One sniper was killed near the Piva River, but most of the Japanese left alive had quietly disappeared into the jungle.[2] By the close of the day on 3 November 2d Raider Battalion had extended the beachhead by almost fifteen hundred yards.

Patrolling would become a daily fact of life for all units involved on Bougainville for the next twenty months, and despite the general quiesence of the Japanese over long periods, it was always potentially dangerous. The thick undergrowth and lack of well-defined trails made it easy for the Japanese to set up an ambush. One addition to some patrols were the dogs of the K9 companies, whose senses were sharper than those of even the most alert Marine. Wilcie O'Bannon was the first patrol leader to have dogs. He recalled how the dogs were used on his patrol:

> One dog was a German Shepherd female, the other was a Doberman male, and they had three men with them. The third man handled the dogs all the time in the platoon area prior to our going on patrol—petting the dogs, talking to them, and being nice to them. The other two handlers—one would go to the head of the column and one would go to the rear with the female messenger dog. . . . If the dog in front received enemy fire and got away he could either come back to me or circle to the back of the column. If

I needed to send a message I would write it, give it to the handler, and he would pin it on the dog's collar. He would clap his hands and say, "Report," and the dog would be off like a gunshot to go to the third man in the rear who had handled him before the patrol.[3]

During the early stages of the Bougainville campaign the dogs located a number of spots where small numbers of Japanese had been. Fortunately there was no heavy fighting or gunfire. In later operations such as at Peleliu these would minimize their use and actually drove many of the dogs mad.

By the close of 5 November the perimeter had been extended inland to a depth of almost three miles. Five battalions held the line: from left to right, 3/9, 3/3, 2/3, 2/9, and 1/9. This last battalion was in direct reserve, while the bulk of the raider battalions were located on Puruata Island and at Cape Torokina as corps reserve troops. Now that all was quiet along the ten-thousand-yard front, the second echelon, comprising eight LSTs and eight APDs carrying 3,548 troops of the 21st Marines and 5,080 tons of supplies and equipment, arrived at 0600 on 6 November.[4] Because the beaches were still crowded with unsorted supplies and still lacked developed facilities, the LSTs landed their cargo on Puruata Island where the beach conditions were better. There was, however, no shore party to organize the unloading, and soon the supply jam on the island became as bad as the mainland.

Echelon 2A brought in the first army troops on 8 November, members of the 148th Regimental Combat Team (RCT) of the 37th Division. They received their baptism of fire on Bougainville just before noon the same day. Kusaka, partially recovered from the beatings of the previous days, sent an estimated twelve to fourteen torpedo bombers and fifty to sixty fighters to attack the transports. One hit on the *Fuller* killed five men and wounded twenty; another bomb struck the *President Jackson* but did not explode. The major result of this air raid and a subsequent attack at 1600 was to delay the unloading of 3,160 tons of supplies. With the beach conditions somewhat improved, the remaining two army RCTs, the 129th and 145th, a total of 10,277 men, were landed with more than eighty-five hundred tons of supplies and equipment on 11-12 November.[5]

Even before the arrival of troops of the 37th Division, General Turnage had almost twenty thousand men available to manage a relatively small perimeter. This local superiority in manpower and weapons makes the Japanese reaction to the landings inexplicable unless one is to believe Japanese statements after the war that they thought there were no more than five thousand Americans within the perimeter. Even so, the thousand-man counterinvasion planned for 1 November and called off by Admiral Kusaka would not have been sufficient to dislodge a force of five thousand marines. It is possible that Rabaul meant only to disrupt marine operations along the beachhead, after which the Japanese landing units would move into the interior to join with reinforcements sent by General Hyakutake to attack the main defenses of the perimeter.

Meanwhile, Hyakutake, the Japanese commander of Bougainville, had been indolent in responding to the Cape Torokina landing, believing that it was a feint similar to the Choiseul operation. Hyakutake continued to believe that the main landings would come later and would target Buka. Under pressure from Rabaul to do something and not having any substantial numbers of troops available near Empress Augusta Bay, he concurred in the plan to land a battalion of specially trained raiders drawn from several regiments of the 17th Infantry Division between the Laruma and Koromokina rivers. This plan was put into operation even after Admiral Omori's decisive defeat on 5 November by Admiral Merrill's cruisers, and after the Japanese should have realized the size of the Allied invasion.

On 6 November four destroyers transported approximately eight hundred men to Bougainville.[6] The Japanese force successfully evaded detection, once reversing course to escape being seen by American ships. Finally at about 0400, the Japanese destroyers doubled back, and from a distance of approximately two miles they unloaded the troops onto a variety of boats for the run in to the beach. The Japanese army commander wanted the destroyers to stand by to give covering fire, but their naval counterparts, showing considerable prudence, decided to leave as soon as the troops were unloaded.

The Japanese landing came as a nearly complete surprise to the marines. Sailors on board one of the American ships reported seeing a strange craft, which they believed to be a Japanese barge, and a PT boat was alerted to check out the report. Before it arrived the Japanese were already ashore and making their first attacks against the left flank of the perimeter. Although doomed from the beginning because of faulty intelligence and planning, the attackers might have had more success had not a number of developments made their situation even worse. First, they were landed at the wrong place. The plan had called for a landing farther north of the perimeter, which would have given time for the units to be assembled into a unitary force. The Japanese planners or perhaps the destroyer commander believed the Allied beachhead was concentrated near the cape. Second bad surf conditions prevented the boats from beaching in one nearly cohesive body.

They came ashore scattered along two miles of beach on either side of the Laruma River. The Japanese senior officer near the Koromokina River then had a difficult choice. He could wait and regroup before attacking with the bulk of his forces or he could gather what men were available and take advantage of the surprise. He chose the latter and attacked the left flank of the perimeter with approximately a hundred men.

The marine unit holding that area was 3/9, the only battalion of the 9th Marines still left in the sector assigned to the 3d Marines after the realignment. Company K, reinforced by a platoon of the regiment's weapons company, met the initial attack. Two of the platoons were directly engaged in a five-hour-long fire fight. Once it had been determined that the Japanese had landed, the guns of the 12th Marines and the 90-mm antiaircraft weapons of the 3d Defense Battalion zeroed in on the attackers, who eventually fell back and took refuge in foxholes dug by the departed marines of 1/9 and 2/9. Thus the men of Company K, attempting to advance, ran into good defensive positions manned by the Japanese approximately 150 yards west of the Laruma River. Hampered by the junglelike undergrowth and the fierce fire from light machine guns and rifles, the men of Company K could not make any headway. At 1315 two companies of 1/3, which had been in reserve, were ordered to advance and Company K was pulled back. During its engagement, five marines had been killed and thirteen wounded, two of whom later died.[7] Company K's third platoon, which had been on patrol inland toward the Laruma River when the Japanese landed, ran directly into them along the east bank of the river. After a brief skirmish in which the Japanese lost a number of men, the patrol leader disengaged and led his troops into the swamp on a wide swing eastward. After almost thirty hours of sweating and cursing, wading through the knee-deep water, the platoon was able to make its way back to the marine lines.

During the early stages of the battle, another patrol, made up of the 2d Platoon of the weapons company and a platoon of Company E of the 3d Tank Battalion, which had been attached for the scouting mission, was caught by surprise and trapped. A Japanese force estimated at company size caught the marines dug in for the night between the ocean and the swamp. Fortunately the Japanese were apparently more surprised than the marines and suffered a number of casualties before they could disengage. The marines' radio was out of commission, and so they could not contact the artillery, but the officer in charge crawled past the Japanese defenses and made his way to the main perimeter area, where he alerted the fire direction center, which

98 Bougainville

then plotted the location and fired a concentration directly on the enemy. Taking advantge of this strike, the marines attempted to break out but were blocked by the Japanese engaging Company K. Finally reestablishing communications, they were instructed to retire to the beach where late in the afternoon two tank lighters dashed in and picked up the sixty marines. Remarkably, only two men of the patrol were wounded, though they claimed to have killed thirty-five of the enemy.[8]

Two other units were also cut off by the Japanese attack. One was a platoon of 1/3, which had been sent ahead to scout the enemy's positions and found itself behind the Japanese. Instead of taking the long island route through different terrain, the patrol leader decided to bring his platoon through the swamp to the beach, where they spent the night. Early on the morning of 8 November they attracted the attention of an Allied plane, which alerted the headquarters to their plight. They, too, were rescued by a tank lighter. The second unit to be isolated was a patrol sent out by Company B of 1/3, which became cut off behind the Japanese lines and spent the night of 7-8 November in place without detection.[9]

Major John Brady's 1/3 had attacked the entrenched Japanese early on the afternoon of 7 November. Company C attempted to flank the right and Company B attacked the left. Each ran into very heavy machine gun and rifle fire from the entrenchments, which were nearly invisible to the attackers. Tanks were ordered in to support the advance and their 37-mm guns firing at point-blank range destroyed many of the emplacements. Meanwhile, 1/21, commanded by Lieutenant Colonel Ernest Fry, which had landed only the day before, was ordered from Puruata Island to spearhead a new assault on the Japanese. Brady's battalion was halted for an artillery preparation designed to support 1/21. The 12th Marines concentrated on a fifteen-minute barrage on the Japanese positions at the same time 1/3 poured machine gun and mortar fire into the emplacements. By the time 1/21 was in place it was growing dark, however, and the decision was made to hold up the attack for the next day. Early on the morning of 8 November, five batteries of the 12th Marines duplicated the firing of the previous afternoon on the restricted area occupied by the Japanese. Following the 20-minute barrage, 1/21, supported by the light tanks, moved through the 1/3 line to find only slight resistance. Most of the Japanese apparently had been killed in place by the two heavy bombardments. More than 250 dead Japanese were found by the marines, whose patrols advanced almost a mile beyond before establishing a firm defensive line behind the Koromokina Lagoon. The total losses to the two marine battalions during the two-day operation were sixteen killed and thirty wounded.[10]

General Hyakutake, in support of the attack by the seaborne troops of the 17th Division, had shifted two battalions of the 23d Division from the Buin area northward. They were to join in the assault on the marine perimeter by first wiping out the roadblocks set up by the 2d Raider Battalion on the Piva Trail, leading northward from the Buretoni Mission. Although this trail was hardly more than a pathway on the high ground, it was the main route inland from Cape Torokina to the more important Numa Numa Trail. If the Japanese could secure the Mission and Numa Numa trails they could negate much of the advance made by the marines after D day and put themselves in a position to wipe out what they still believed to be only a diversionary thrust. Hyakutake thought he could deal with a lodgment of five thousand marines without greatly weakening his garrisons at the points of greatest danger.[11]

The first indication the raiders had of enemy intentions was during the night of 5-6 November, when the Japanese hit Company E of the 2d Raider Battalion, which was maintaining the block. The marines beat off two sharp, probing attacks. Colonel Craig, who at this time commanded both the 9th Marines and the 2d Raiders, expected further attacks and immediately moved most of the raiders north in support of the block. His suspicions of a major attack were justified in the early afternoon of 7 November when the Japanese commander launched a company-sized attack directly at the roadblock manned by Company H. The marine defenders, supported by heavy mortar fire from units of the 9th Marines, beat off the first attacks. Raider Companies H and G rushed to reinforce the defensive perimeter, and by midafternoon the three raider companies had driven the Japanese back toward Piva village where they were observed digging in. Further probing attacks by the Japanese proved fruitless, and they contented themseves during the night with harassing fire from their heavy mortars sited along the trail area.

Although the Japanese had suffered a number of casualties, the commander, Major General Shun Iwasa, had no intention of aborting his mission without pressing home a more serious attack in order to dominate the junction. Early on the morning of 8 November he launched a new assault with both his 1st and 2d battalions behind a very heavy mortar barrage. Companies G and E of the 2d Raider Battalion, located astride the roadblock and extending approximately four hundred yards along the Piva Trail bore the brunt of the assault. Units of the 3d Raider Battalion had been brought in from reserve and formed up on either side of the units being attacked. In addition, the position was reinforced by mortars from 2/9, heavy weapons from the regimental weapons company, and a number of light tanks from the 3d Tank Battalion. By noon the marines' position was roughly a horseshoe with two companies connecting the roadblock to the main perimeter. The swampy area on either side of the trail prevented the Japanese from attempting flanking movements. Thus they were forced into frontal attacks, which were beaten off, the Japanese suffering heavy casualties. Early in the afternoon, Companies E and F of the 2d Raiders attempted a flanking movement through the swamp. After advancing with great difficulty a few dozen yards, they hit a large force of Japanese and the fight began once again. The tanks and half-tracks proved useless except to evacuate the wounded, and by 1600 the fight was a stalemate and the two companies were pulled back to the original lines before nightfall. This action had cost the marines 8 killed and 27 wounded, compared to estimated Japanese casualties of 125 dead.[12]

General Turnage was concerned that if the Japanese held their positions along the trails they would at the very least delay the building of the planned airstrips. He therefore ordered a new advance to clear the trail. He moved Lieutenant Colonel Robert Cushman's 2/9 forward into a support position and ordered Major Alan Shapley's 2d Raider Battalion to spearhead the attack, with Lieutenant Colonel Beans's 3d Battalion in the lead. Beginning at 0730 on 9 November, the guns of 1/12 began to pound the trail area ahead of the proposed advance. Some Japanese, however, had moved at first light to within twenty-five yards of the marine position, roughly a hundred yards ahead of their main defensive lines. Surviving the artillery barrage, they were in excellent position to hold up the marine attack.

The two raider companies, forced to move along a narrow front between swampy areas, ran directly into heavy machine gun and mortar fire. After one and a half hours, the raiders had advanced only a few yards. As in the attack of the previous day, the tanks and half-tracks could not maneuver and therefore were of little help to the riflemen. The action came down to a series of thrusts and counterthrusts at point-blank range: the Japanese were attempting to break through the marine defenses just as the raiders were trying to smash those of the Japanese. It was in this desperate fighting that the second marine on Bougainville won the Congressional Medal of Honor. Private First Class Henry Gurke of the 3d Raider Battalion was in one of the two-man foxholes at the forefront of some of the most serious

Japanese attacks. To protect his partner who was operating a BAR, Gurke threw himself on a grenade tossed into their foxhole.[13]

Just before noon, the Japanese attempted a major flanking movement on the right of the roadblock. The regimental commander of the 3d Marines, Colonel Craig, who had assumed direct control of the defenses, shifted one company into position to bolster the right flank and positioned the weapons company of the 9th Marines to support them. Later he would reinforce the right with an additional platoon from the 3d Raiders. These moves checked the Japanese counterattack. The marine fire power ultimately proved too much for General Iwasa's attackers, and by 1230 Japanese resistance had crumbled, and the survivors retreated past Piva village. By midafternoon the marines had reached the junction of the Piva and Numa Numa trails. Patrols began to move cautiously northward along the Numa Numa Trail and in the adjacent jungle area without making further enemy contact. The bulk of the marines engaged in the day's action were ordered to dig in for the night considerably in advance of their previous defensive lines. The fighting on 9 November had killed twelve marines and wounded 30. More than a hundred Japanese bodies were found in their positions, and the next day an additional forty Japanese were discovered along the trail leading to Piva village.[14]

During the night a patrol from the 3d Raiders was sent to scout forward to Piva village. It returned early in the morning with the report that no Japanese had been encountered. Nevertheless, a previously ordered air strike was carried out by bombers from marine air squadrons from Munda. The planes bombed and strafed a fifty-yard strip on either side of the trail as far north as Piva village. Only then, shortly after 1000, did 1/9 and 2/9 pass through the raider lines and move unopposed through the village. Patrols from these units moved well beyond, toward the coconut grove at the junction of the East-West and Numa Numa trails. By nightfall of 9 November the marine perimeter had been extended approximately eight hundred yards inland. The Japanese had lost a large portion of their force attacking the roadblock and were no longer an immediate threat to the beachhead from the interior. The Koromokina landings of 6 November had failed dismally, and in the battle on the Piva Trail, more than eight hundred Japanese troops had been killed without gaining an iota of tactical advantage.

Even while preliminary work was being done at Cape Torokina on the fighter strip, higher headquarters had decided to investigate the possibility of an airfield in the interior that could handle bombers. A group of navy and marine engineers and construction personnel, protected by a combat patrol, had been sent forward even while the battle for the Piva Trail was going on to survey possible sites for one or possibly two airfields. Utilizing aerial photographs, the surveyors selected an area about three miles inland and almost a mile beyond the existing perimeter, where they found suitable sites for two airstrips and cut long survey lanes on an east-west axis. This work went on without incident, although on 12 November a combat patrol encountered a Japanese patrol in the vicinity of the survey lanes. General Turnage knew that the main divisional perimeter could not be immediately extended to include the proposed airfields and decided to create an interim combat outpost at the junction of the East-West and Numa Numa trails. From there, patrols could fan out and, he hoped, keep any Japanese troops east of the juncture off balance until the main marine elements could be moved forward. He alerted Colonel Evans Ames, commander of the newly arrived 21st Marines, to move a company-sized unit forward along the Numa Numa Trail to establish a block.[15]

At that time there were only two battalions of the 21st ashore and one, 1/21, was still on the left flank of the perimeter in support of the 37th Division. Thus, only 2/21 was available for action. Its commander, Lieutenant Colonel Eustace Smoak, was notified of the plan early on 12 November, and the battalion was moved forward about four hundred yards behind the front lines held by the 9th Marines. Division command modified the original order that evening, enhancing the outpost to two companies and artillery observers. Smoak requested that he be permitted to use the entire battalion, so he would have one company in immediate reserve. His suggestion was approved but did not appreciably change the plan to occupy the junction.

At 0800 on 13 November, Company E crossed the line and moved up the trail toward the coconut grove lying athwart the Numa Numa Trail approximately three hundred yards south of the junction. The area had not been scouted, since the observer party had been late in arriving, but Smoak didn't believe the scouts would be needed immediately. He sent Company E ahead. The rest of the battalion was still in process of drawing ammunition and preparing for what they thought would be a leisurely advance northward. However, the Japanese commander, by what was probably a coincidence, had also recognized the tactical value of the junction and had sent forward a considerable force, which had occupied the grove on the previous day and had established a fairly strong defensive position. Company E ran into the ambush at approximately 1105 and began to take casualties from the concentrated Japanese machine gun and mortar fire and from snipers located in the trees. The company commander sent back a report of his situation. This was just the first of many messages on the situation in the grove that Smoak would receive, most of them inaccurate and some tinged with panic. It should be remembered that this was the first combat experience for 2/21.

Smoak hurried forward, established his command post close to the action, and sent Company F up to relieve Company E, which he believed had suffered more heavily than was actually the case. Company F missed making contact with the supposedly beleaguered Company E, but continued forward, suffered a number of casualties, and became disorganized. By 1630 the communications between Smoak's command post and the regiment commander had failed, nor could he contact the artillery. Therefore, he ordered his units out of the grove, withdrew a few hundred yards, and set up a defensive position for the night. Company E was not hurt as badly as he had thought, and Company F, after making a circuit of the battalion's right flank, joined the defense at 1745. A few minutes later communication to regiment was restored and a number of harassing rounds were fired into the grove during the night. Except for occasional ineffective sniper fire, the night passed without incident.

The next morning five light tanks joined 2/21 and Smoak sent patrols forward to try to determine more about the enemy's strength and disposition. Division command had also decided to reinforce the sector and had detached 1/21 from operational control of the 148th RCT and sent that battalion forward. This unit reached the bivouac area just south of the regimental command post at 0900. Regiment had arranged for an air strike to coordinate with a renewed attack on the coconut grove at 0905. Directed by a marine ground liaison team, twenty Avengers, carrying hundred-pound bombs with .1-second delay fuses struck a corridor a hundred yards ahead of 1/21, extending well into the grove. Unfortunately the marines on the ground were being supplied with water and Smoak did not feel he could launch an attack to take maximum advantage of the air strike. The assault on the Japanese positions did not come until 1155, following a twenty-minute artillery barrage. The Japanese had had plenty of time to resume their forward defenses and poured a heavy fire on the assault companies. The tank commanders became disoriented, at one time even firing on the marine left flank. Two tanks were soon disabled, one from a mine and the other from a shell. Smoak halted the disorganized attack, regrouped his forces, and reattacked, and this time the marines overcame the slackening Japanese resistance. Mopping-up operations were continued in the grove and up the two trails until 1545, when a perimeter defense was established. Forty Japanese bodies were found, but the size of the defenses and the resistance given indicated that a much larger force, estimated at the time as at least a reinforced company, had occupied the position. The Japanese commander had skillfully pulled the remainder of his force out of the grove, and they escaped eastward along the East-West Trail. The baptism of fire of 1/21 had secured the vital road junction, but at a cost of twenty dead and thirty-nine wounded.[16]

With the routing of the Japanese in the coconut grove, the perimeter had been extended forward by almost a mile to reach what staff had labeled Island Defense Line D. The extreme left of the perimeter was assigned to the army's 37th Division, which had the 129th Infantry on line, reinforced by one battalion of marines, 2/3. The central and most active part of the front was the responsibility of the 3d Marines commander, Colonel George McHenry, who, however, had only one of his own battalions, 3/3, on line just west of the critical Numa Numa and East-West road junction with 1/3 in direct reserve. Tied into 3/3 was 2/21, temporarily assigned to McHenry, which was in turn supported by 1/21 in reserve.

The USS Fuller was transporting 3/21 to Bougainville on 17 November, when Japanese planes attacked and sank the vessel, killing thirty-eight marines. When the survivors landed, the battalion was ordered forward to a bivouac area. Hostile aircraft strafed the position two days later, killing five and wounding six. Thus, before going into action, 3/21 already had as many casualties as most of the frontline battalions.[17]

The 9th Marines occupied positions along the west bank of the river. In this low swampy area, the most serious problem concerned supply. Only LVTs could negotiate the swamps and large numbers of marines in this sector were taken off the lines to hand-carry supplies to the front.

With few exceptions, the period 15-20 November was quiet in the frontline areas as the army and marines improved their defenses, reorganized their units, and brought forward needed supplies. All battalions sent out patrols probing into the jungle and through the swamps. There were a few minor skirmishes in the 9th Marine sector, and patrols warned that Japanese activity seemed to be increasing. The army patrols generally found little evidence of Japanese anywhere to their front. The 3d Marines in the center had the most hostile contacts. One such involved a patrol from 3/3 which ambushed a Japanese unit on the East-West Trail, killing eight. One of the dead, an officer, had a

Above, Torokina Airstrip from the southwest, with Empress Augusta Bay in the background. Below, Marines of the 3d Marine Division race from their landing craft on D-Day, 1 November 1943.

All photos are courtesy of the National Archives, groups 127-N and 111-SC.

Above, the entrance to a Japanese dugout showing log and earthen construction with palm tree camouflage. Below, a large log dugout and interconnecting trench line.

Above, troops of the Army's 37th Division cross Piva River on a makeshift log bridge. Right, soldiers of the 1st Battalion, Fiji Regiment, on patrol.

Above, Marine paratroops move through typical swamp terrain inland from the northern beaches. Left, black troops of the 25th Regiment, 93d Infantry Division, on the march in a rear area.

Above, troops of Company E, 2/132 of the Americal Division, cross a small stream after heavy artillery bombardment of the area. Below, an American noncommissioned officer poses with Fiji troops of the 1st Battalion, Fiji Regiment.

General Robert Beightler, commander of the 37th Division.

General John Hodge, Commander of the Americal Division.

Above, Admiral William F. Halsey, COMSOPAC, General Oscar Griswold, commander of XIV Corps, and future senator Henry Cabot Lodge, then a staff officer, on an inspection trip to Bougainville. Right, Commodore L.F. Reifsnider, commander of Transport Divisions A and B, and General Allen Turnage, commander of the 3rd Marine Division.

The surrender ceremony at Cape Torokina, 21 August 1945. Above, Lieutenant General Masantane Kanda, commander of Japanese Army units on Bougainville, and below, Vice Admiral Baron Tomoshige Samejima, senior Japanese officer on Bougainville, sign the surrender documents.

map which was immediately sent back to higher headquarters. Although it was difficult to orient the map, it clearly showed the terrain around the forks of the Piva River. This, along with other intelligence information, indicated the Japanese intention of building up considerable defenses along the Numa Numa and East-West trails.[18] It became imperative for the marines to move swiftly in pushing forward to their next phase line.

Another patrol of 3/3 on 18 November began the opening moves in what was to become the week-long Battle of the Piva Forks, the most serious engagement fought by the 3d Marine Division on Bougainville. This patrol discovered a Japanese roadblock on the Numa Numa Trail approximately 5/8 of a mile beyond the marine perimeter (Map 7). A patrol of 1/21 at about the same time discovered a block on the East-West Trail between the two forks of the Piva River. The 3d Raider Battalion was moved up in support and Lieutenant Colonel Ralph King on 19 November was ordered to take his 3/3 with light tanks in support and knock out the Numa Numa roadblock. Following an artillery barrage, 3/3 cut to the left of the trail, took the Japanese in the flank, and routed them, killing sixteen.[19] The battalion took over the Japanese defenses, and soon 1/3 and 1/21 arrived and took up positions along the trail facing eastward toward the block discovered earlier by the patrol from 1/21.

In the morning of 20 November the Japanese attacked the defenses of 3/3 and were driven back. Colonel King then moved his battalion eastward along the trail. At the same time Lieutenant Colonel Hector de Zayas's 2/3 on the right moved ahead and crossed the west branch of the Piva over a bridge hastily rigged up by the engineers. By midafternoon his battalion had captured the Japanese outpost and was in a strong defensive position between the forks of the river. An advanced patrol of 2/3 located a ridge rising about four hundred feet out of the jungle off to the left of the East-West Trail, the first high ground encountered by the marines. Its value for observation was not lost on de Zayas. He ordered First Lieutenant Steve Cibek to take his 1st Platoon of Company F, augmented by a section of heavy machine guns, and occupy the ridge. As they were assembling, the company was hit by a heavy mortar attack. Nevertheless, Cibek led his men quickly out of the perimeter because it was already late in the afternoon. Signalmen attached to the platoon reeled out telephone wire, the scouts found a good approach to the top of the ridge, and the men, tired from a long day of marching, crawled up the slope. Surprisingly, considering its obvious value as an observation post, there were no Japanese to guard the approach or the ridge itself. Before darkness, Cibek's ma-

Map 7. BATTLE OF PIVA FORKS
19-25 November 1943

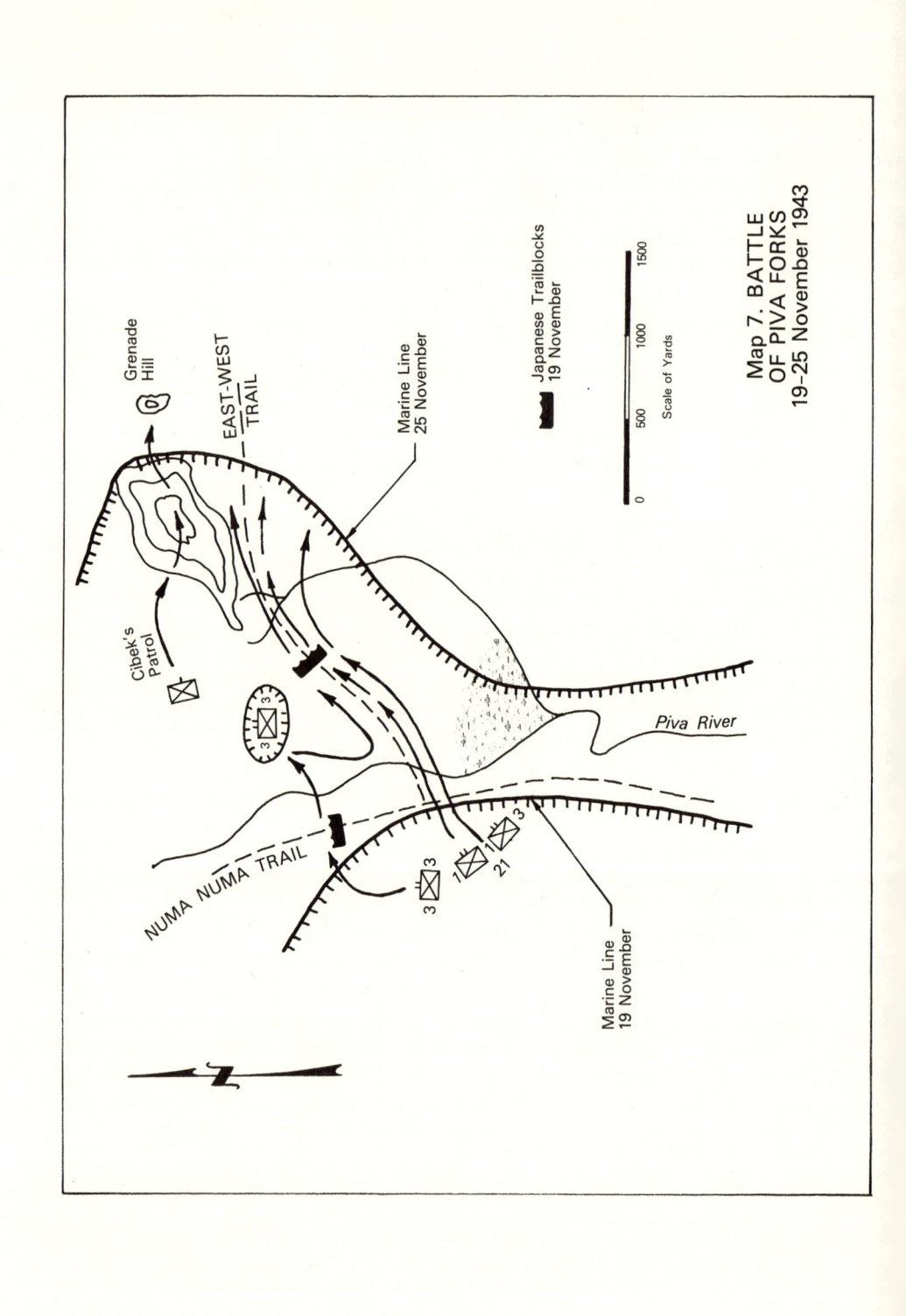

rines had dug in and sited their weapons along the most likely lanes of approach. The next day he moved his platoon to another area to take advantage of the Japanese foxholes already dug there. His superiors, recognizing the importance of the ridge, hastily reinforced Cibek's platoon, and by the evening of 21 November, he had sixty-eight men, a mortar platoon, and more machine guns. Despite fanatical attacks by the Japanese during the next three days, the marines held on to the valuable height.[20] On 25 November, as part of the general forward movement, 1/9 took over the ridgeline, which by that time was referred to as Cibek's Ridge.

The general expansion of the beachhead began on the morning of 21 November. General Geiger's plan was for the 21st Marines to move through the lines at the boundary of the 3d and 9th Marines with the objective of placing the 21st Marines on line between the other two regiments. The two assault battalions, 1/21 and 3/21, moved ahead in a controlled approach march and extended to the right and left until they reached their designated objective at 1425. There was Japanese resistance to the forward displacement only on the left flank, where a platoon of 1/21, which was the contact with the 3d Marines, was attacked by a strong Japanese patrol. This assault was beaten off with no great difficulty. The 3/21 was tied into the 9th Marines on its right. During the advance the 9th crossed the Piva River and moved approximately a thousand yards eastward before halting, confronted by nearly impassable swamp. At the same time, to the far left of the perimeter the 129th Regimental Combat team also advanced another thousand yards without opposition.

The 3d Marines, now sandwiched between the 37th Division on the left and the 21st Marines, on the right had to fight its way forward against unexpectedly heavy Japanese resistance. All three battalions ran into problems. The 3d, on the left, was pinned down by heavy mortar fire soon after it had crossed the Piva River. The battalion was halted and the marines took shelter in foxholes dug by the Japanese. The 2d, in the center, ran head-on into a very well constructed Japanese defense line astride the East-West Trail, where the Japanese had built about twenty pillboxes and committed a relatively large force to man them. Attempts to take the position head-on failed, as did flanking movements. De Zayas then pulled back his battalion to the lines of the reserve, 1/3, to give the artillery room to operate. The Japanese tried an attack, a double envelopment of 1/3, which failed miserably, the attackers being cut to pieces by the marine machine guns sited along the trail. The 1st Battalion then extended its lines northward toward Cibek Ridge.

General Geiger halted the forward movement on 22 November; he shifted units and the following day plugged gaps in the line in preparation for a larger, more concentrated assault on 24 November, Thanksgiving Day. The artillery observers plotted targets and adjusted the batteries. Every available machine gun unit was brought on line, and the marines also used several Hotchkiss and Nambu weapons captured from the Japanese. By the evening of 23 November all was in readiness. Men of 1/3 in reserve had sited forty-four machine guns and also had twelve 81-mm and nine 60-mm mortars zeroed in on the area of the front to be attacked by the other two battalions of the 3d Marines. In addition, seven battalions of artillery, four of the 12th Marines and three of the 37th Division, were scheduled to begin firing their 75-mm and 105-mm howitzers at 0835 the next morning into an area roughly eight hundred yards square. Also the heavy corps artillery, 155-mm howitzers and guns, had registered in on more distant targets.[21]

At precisely the appointed time the artillery opened fire with the greatest concentration of artillery fire yet seen in the Pacific theater. For twenty minutes the guns hammered away at the Japanese defenses, pumping 5,600 rounds into their positions. In the meanwhile, 2/3, on the right of the East-West trail, and 3/3, on the left, moved into assault position, and the men of 1/3 laid down devastating machine gun and mortar fire. As H hour, 0900, neared, a Japanese battery located on the forward slope of a coconut grove began very accurate firing at the assembly locations and at 1/3 positions. One observer noted the effect of this unexpected fire:

> Shells poured into the first lines, into the attacking battalions' areas, the forward Regimental C.P. area, the rear C.P., the trail. The noise was much greater now—not only the deafening roar, but, added to it, the sharp terrifying sound of a shell exploding close by . . . the agonizing moans of men shouting for corpsmen, for help, for relief from burning torture . . . the maniacal screams and sobs of a man whose blood vessels in his head have burst from the blast concussions of high explosives devised by the clever brain of civilized man. The Third Battalion took it. The C.P. area took it to the tune of fourteen men killed and scores wounded in a period of five minutes.[22]

Fortunately the forward observer team on Cibek Ridge located the Japanese battery and requested counterbattery fire from the 37th Division's 155-mm howitzers. Fire was adjusted, and in a matter of minutes the offending battery was destroyed.

Despite the pounding by the Japanese guns, the men of 2/3 and 3/3 moved out at 0905 in what has been described as an eerie silence. At first there was no resistance; the artillery had done its work. The scene ahead of the marines has been aptly described by one historian of the 3d Marines: "For the first hundred yards both battalions advanced abreast through a weird, stinking, plowed-up jungle of shattered trees and butchered Japs. Some hung out of trees, some lay crumpled and twisted beside their shattered weapons, some were covered by chunks of jagged logs and jungle earth, a blasted bunker, their self-made tomb. The Marines pressed forward on their destructive mission toward their clearly defined day's objective."[23]

As the two assault battalions moved past the devastation of the beaten zone they began to encounter heavier Japanese resistance from reserves, which had been rushed forward from behind the fire zone. Extremely accurate artillery and mortar fire hit the advancing marines, causing many casualties. De Zayas's 2/3, after moving slowly beyond the devastated area, suffered more than seventy casualties by the time it had advanced a quarter mile. In addition to the woods and knee-deep swamps the men had to traverse, they encountered a small winding stream, which they had to cross and recross eight times during the morning. At the bend of the stream, the Japanese had sited earth-covered log bunkers housing multiple machine guns and connected by interlocking slit trenches and foxholes. The bunkers had to be destroyed one by one. The Japanese concentrated their fire on the engineers carrying flame throwers, and a number of them were killed. Despite all problems, 2/3 had reached its initial objective line by 1200.

Meanwhile, King's 3/3, to the left of the East-West Trail, had also run into fanatical Japanese defenses. At every defensive point were snipers in the trees, some on prepared platforms with Nambu machine guns and plenty of ammunition. Approximately one-third of a mile beyond the line of departure the marines were hit by a strong Japanese flanking attempt at a place where the marine advantage in artillery and mortars was of no avail. The terrain dictated that this attack had to be halted by hand-to-hand, tree-to-tree fighting. Company L was particularly hard pressed, and its wounded littered the swamp. Despite the terrain and the fierce assault, however, the flanking movement was halted, and by 1200, 3/3 had also reached its initial objective line.[24]

The two battalions halted briefly for rest and reorganization and then pushed ahead through the same type of terrain that had been such a handicap in the morning. This movement to the final objective line was preceeded by a heavy artillery bombardment of the front and by a barrage from 81-mm mortars. Although the intensity of Japanese resistance had slackened, the survivors of the earlier actions were still determined to make the marine advance as costly as possible. Company L of 3/3, on the extreme left once again, bore the brunt as the Japanese from a slight rise ahead of the swampy area poured fire at the marines. Company L was reinforced by Company I and a platoon from Company K. Together, these rushed the high ground in midafternoon and killed the Japanese defenders. The 2d Battalion had also encountered problems as it neared the final objective line. Reduced in numbers and weakened by a heavy mortar concentration, the Japanese defenders nevertheless contested every yard of territory. Eventually the resistance collapsed, and the marines moved forward, mopped up the survivors, and drove three-quarters of a mile beyond the objective line before halting. They then prepared defenses for the night. Because of the swampy conditions, it was impossible for most to dig in. They set up their machine guns and lay down beside them in the water.[25]

This battle in the swamps for domination of the Piva Forks witnessed many macabre events. Perhaps none was more so than the celebration of Thanksgiving. General Geiger and his staff could not postpone the attack to secure the terrain above the proposed airfield site. The Marine advance had to be scheduled for Thanksgiving Day. Higher command had decided beforehand to provide all the troops with real honest-to-goodness turkey in lieu of the usual rations. The turkeys had arrived on 23 November, and the regimental cooks had spent the night before the attack cooking them. There was no thought of saving the birds for later, for it was hot and there was no refrigeration. The marines and army service personnel in the rear echelons could have their dinner warm and eat in relative comfort, but what of the frontline troops? The 3d Marine commissary officer decided to try to send the turkey forward. Carrying parties were organized and, braving sniper fire late in the afternoon, they carried it to the advance areas. An observer recalled:

> Some of the meat got there, some didn't. But it was a good stunt and a necessity; no one would have been forgiven if it had been left to rot down at the Division Commissary just because we had a battle! The men sat on logs eating their turkey. Near by a Jap lay rotting in the swamp. Heads and arms of dead Japs floated in the near-by jungle streams. Not a very enjoyable setting, but these were tired, ravenously hungry men who had been fighting all day.

And it was Thanksgiving. Those who were able to get it enjoyed their turkey.[26]

Although by nightfall of 24 November Japanese resistance had dwindled to almost nothing in front of the assault battalions, there was still danger to the rear. Individual Japanese who had been bypassed during the advance fired at anyone who moved along the paths, making it very dangerous for ammunition carriers and stretcher bearers. Action to eliminate these stragglers went on well into the night. In fact, days after the conclusion of the battle for Piva Forks isolated Japanese still posed a danger to anyone attempting to move forward. With this exception the battle for control of this vital sector was over when the marines established their perimeter in the late afternoon of Thanksgiving Day. The Japanese retired from the high ground that had given them control of the site of the projected bomber fields and had allowed them the opportunity of harassing the entire Allied lodgment. The battle had been costly for the Japanese. Their 23d Infantry had ceased to exist as a well-organized fighting unit. The marines counted 1,107 Japanese dead at the conclusion of the fighting, although it is probable that many more were killed in the engagement.[27] Given the nature of the trails, the unbelievably difficult terrain, and the primitive Japanese medical service for frontline troops, almost all their wounded probably died before reaching medical aid. One indication of how intense the fighting had been is seen in the marine casualties, a total of 115 dead and wounded.[28]

The 3d Marines had borne the brunt of the fighting since D day. Casualties and sickness had by 25 November seriously reduced their numbers, yet they still occupied the most active area of the front. Two days before the attack, General Turnage had decided to shift other units to take over the 3d's positions. This movement had begun even while the battle for Piva Forks was going on. The 1/9, which had been the reserve battalion of the 9th Marines and the 2d Raiders, was moved up on 25 November, preliminary to pulling the 3d Marines out of that sector and replacing them with the 9th Marines. Through a complicated reshuffling of units, this exchange was completed by the evening of 27 November. At that time the 148th and 129th Regimental Combat Teams of the 37th Division were holding the extreme left of the perimeter, tied into the 9th Marines on the left of the marine sector. The 21st Marines were in the center of this sector, and the 3d Marines held the right in positions very close to those they had occupied at the end of D day. Actually, a makeshift battalion comprising marines from several support units and 1/145 held the line while the battered battalions of the 3d Marines rested and were reorganized. This sector bordered on deep swamps, extensions of which cut across the supply routes, making it difficult to maintain the frontline troops in position. Patrols sent out into the swampy area could find no signs of Japanese, and the marines concluded that the Japanese intended only to keep the sector under observation.[29]

While these shifts in IMAC dispositions were occurring, General Turnage decided to advance his lines to occupy some high ground eastward, which dominated a portion of the East-West Trail. The assault units for this advance were the 2d Raiders on the left flank and 1/9 on the right. These were to attack from Cibek Ridge at 1000 on 25 November along a twelve-hundred-yard front after the artillery fired a ten-minute preparation for the advance.

Battalion 1/9 at the base of Cibek Ridge ran into unexpectedly heavy machine gun fire from a small hill directly in front. The Japanese, estimated at seventy soldiers, were well dug in with an all-round defense and many machine guns sited to cover all avenues of approach. They also had an excellent supply of grenades, which they used to good effect against marine attacks all during the day. Impressed with the Japanese effectiveness with this weapon, marines named this knoll Grenade Hill. The defenders beat back every flanking attempt, and the nearest the marines came to reaching the top was when a platoon from Company A on the left almost made it to the crest before having to fall back because of intense concentrated fire. The reserve, Company B, was ordered from Cibek Ridge to block the gap between Company C and the left flank of the 3d Marines. It ran into a strong Japanese force that controlled the high ground ahead of them and was forced back to a more defensible line near the base of Cibek Ridge. The other two companies of 1/9 by late afternoon had given up the attempt to take Grenade Hill that day. The marines dug in and waited to resume the attack on 26 November. The 2d Raiders, extending the perimeter on the left of 1/9, had encountered only sporadic resistance from scattered Japanese groups that gave way before their advance. By midafternoon it had reached the objective, a small hill mass from which the enemy could have brought the East-West Trail under fire.

Scouts from 1/9 were sent out on the morning of 26 November, and they reported that the Japanese had withdrawn from Grenade Hill during the night, inexplicably giving up a very strong defensive position—just how strong the marines discovered when they occupied the knoll. The Japanese had dug three-man foxholes all over the crest, which was only sixty feet across. They also had bunkers from which some of their many machine guns could operate. The marines discovered thirty-two dead Japanese left behind by the retreating survivors. The attacks by 1/9 and the 2d Raiders had cost the marines five dead and forty-two wounded.[30]

The fighting after 24 November had broken the back of organized Japanese resistance in the area of Empress Augusta Bay. On 28 November, General Geiger ordered a further forward displacement to better defensive positions, particularly in the sector of the 9th Marines. The army troops on the left flank had already reached their final inland line by 25 November. There were minor adjustments to the line, particularly in front of the 21st Marines, to make certain that the defense line occupied the most favorable positions on whatever high ground could be found in the predominantly swampy areas. Artillery units were moved forward into better positions to cover the now all but static front. The frontline positions were improved as much as possible, automatic weapons sighted in on every avenue of approach, and possible routes of attack mined. Daily patrols from platoon to company strength scoured ahead of the front, locating the many Japanese outposts to the east and north of the American positions. In general these outposts were let alone, the patrols bypassing them. However, a decision by corps to move the final inland line eastward toward the Torokina River brought on a serious conflict.

Although there had been little action along the right flank after the initial landings, General Geiger and his corps staff worried about a possible Japanese counterthrust against that sector. They decided, therefore, to mount a raid against the Japanese in the southern portion of Empress Augusta Bay in an operation similar to that conducted by Colonel Krulak on Choiseul. The 1st Parachute Battalion, commanded by Major Richard Fagan, which had only arrived on 23 November, reinforced by Company M of the 3d Raider Battalion and a forward observer team from the 12th Marines, was chosen to conduct the raid. The original plan was for the marines to be landed on a beach near Koiari approximately ten miles down the coast from Cape Torokina. Because of embarkation delays, the operation was postponed for two days. This delay meant that the destroyers from a shipping echelon would no longer be available to provide preliminary and covering fire for the landing teams. The commanders were not concerned, since a trial landing near the target area had been made on the evening of 27 November, and a reconnaissance boat had surveyed the beach the following day. Both times the report was the same—no enemy sighted anywhere near the target area. IMAC staff therefore believed that the raiding party could surprise the Japanese near Koiari, blow up any supply dumps, disrupt communications, and harass the enemy as far into the interior as the East-West Trail. A boat would be sent in to the beach each night to check on the progress of the operation.[31]

Unfortunately, the reports of the number of enemy in the area were faulty. It is likely that neither scouting patrol had even surveyed the actual landing sites. The marine paratroops landing from the LCMs and LCVPs at 0400 on 29 November found themselves almost in the center of a Japanese supply dump, but the Japanese were just as surprised as the marines, who quickly overran the dump and established a perimeter approximately two hundred yards inland. The raider company and battalion headquarters company had landed more than a half mile south of the main force. Major Fagan later estimated that he was opposed by at least twelve hundred Japanese in much better defensive positions than the marines. Almost immediately the Japanese began to pound the marine beachhead with mortar, machine gun, and rifle fire. Fagan notified corps headquarters of his predicament and requested that his force be withdrawn. Although Geiger immediately put a rescue into operation, his return radio communication to Fagan was never received. Later the forward observer team managed to raise artillery headquarters, and thus Fagan was kept apprised of the rescue plans. At 0930 the marine main body was joined by the two companies that had landed farther south, which had sustained thirteen casualties during the move. The Japanese continued during the day to try to break through the flanks of the perimeter but were kept off balance by 155-mm guns of the 3d Defense Battalion at Cape Torokina. Later in the afternoon Fagan heard trucks approaching from the south, indicating that reinforcements were being brought up.

The desperate nature of the marine position was again communicated to corps, which sent landing craft south, but Japanese artillery prevented the boats from coming in to shore. Geiger then sent an emergency message to the destroyers escorting a convoy on its way back to Guadalcanal. Three of these were detached and reversed course at full speed back to Bougainville. They arrived just at dark, took up their positions, and using radar began firing ahead of the marine perimeter. At the same time the "long toms" were firing parallel to the beach. This rain of shells kept the Japanese pinned down so the rescue boats could make their run in to the beach. The marines who were out of ammunition by this time staged an orderly retreat to the boats, and all marines were off the beach by 2040. Navy and marine guns continued to fire randomly along the beach area for some time after the evacuation was complete. Measured by any standard, the raid was a failure. The marines had 15 killed, 99 wounded, and 7 missing out of a force of 614 officers and men.[32] They estimated 291 Japanese casualties, but this was probably more of a guess than an accurate count. Any serious damage to Japanese installations at Koiari was due to the artillery and naval bombardment. The raid was in retrospect a good plan marred by the lack of good intelligence information. More men, backed by naval and air support could possibly have achieved the objectives, but Fagan and his men had been blindly committed to an action against what proved to be a much superior force. The raiding party was very lucky to have escaped total destruction.

General Geiger had planned to advance to the final inland defense line in the east by 30 November, but action elsewhere and the difficulty of moving troops and supplies had postponed this move. This line would be anchored in the north by Hill 1000 and then extend southward roughly paralleling the Torokina River to Hills 600 and 500. The move forward would considerably strengthen the marine positions and would deny the Japanese access to the high ground from which they periodically shelled the airfields and beachhead. A fierce artillery duel was fought on 3 December between the Japanese 150-mm guns on the forward slopes and regiment, division, and corps artillery. Aided by spotting planes, the marine fire forced the Japanese to pull back their remaining guns quickly. While amtracs were busy cutting trails through the jungle and swamps preliminary to a general forward movement, a patrol of twenty-two men from the 21st Marines occupied Hill 600 on 27 November. The 3d Parachute Battalion, the weapons company and headquarters of the 1st Parachute Regiment, was ordered from Vella Lavella on 3 December. Two days later the marine paratroops had occupied a line stretching from the military crest of Hill 1000 across a whole series of ridges and ravines to the junction of the East-West Trail and the Torokina River. Lieutenant Colonel Robert Williams, commanding the parachute battalion of approximately nine hundred men, held ground extending more than three thousand yards. Meanwhile the patrol on Hill 600 had been reinforced by a machine gun platoon, a rifle company, and a rocket platoon. Then on 6 December the 3d Marines occupied Hill 500. This forward displacement was done with minimal contact with Japanese infantry. The one serious fire fight was in the 9th Marines' sector, to the left of Hill 1000, where a small patrol of 2/9 was ambushed on 5 December.[33]

On 6 December the war was relegated to second place as nature decided to put on a show. Few, if any, of the planners were aware of

Map 8. THE PERIMETER TO 15 DECEMBER 1943

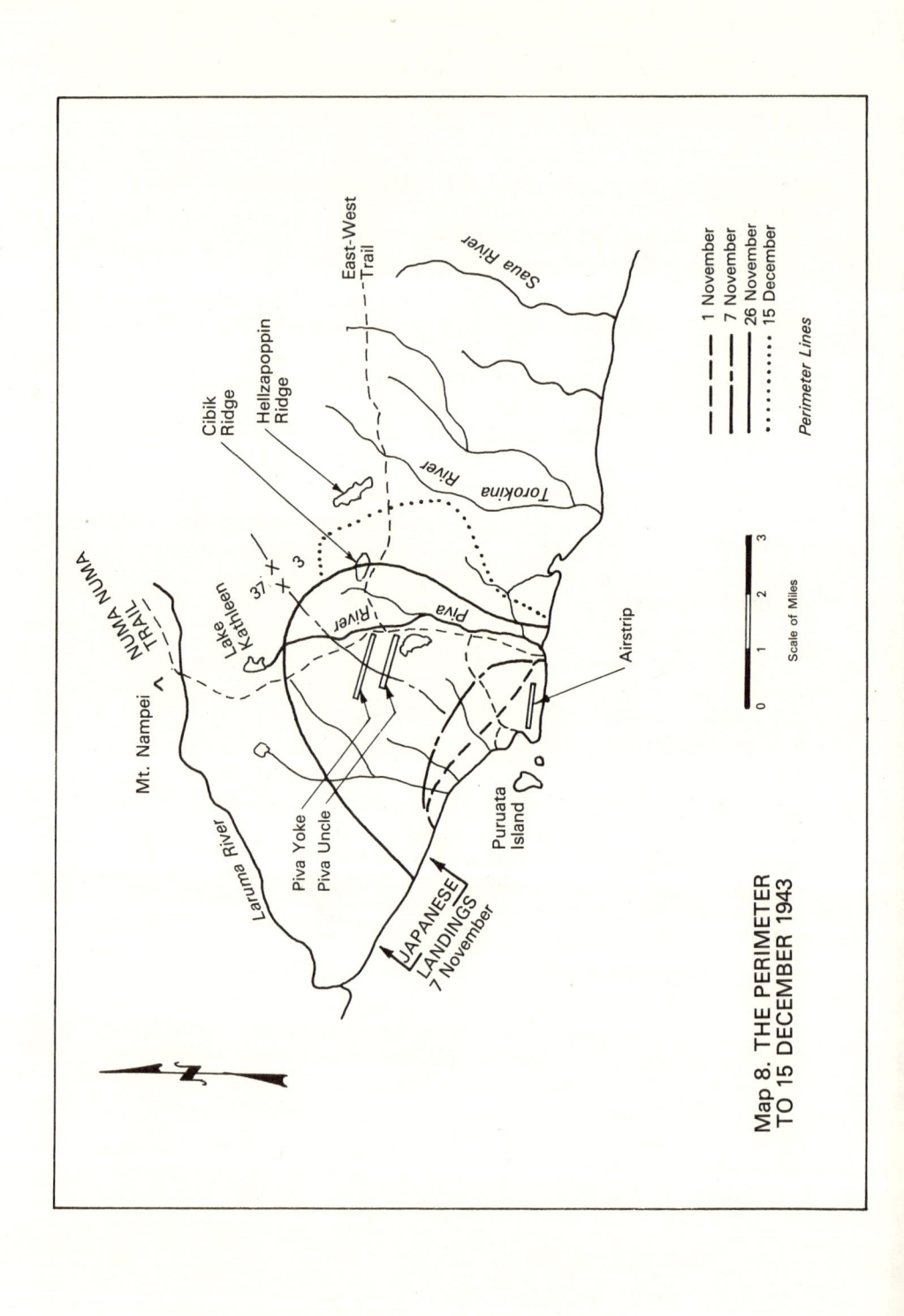

the extensive rift lines radiating out from the central highlands and Mount Bagana, an active volcano. Everyone was therefore surprised when the entire island was shaken by a major earthquake during the morning of 6 December and then by a series of sharp aftershocks. Frazer West, commanding a company of the 9th Marines, recalled the event:

> Being raised in Nevada I'd been through a lot of earthquakes so they were nothing new to me. We had one really severe earthquake on Bougainville. The big trees were just swaying around and we had built this fortification on this ridge, pillboxes, and such out of coconut logs and the roofs fell in on the pillboxes and some of the trenches caved in. The men got down and hugged to ground. It was impossible to stand up while it was going on. They were scared to death when these huge trees were breaking down around them. This went on it seemed for several minutes. The ground really rumbled and shook. It was the worst earthquake I'd ever been in.[34]

The day following the earthquake a patrol from the parachute battalion scouted a spur extending eastward from Hill 1000, which was not shown on any of the maps at corps headquarters. No Japanese were discovered there, but the patrol found a number of well-dug-in positions on the ridge. As events developed it was unfortunate that Williams postponed taking and holding the ridge till the following morning, for when he led a patrol forward on the 8 December, he found that the Japanese had reoccupied it in force. Williams encountered a reinforced company of the Japanese 23d Infantry numbering by later estimates over two hundred men. Williams's patrol made two attempts to seize the ridge but was driven back both times. Williams and seven of his men were wounded before retiring to the marine lines.[35]

The spur was almost three hundred yards long, with steep slopes leading up to a narrow crest, and the Japanese commander had sited his defensive positions very well. It would take eleven days of intense fighting before the Japanese would surrender the ridge, which by then had earned the nickname Hellzapoppin Ridge (Map 8). On 9 December three separate patrols from the parachute battalion attacked the spur and in confused close fighting a number of marines were wounded without gaining any advantage. Then in the late afternoon the Japanese made a sudden direct attack on the marine positions on Hill 1000. The paratroops were supported by 105-mm and 75-mm howitzers, whose fire struck the attackers as they advanced across the saddle linking Hill 1000 and its spur. A combination of intense rifle and machine gun fire in conjunction with the artillery ended the attack, but twelve marines had been killed and twenty-six wounded during the fire fight.[36]

On 10 December the parachute battalion was pulled off Hill 1000, and the responsibility for taking Hellzapoppin Ridge fell to 1/21 and 1/9. At first the Americans tried to neutralize the Japanese by artillery fire, but because of the location of the ridge on the reverse slope of Hill 1000 it was difficult for the guns firing almost due east to hit the position. A number of marines were wounded from friendly rounds falling short. Mortar fire, although more accurate, appeared to have little effect on the enemy. General Geiger then called for air strikes. The first of these, on 13 December, by three dive bombers and three torpedo bombers left much to be desired. Some of the bombs hit the target, marked by smoke shells, but one bomber dropped its load on marine positions north of the ridge, killing two and wounding five. Lieutenant Colonel Arthur Butler, the 21st Marines' executive officer, not only plotted the air strikes but flew on the last two missions with the flight leader to zero in on the enemy positions.[37] On these, the marine lines were outlined by colored smoke grenades, while the enemy area was marked by white smoke. On 14 December, seventeen torpedo bombers struck the ridge, and the next day another eighteen torpedo bombers successfully struck the Japanese positions. Finally on 18 December, loaded with hundred-pound bombs with delay fuses, six torpedo bombers attacked, followed by five more TBFs, which dropped all their bombs in the target area. The planes then swooped across the ridge in low-level strafing runs in order to pin the enemy down.[18] The air strikes were complemented by fire from a battery of 155-mm howitzers, which had been moved by LCMs to a point near the mouth of the Torokina River. At midmorning, they began firing almost due north into the ridge. By noon the fire from the heavy guns had cleared much of the tangled jungle that covered the crest of the ridge.

Immediately after the second air attack, riflemen of 1/21 and 3/21 attacked the ridge from Hill 1000 in a double envelopment. The air and artillery poundings had succeeded. There was but token resistance offered by the dazed survivors, who were quickly eliminated. The marines counted more than fifty Japanese dead; the remainder of the company, including wounded, had fled to the east. The eleven-day battle for Hellzapoppin Ridge was over. It had cost the marines twelve killed and twenty-three wounded. Without the excellent cooperation with marine air from the airfield at Cape Torokina these casualty figures would have been much higher.[39]

There was no further serious contact with the Japanese as the marines consolidated their positions along the hill lines until 21 December. Then a combat patrol of the 21st Marines encountered a few Japanese on an elevation east of Hill 600. One marine was killed and one wounded in the skirmish. Early the next morning a platoon from 3/21 moved out to drive the Japanese from the rise, now called Hill 600A. They ran into heavy fire from the Japanese entrenched on the hillock. Company I was then ordered forward and tried a double envelopment but was pinned down by heavy fire from the defenders and forced to retreat. The next day Company K, reinforced by a heavy machine gun platoon attempted a direct assault but was driven back. The artillery then pounded 600A, and the marines moved forward after the barrage lifted, only to be driven back again. Another heavy artillery concentration was directed at the defenders and once again the men of Company K were repulsed and retreated back to the defense line on Hill 600. Scouts were sent out early in the morning of 24 December and discovered that the Japanese inexplicably abandoned their strong position and silently slipped away during the night.[40]

The neutralization of Hill 600A was the last offensive by the marines on Bougainville. Already General Geiger had relinquished command to Major General Oscar Griswold, commanding the army's XIV Corps on 15 December, and the Americal Division was moving in to relieve the 3d Marine Division. By this time the inland perimeter extended for approximately twenty-three thousand yards, and behind its ever-strengthening defenses were more than fifty thousand troops. Although aware of the possibility of a future Japanese counterthrust, General Geiger and his staff, even before the attack on Hellzapoppin Ridge, were convinced that the perimeter was secure and the air bases could be successfully defended.

7. The Rear Areas

As the army and marine riflemen at first expanded and then consolidated the perimeter, personnel in the rear areas were engaged in a variety of tasks that enabled the frontline troops to carry out their missions. Of all the noncombat troops, the ones most directly involved with the men on the line were the medical personnel. From the beginning, aid stations were located as near the front lines as possible in order to give the wounded emergency treatment quickly while minimizing the trauma of carrying them on stretchers for long distances. These stations were moved forward as the perimeter was extended. The wounded would be given blood plasma and emergency care at the aid stations before being sent back to the field hospitals for more thorough care. Even under the best of conditions movement of the wounded to a field hospital was a long, traumatic experience for nonambulatory wounded. Evacuation to the rear areas was speeded up as the engineers cut roads through the jungle and swamp that enabled jeep ambulances to move closer to the front. Early in the fighting, amtracs were used whenever they were available to bring the wounded back over otherwise nearly impassable semitrails. In the most inaccessible regions the stretchers had to be carried for long distances, and in most cases the transport proved hellish for the wounded. In steep, wooded areas it took more than the usual numbers to carry and drag the stretchers back to the rear. During the attack on Hellzapoppin Ridge in December, sometimes twelve men were needed to bring down one wounded man from the heights.[1]

Field hospitals were set up as close to the front as was deemed relatively safe. Here the less seriously wounded were treated and put into hospital tents for recovery. The more grievously injured, once their conditions stabilized, were evacuated by ship to the more extensive facilities at Vella Lavella. Many of the activities of the medical personnel made a joke of their supposed noncombat status. Corpsmen from the first landings were directly involved in the very dangerous work of giving first aid and moving the wounded from the front lines to safer locations to the rear. They were as exposed to enemy fire as were the riflemen. Even later, when the perimeter was advanced, so-called safe areas adjacent to the trails could be infiltrated by the Japanese. Sniper fire was an ever-present hazard to everyone. All field hospitals were subject to air attack, and the medical personnel, particularly during the early stages of the invasion, had to work under extremely dangerous conditions. The Japanese landings and subsequent attacks along the left flank on 6 November were particularly hazardous to the rear echelon. The reaction of the medical personnel during this period showed most clearly both the dangers involved and also their dedication to the sick and wounded.

Company E of the 3d Medical Battalion was located a mere thousand yards to the rear of the left flank of the 3d Marines when the Japanese began their Koromokina assault. By 1300 on 8 November the first casualties began to arrive, and in the hours that followed more wounded were brought in. The five doctors and their assistants worked frantically, ignoring the increasing volume of rifle fire that tore into the tents from snipers who had infiltrated the dense jungle between the hospital and the marine lines. Commander Bruce, the commanding officer of the medical battalion, after ordering his personnel to carry on, in spite of the dangers, rushed to the beach and salvaged two machine guns from a landing craft, brought them back to the hospital area, and placed them near the banks of a small stream. Aided by corpsmen, he set up a semicircular defense position. Returning to the beach, he managed to find two marines and seven seabees, whom he brought back to relieve the corpsmen along his ad hoc defense line. Although the Japanese got close enough to the field hospital to cause casualties, they did not break through. By evening a platoon of marines from the 21st Marines was detached to set up a stronger defense of the hospital area. The doctors of Company E continued to operate all through the night as more wounded from the 9th Marines were brought to the hospital area.[2]

However dedicated and compassionate were the medical personnel, there were some things over which they had no control. During heavy combat there would be more wounded than could be treated immediately. The more serious cases were identified and moved ahead to be operated on first. Less seriously wounded men simply had to bear their pain and wait their turn. From time to time, moreover, Japanese planes harassed the rear area and, although they did little damage, nevertheless posed a threat to all who were hospitalized. Lieutenant Orville Freeman, a future governor and cabinet officer, leading a platoon on a routine patrol was struck in the jaw by a machine gun bullet. Aided by his men, he managed to find his way back to the perimeter. His remembrance of the field hospital was probably shared by many:

> The jeep finally showed up and took me to our field hospital where they started to go to work on me.
> But this place was no great shakes either. The two nights I was at the field hospital—it was really more of a sick bay—Jap bombers came over. I had to spend those nights in a slit trench right next to two 90-mm antiaircraft guns that we had firing at the Japs. What a sound! My ears were sore for days.
> On the third day after I'd reached the beachhead one of those destroyer transports arrived, picked up several of us who needed more attention and took us down the slot to Guadalcanal, where they had a base hospital.[3]

Although not as dramatic as the experience of Company E, the work of the doctors and corpsmen in all the field hospitals continued unabated during the expansion of the perimeter, but the conditions under which they worked became much better as the front was pushed inland and more permanent installations were constructed at the field hospital locales. By the end of November the major problems faced by the medical corps concerned non-combat-related diseases. The work of the marine and army medical units had been so well done that fewer than 1 percent of all battle casualties died of their wounds.[4]

Even while the marines were making their first advances inland, some began to feel the effects of living in the jungle and swamps. It had rained on seventeen of the first eighteen days after the landings. Everyone who was there would agree with Orville Freeman's assessment of the weather:

> We finally set ourselves up and around four o'clock that first day we had our first experience with what I soon realized was a Bougainville ritual. It rained. As a matter of fact I think it rained at four o'clock every day that I was on that goddamn island. It was almost impossible to keep dry.

Then at night, with the sun gone, it would get chilly. It was always hot and humid during the day but not too bad as long as you were by the water. But then that rain would come, followed by the chill. It was miserable.

There you would be, lying in a hole in the sand with a wet poncho. You'd be soaked and you'd get so goddamn cold you thought you were going to die. Hell, I'm from Minnesota; I'm no stranger to cold. But this was different. It was so bad you'd try to keep your teeth from chattering because you wanted complete silence.[5]

Daytime temperatures would reach 100°, and men were forced to live in swampy areas where it was impossible to keep feet and legs dry. In conditions like these it was to be expected that men would get trench foot and other fungus diseases. Eugene Edwards, a sergeant in an amphibious tractor battalion, recalled:

Your feet began to rot, your clothes were stinking, you would get skin ulcers between your legs to the point where you ran around with Kotex on and were just downright miserable. That's just everyday living, and thats just the normal situation to say nothing of the other goings on.

Bugs, spiders, an ungodly number of insects biting on you. We used to put repellent on; I don't know whether it did any good but we used it.[6]

Colonel Frazer West, then commanding a company in the 9th Marines, was even more explicit:

Jungle rot was the major problem. We had very little change of clothes. That sand rubbing against your skin and the heat and wet combined made it easy to get jungle rot which is a form of fungus. Got it primarily on scalp, under arms, and in genital areas. I had it all above my knees. And it was miserable—no other word for it. No real cure for it. The only thing you could do was with the jungle ulcers. I'd get the corpsman to light a match on a razor blade, split the ulcer open, and squeeze sulfanilimide powder in it. I must have had at one time 30 jungle ulcers on me. This was fairly typical. I think the lower ranks even had more. At least I could get a little bit more being a company commander although I was right with them. The kids were miserable.[7]

Another chronic, although not life-threatening, problem was directly related to diet and water. After the first day the water supply for rear area troops was adequate. Good water was brought to the beach in drums and also in five-gallon jerry cans. The men carried two canteens. The water supplied to them on board ship had been chlorinated, and they were supposed to use halogen tablets for all other water. Given the heat and high humidity and the physical demands of combat, there were amazingly few cases of heat exhaustion. Most of the marine and army troops were aware of the necessity to maintain an adequate water level for their bodies. As they moved farther into the jungle, however, the good water became more difficult to find, and the men began to fill their canteens from the streams. Some obviously did not use the halogen tablets, and drinking the untreated water contributed to the high rate of diarrhea, particularly among the frontline troops. Frazer West commented on this:

> We had diarrhea so bad at this time that I talked Bob Cushman [CO 2/9] into allowing us to have a company mess. By bringing up water—the engineers had built a jeep road—lots of rinse water, in about two or three days I got rid of everybody's diarrhea. It wasn't dysentery; it could have gone into dysentery. It was bad rain diarrhea—bad water—and when you eat over a prolonged period of several weeks (unless you are putting it over the little alcohol thing) you can develop diarrhea real quick. All we had was K rations and C rations. Undoubtedly stress played a big part in it. We didn't even know the meaning of the word stress then but now we do. That played a part.[8]

There were also a few cases of more esoteric tropical diseases such as filariasis and even elephantiasis. Nothing could be done for victims of elephantiasis on Bougainville. They were evacuated as quickly as possible to Guadalcanal and then usually sent on to Pearl Harbor for the necessary treatment and long convalescence.

Experience on Guadalcanal had early taught the higher command about the debilitating effects of malaria. As noted, much of the terrain in the Empress Augusta Bay region was low, marshy ground with deeper holes of stagnant water, overgrown with trees, vines, and water plants. Through the swampy areas ran a number of sluggish streams, the largest being the Koromokina and Piva rivers. In addition, four creeks lay between the two rivers, of which Dead Jap, Buir, and Seabee creeks were the most important. These streams would have provided drainage for the swamps except that their flow was impeded by vegetation. Thus the entire area of the perimeter provided excellent breeding grounds for the malaria carrier, the *Anopheles* mosquito. Surprisingly the numbers of mosquitoes increased as the front lines moved forward and earlier campsites were abandoned. By the end of November mosquito larvae could be found everywhere in the occupied zone.[9]

To deal with sanitary problems, particularly control of malaria vectors, the marines landed three combat teams between D day and D + 3. One combat team was assigned to each regiment. They brought with them supplies to be issued to the companies including sixty Atabrine tablets for each man, four bottles of insect repellent per man, and one dispenser of freon-pyrethrum bombs for every four men. In addition they had chests of tools and eventually twenty-five thousand gallons of diesel oil for spraying suspected areas. Unfortunately for the control of malaria, a number of factors were working against the success of the plans made at Guadalcanal. One was the problem of working in a combat zone, where killing mosquitoes was not as high a priority as killing Japanese. The marine sanitary combat units and their army counterparts did not begin to do any really effective work until D + 10. Then there was the problem of lack of heavy equipment to help dig ditches and remove obstructions from the streams. The sanitary personnel had either to use hand tools and recruit native labor to help or to depend on the seabees and engineers in draining the swampy areas. Finally there was the problem of getting the troops to observe the most rudimentary precautions. The report of the sanitary team was quite frank: "Troops in combat are very lax about personal measures. In general, the men in the front lines protect themselves better than those in the rear areas. They are forced to do so because of camouflage, flash burns, and sleeping conditions. The men in the rear areas wore very few clothes and did not use bed nets, repellents, nor Freon-Pyrethrum dispensers to any appreciable extent."[10]

By the end of November, utilizing extra personnel from the 12th Marines, 71st Naval Construction Battalion, division headquarters, and forty-one native workers, in conjunction with the 37th Division Malaria Control Unit, the Malarial Control Construction Battalion had cleared the obstructions in the four creeks. The swamp through which Seabee Creek passed was lowered from an average depth of three feet to only six inches. By the end of the year the various malarial control units had cleared approximately sixty-one thousand linear yards of creeks, of which eight thousand yards were through swamp or marshland where there was no actual stream. The channels dug by hand were three to five feet wide and approximately two feet deep and the added water flow through them continued to increase their size. Approximately four million square yards of swamp were drained, thus eliminating a large area of potential breeding places. In addition, malarial control was aided by the good drainage ditches cut by the engineers as they built the lateral and inland roads. A large ditch along the fighter strip also helped lower the water table there.[11] All this, in conjunction with oiling of swampy areas and the attention paid by unit commanders in having their troops take Atabrine, had by the time of the army takeover of the enclave considerably reduced the most deleterious effects of malaria. Although some troops of the 37th and Americal divisions contracted the disease, the living conditions, even for first-line troops, by then were far superior to those suffered by the marine and army units in the first month after the invasion.

Another major problem area, which developed on D day, was that of supply. The planners had envisioned a supply dump for each of the three regiments. Each regiment would be responsible for handling and transporting the needed material from its own dump to its frontline troops. The chaotic landings and subsequent shifting of marine units made any such plan inoperable, however. Instead, the beaches were cluttered with supplies of all types. As the front moved inland, some semblance of order was obtained by using large numbers of combat troops along with shore-party units to shift the materiel around. The dumps were then used by the frontline units on a first-come-first-served basis. Ammunition, water, and rations were simply taken by most units from the nearest available source. Within a week the situation had been clarified and all shore-party dumps reverted to control of the marine division quartermaster. Later a division dump was established and all supplies elsewhere along the beach were gathered up and moved there. As new supplies arrived, either directly or from Puruata Island, they were shunted to this division supply dump. The army's 37th Division adopted a similar central distribution point, establishing regimental and battalion supply dumps forward as the situation became more settled. This system allowed for a much more efficient and equitable distribution of supplies. Puruata Island, because of easier access and its safer location, became the major permanent supply depot, under direct corps control. By January so much was concentrated there that General Harmon could joke that he believed the island was in danger of sinking because of the weight of materiel.[12]

Delivery of supplies to the front lines was an arduous and hazardous task. Before the completion of the lateral road, most supplies were delivered as far forward as possible by truck or jeep and then transferred to amphibious tractors of the 3d Amphibious Tractor Battalion. There were twenty-nine LVTs landed with the first waves on D day. Eventually 124 of these early alligators were landed in the marine sector, but because of problems with their track design and the demands made on the machines, normally only a few were available for use each day. At the time of the Battle of Piva Forks, the same number were operating as had landed on D day. Despite all the difficulties in keeping them running, the LVTs played the key role in supplying the frontline troops during the first weeks of the operation. They could easily operate in the swamps and on the muddy trails, where any wheeled vehicle would have been mired down. They broke trail through the swamps and marshes, delivering all types of supplies as close to the front lines as possible. In all, the men of the 3d Amphibian Tractor Battalion delivered almost twenty-three thousand tons of supplies of all types. Without the LVTs, supply to the forward companies would have been all but impossible during the first weeks. They played a major role in the rapid expansion of the perimeter.[13]

It fell to the marine and army engineer units, in conjunction with the seabees, to make the Empress Augusta Bay lodgment more livable while they were constructing roads and the airfields that were the main point of the invasion. At first the major task was simply to help bring some kind of order out of the chaotic beach situation and then to begin constructing roads that would expedite both supply and movement of troops. The trails into the interior were widened, but the main focus of construction activity was on the lateral road begun on D + 2 and gouged out in two weeks. This rough one-lane road began near the Koromokina beaches, wound into the interior for several thousand yards, and then turned southeastward toward the coconut grove and the Piva River. The small streams were bridged by hand-hewn timbers. Extremely swampy areas were drained and coconut logs laid down to minimize difficulty in transit. Although much work remained to be done on this road, it did connect the two sections of the beachhead and was ready for use by the time of the Piva Forks engagement.

By 10 November the 117th Combat Engineer Battalion of the 37th Division was ashore with most of its equipment. At first it was kept busy cutting supply trails east of the Koromokina River, but by late November it had completed a three-span all-traffic bridge across the river. The men then turned their attention to improving the lateral road in the army's section. Army and marine engineers used bulldozers and explosives to clear a strip one hundred feet wide. Then they scooped out drainage ditches on either side of the planned thirty-foot roadway.

128 Bougainville

These were ten feet wide and five feet deep. Topsoil adjacent to the road was removed, uncovering volcanic sand adequate for surfacing. This was piled up alongside the road to be smoothed out by bulldozers and graders. By the time responsibility for actions on the island passed from IMAC command to the XIV Corps on 15 December most of the road construction within the perimeter had been completed. After that date a service command was established for Bougainville, which thereafter directed all engineering work on the island.[14]

Additional engineering units arrived soon after the army had assumed command. Elements of the 131st Engineering Regiment arrived between 15 and 21 December, to be joined later by the 57th Combat Battalion. Part of the 131st and all the 57th joined the 117th in supporting the infantry. Men of these units cut more trails, built timber bridges, and aided in strengthening the perimeter defenses. Many were put to work in the service command area at first, clearing the jungle by hand and cutting drainage ditches to lower the water table. Heavy equipment was brought in to finish the tasks. After the ground had been cleared and drained, construction could begin on the major projects, particularly on the supply dumps for all sections of the command. The largest jobs by far were constructing the storage areas for quartermaster, ordnance, chemical warfare, and air force units.[15]

One of the largest projects was the ration dump for the Quartermaster Corps. For two months four hundred men of the 131st Engineers worked on this project with six bulldozers, two clamshells, and twenty dump trucks. The area cleared was equal in extent to four large city blocks. The storage platforms were placed on man-made elevations. Each platform was sixty by thirty feet and was designed to support a hundred tons of rations. These platforms were constructed from lumber from coconut trees sawed at sawmills set up at different locations. By the end of April 1944, ten such platforms had been built on each elevation. In addition, a 4.5 square-mile area was cleared for gasoline storage tanks, and a chemical warfare dump measuring over one square mile was also developed. Better living quarters were built in selected camps and in the areas of the tent hospitals. Eventually ten more-permanent buildings of a simple design were erected to house such organizations, the chaplain's offices, and the Red Cross. A movie theater called Loewe's Bougainville was built, as were three tennis courts and a baseball diamond.[16] Thus by the spring of 1944 most of the troops in the rear echelon had amenities that would have been inconceivable to the marine and army troops who had made the initial landings the previous November.

The men of the 37th and Americal divisions up forward could not boast of any such luxuries, although the living conditions had improved considerably. By the time of the major Japanese counterthrust in March there were tent cities behind the perimeter lines. Improvised showers had been set up, and movies were shown on a regular basis. The frontline troops had also been involved in construction work on the system of bunkers or pillboxes and interconnecting trenches that defined the perimeter. One former rifleman of the 129th RCT recalled:

> The engineers were with us all the time; I remember them building bridges over these little streams that we couldn't get over otherwise, and we didn't have to do any of that kind of building at all, although we built our own pillboxes. We dug the holes and built them with the trees we cut down. These were almost square—12 to 15 feet square—and they were not more than eight feet deep. Of course it was easy to dig; the soil was mostly sand and easy to dig into. We would then reinforce them with other trees. We left firing ports to the front and we left inclines to the rear to crawl out of. Some of the pillboxes were connected by trenches and some by a tunnel you would have to crawl through. The main ones were connected. These normally had four to six men to a pillbox and we made little cots from the strong vines. . . . We also strung out some barbed wire in the danger areas where we thought the Japs might come through.[17]

The most important construction effort on Bougainville was begun immediately after the landings by the seabees of the 71st Naval Construction Battalion. Survey teams and workers were sent out on D + 3 to begin preliminary work on the proposed fighter strip at Cape Torokina. The plans for this airfield called for a runway 200 feet wide by 5,150 feet long. With some assistance from the 53d Construction Battalion and a marine labor party of a hundred men, the work of clearing the jungle and removing the muck down to an acceptable subgrade proceeded rapidly. The seabees, despite the danger of snipers, worked at night to cut out the runway and lay down the steel matting. Enough of the strip had been completed by 24 November that a damaged navy dive bomber was able to make an emergency landing. The field was completed on 10 December.[18] Seventeen F4Us of Marine Squardron VMF-216 were the first to land on the new strip, followed by six SBDs and four SCAT transport planes. From this time on, the Torokina field would play an important role in the support of the army units on the perimeter and in the sweeps against Rabaul undertaken by VMF-216 and VMF-214, led by the brash, swashbuckling Major

Gregory Boyington.[19] Simultaneously with the construction of the Torokina airstrip and its direct support facilities, camps were erected for the aviation personnel, who began to arrive a few days before the planes of VMF-216 landed. These facilities ultimately included two galleys and mess halls, storage buildings, and a hospital with three wards and an operating room with all utilities.

The 36th Construction Battalion arrived on Bougainville on 26 November 1943 and immediately began work on the two longer airfields in the interior. The first bomber strip, code named Piva Uncle, was planned to be eight thousand feet long and three hundred feet wide, complete with warm-up aprons at each end. Progress was rapid in spite of intermittent artillery fire from the Japanese, the never-ending rains, and the jungle that had to be cleared. The first airplane landed on the strip on 19 December, and Piva Uncle was officially opened as a staging field on 30 December. With the arrival of heavier bombers, it was found necessary to extend the runway two thousand feet. By the time the seabee units were removed from the island in July and August 1944, they had constructed at Piva Uncle three taxiways with 35 hardstands, a shop area, seven nose hangars, three prefabricated large steel buildings, and twenty-six frame buildings. The 77th Battalion had also constructed a five-thousand-man camp for the marine air group, and the 36th Battalion had constructed camp facilities for two thousand more troops.[20]

The 77th Naval Construction Battalion had arrived on 10 December and was assigned the task of constructing the second airfield, another fighter strip, code named Piva Yoke. The difficulties were similar to those involved in building Piva Uncle. Grading was completed by 28 December, but final completion was delayed until 3 January because of the late arrival of the steel matting. When this second interior field became operative, marine and army midweight bombers and torpedo and dive bombers from the two new fields were able to strike directly at Rabaul early in the morning before cloud cover obscured the targets. Each of the fields, like that at Cape Torokina, also acted as a support strip for AIRSOLS planes operating out of Vella Lavella and Munda. The presence of a large number of P-39s, Corsairs, SBDs, and TBFs on Bougainville proved a godsend to the 37th and Americal troops struck by the Japanese counterattack of early March 1944.

The 75th Battalion was working simultaneously to build a complete tank farm for the two airfields. Problems with shipping and loss of supplies in November complicated the task since many of the needed fittings simply were not available, and pipes had to be welded together at the joints. Despite the usual difficulties of working in the marshy jungle, the tank farm, comprising one 10,000-barrel tank and eighteen 1,000-barrel tanks, tanker moorings, submarine pipelines, and five miles of overland pipe, was completed in time to support air activities from the new airfields. Enemy shelling damaged the pipeline eighteen times, but in each case the break was quickly repaired, and delivery of fuel was not interrupted.[21]

The 75th Battalion was also busy constructing a PT boat base on Puruata Island. Wood pilings and timber were used to build a main pier, a fueling pier, and a crash boat pier. Eighteen small boat landings, using three-pile dolphins driven in and lashed, were provided and LST landings installed. The seabees also built complete camp facilities on the island, including quarters, mess halls, five prefabricated steel warehouses, and an emergency hospital with all utilities. By April 1944 seabees of the 36th Battalion had built a main hospital facility supplementing the emergency installations farther forward. This hospital consisted of seventy standard quonset huts and one forty-by-one-hundred-foot mess hall with accommodations for five hundred patients, an administration building, a general and an underground emergency surgery, and quarters for the medical personnel.[22]

The Japanese after their naval defeats in November and with Rabaul under constant attack from New Guinea and the Solomons bases were in no position to halt or even delay this construction of what amounted to a fortress enclave. The various Japanese airfields had been rendered inoperative even before the invasion. Therefore General Hyakutake, once his blocking force was beaten back at Piva Forks, was unable to interfere in any significant way with the many construction projects that made the American perimeter not only more livable but daily more impregnable. Time was against the Japanese commander. The longer he waited to launch another major counterattack, the stronger his enemy became. By the time he seriously considered moving troops forward for another attempt to destroy the American enclave, there were two full army combat divisions and thousands of shore-party, seabee, and medical personnel ashore. The American commanders could operate on interior lines with good lateral and connective roads and had total control of the air over the battlefield. Even the fanatical loyalty of the Japanese soldier and his ability to endure hardships could not even the balance. Any Japanese attack was foredoomed to failure.

8. Consolidating the Perimeter

The forward movement of the 3d Marine Division and the subsequent fight for Hills 600 and 600A had taken place under a new corps commander. Major General Oscar Griswold, commanding the army's XIV Corps, had replaced General Geiger on 15 December. This was the first step in Admiral Halsey's revised plan to relieve all marine units on Bougainville and replace them with army troops. Originally the army's Americal and 40th divisions had been slated to land on New Ireland with the objective of taking the strong Japanese air and naval base at Kavieng at the north end of the island. Halsey was opposed to the New Ireland operation and would ultimately be responsible for the decision in early 1944 to bypass Kavieng, but in November 1943 he and his staff were planning for that operation. Despite the fact that the Americal Division had acquitted itself very well in the later stages of the Guadalcanal campaign, Halsey was convinced that a marine division should spearhead the Kavieng operation. The 1st Marine Division was already scheduled for the Cape Gloucester landings and the 2d Division was recovering from its losses in the Gilberts, leaving only the 3d Division available. Halsey believed it would not be too battered after the Cape Torokina landings, but General Millard Harmon, commanding all army units in the South Pacific, disagreed with Halsey's reasoning. He felt that the disruption in the Bougainville operation that would be caused by a change of command and withdrawal of the marines might "jeopardize the success of this operation."[1] Halsey was not convinced by his subordinates' arguments, and the November order stood. He would have the 3d Marine Division for the projected New Ireland landings.

Headquarters of the Americal Division was notified on 25 November to prepare to move to Bougainville. On 5 December, Americal received the basic outline of the move, which was to occur in four echelons, each to be loaded on three APAs and two AKAs. The first elements of the Americal Division, the 164th Infantry Regiment, commanded by Colonel Crump Garvin, left Fiji on 19 December and arrived at Empress Augusta Bay on Christmas morning after an uneventful but long voyage from Viti Levu in the Fiji Islands. After reassembling in an area just beyond the beach, the 164th moved to the front and, unit by unit, relieved the 9th Marines on the left flank of the 3d Division's perimeter. Garvin arranged his troops along the static defense line, with the 1st Battalion on the right, the 3d in the center, and the 1st tieing into the right flank of the 37th Division. The relief of the 9th Marines was completed by 28 December. The second echelon of the Americal, the 245th Artillery (105 mm) and the 182d Infantry Regiment, commanded by Colonel William D. Long, arrived on 28 December and by 2 January 1944 had replaced the 21st Marines in the center and were tied into the 164th on the left and the left-flank elements of the 2d Marine Raider Battalion. The last regiment of the division, the 132d Infantry, commanded by Colonel Joseph Bush, arrived on 9 January and within two days had relieved the marine paratroops on the extreme right of the lodgment. With the arrival of the last of the artillery units on 14 January, Major General John Hodge, who had relieved General Turnage on 28 December, had his division firmly ensconced on the defensive line along the heights from just east of Hill 700 to the Torokina River and thence southward to the bay.[2] The last of the marine infantry units had left Bougainville by the end of January, leaving only a few specialized marine units including the 3d Marine Defense Battalion behind.

Supporting the infantry units of the 37th and Americal divisions was a strong backup of artillery, although XIV Corps did not have its own organic artillery. Brigadier General Leo Kreber, the artillery commander of the 37th, acted as corps artillery commander. He could call upon six 105-mm howitzer battalions and one 155-mm howitzer battalion organic to the two army divisions. In addition, he had provisional corps artillery consisting of two 155-mm gun batteries of the 3d Marine Defense Battalion and light 90-mm antiaircraft batteries. In early March six cannon companies with their 75-mm pack howitzers reached Bougainville and joined the infantry regiments.[3] A number of

L-4 Cub light aircraft were available to each of the divisions to be used for artillery spotting. By mid-January the pilots were flying from dawn to dusk reconnoitering the areas in front of the perimeter and adjusting fire on targets of opportunity.[4] Later some of these planes would be used to fly in supplies and evacuate wounded from advance posts established far beyond the perimeter lines.

General Griswold on 6 January ordered the 164th Regiment of the Americal Division to occupy Hill 700 located just in front of and beyond the left flank of the Americal sector. Within five days the 2d Battalion had pushed forward almost a thousand yards through nearly impenetrable undergrowth and up the steep slopes to occupy the crest of Hill 700, which was the highest point held by the Americans. After the hill was secured, men of the 37th Division's 145th Infantry relieved the 164th, and the boundary between the divisions was moved more than a mile eastward. On the right flank the low, swampy ground was difficult to defend. On 17 January units from 2/132 moved forward to set up positions nearer the Torokina River at the jungle fringe. After a number of reconnaisance patrols had scoured the area in search of higher ground, the 132d displaced forward to the west edge of the river, thus straightening out the previously crooked defense line. Outposts were then established one-quarter mile east of the river.[5] There they remained until 29 January, when corps headquarters decided to negate the Japanese defenses east and north of the 132d's forward lines.

In the weeks following the arrival of the Americal Division, activity along the front of the lodgment was mainly confined to improving the defenses and to aggressive patrolling. In all areas units were hard at work constructing earth, log, and sandbag pillboxes and interlocking trenches and rifle pits. Each of the bunkers was large enough to accommodate from three to five men, whose major responsibility was to man or protect an automatic weapon. Trees and undergrowth ahead of the line were cut down so that an approaching enemy was exposed at least fifty yards ahead, mainly to prevent the Japanese from using cover to throw grenades. At key points, particularly in front of the pillboxes, a double apron of barbed wire was laid out, in front of which pressure mines were laid. A variety of booby traps were also constructed, the simplest of which were grenades attached to trip wires along the most obvious approach lanes. In some areas oil drums were loaded with scrap iron packed around a bangalore torpedo and set up to be triggered by a simple electrical device. Searchlights were brought forward and stationed near the front, and various improvised illumination devices were constructed using flares, gasoline, and

Consolidating the Perimeter 135

thermite grenades to provide light if the Japanese decided to attack at night. Almost all units were issued extra machine guns and each rifle squad had two BARs. In some areas, such as that occupied by the 129th Regimental Combat Team of the 37th, these defenses were organized in depth, so that if the front were penetrated, the attackers would find themselves facing a new line that had to be broken.[6] General Griswold, operating on interior lines, could shift troops quickly from one sector to another and also reinforce areas from his corps reserve, which included infantry units from the various service battalions.[7]

Both divisions continued the aggressive patrolling that had been standard procedure since the first days of the invasion. All patrols were conducted during daylight hours, since it had earlier been discovered that night patrols could be successful in jungle terrain only if the route had previously been reconnoitered and marked. Movement at night was attempted only to put a patrol in a better position to begin its mission once daylight came.

There were basically four different types of patrol. Usually a reconnaissance patrol would be of squad or platoon size, never fewer than twelve men. A patrol of this size could move quietly and quickly through the underbrush and junglelike growth but still had enough men to defend itself if attacked. Combat patrols, as described in the Operations Report of the Americal Division, "should be the size of a company, or possibly larger. Although this may seem to be a large unweildy group, if all members of the company had been adequately trained, they can move rapidly and silently. A patrol of this size, if aggressively handled, can raise havoc with an enemy battalion, and vanish into the jungle before strong resistance can be organized."[8] The other two types of patrols were the ambush and sniper patrols, which were used sparingly and only after the location, size, and capabilities of the enemy in a given location had been assessed.

The actual distance covered by a patrol depended on its mission and the type of terrain. The rule of thumb for movement of all types of patrols on Bougainville was that without resistance they could cover only seven hundred yards an hour. Each patrol was provided with enough food and ammunition to enable it to stay out on its mission for as long as eight days.[9] Most of the patrols sent out during January and the early part of February met no Japanese. The major function, to gather information on features of the terrain, was accomplished without many serious fire fights.

Although the information obtained was invaluable for the divisional staffs and particularly for the artillery, the men involved considered it foul duty, repeated over and over again seemingly without

136 Bougainville

purpose. However, American patrols had pushed far into the interior across the flatlands to the forward slopes of the Japanese-held Hills 1111, 1000, 600, and 250—all of which overlooked the beachhead.

One of the first heavy actions involving the Americal Division occurred on 7 January when a large patrol of more than a hundred men of 1/164 moved out toward Hill 250 located approximately three thousand yards northeast of the regimental lines. After precautionary artillery fire had been directed against the east side of this hill, the patrol began to work its way around it to scout the area to the north. The Japanese entrenched on the slopes opened heavy fire on the Americans, and a large number of Japanese maneuvered behind the patrol, forcing it to fight its way back to the perimeter. After a two-hour fire fight in heavy undergrowth, the patrol forced the Japanese roadblock and reached the safety of the regimental lines. The patrol had suffered only four wounded but reported killing about twelve Japanese during this engagement.

Other January actions included one on 10 January, when a large patrol of the 182d operating a mile beyond the Torokina River discovered a strong Japanese position. They attacked and drove the Japanese back, killing twenty-five men. On 17 January patrols of the 164th Infantry operating near the southeast slopes of Hill 600 made contact with groups of Japanese, amounting to battalion strenghth. The main elements of 1/164 moved into this area and with heavy artillery support drove the Japanese from their strongpoints.[10]

The 37th Division had been in its fairly secure positions since early December and had been very actively pushing its patrols out far beyond the lines. One such excursion took a reinforced platoon of 2/145 approximately thirty miles up the coast to scout a reported Japanese bivouac area near Cape Moltke. Other patrols pushed deep into the central area of Bougainville up the Numa Numa Trail. By mid-February General Beightler and his staff became concerned about mounting evidence of increased Japanese activity in front of the 37th. Intelligence information from the Americal front also indicated stepped-up activity. One example was the strong Japanese reaction to the occupation of an outpost six miles beyond the perimeter on 14 February. Initially, Lieutenant Colonel Cecil Whitcomb, commanding the 145th, sent in a reinforced platoon from Company A of 3/145 and two platoons from the Fiji Infantry Regiment. Initial contact with the enemy forced the patrol to establish a defense; they positioned mortars, communications, and the native carriers in the center and the riflemen and automatic weapons along the perimeter. The Japanese, estimated by the Fiji scouts to be in excess of three platoons, occupied ridge lines across the riverbank and from this superior position poured rifle and mortar fire into the American defenses. This forced the patrol to abandon its position by midafternoon and retire approximately one and a half miles to the rear of the contact area where the wounded could be evacuated. Division headquarters decided to contest the river area with the Japanese, and two companies from 1/145 were ordered to reinforce those still in position beyond the main perimeter. This combined force of almost five hundred men then advanced approximately half a mile, set up a defense, and requested artillery fire for the morning of 16 February to neutralize the Japanese defenses before the attack. Unfortunately, some of the rounds landed short, right in the area held by the Americans. Three members of the 145th and one Fijian soldier were killed and twenty more wounded. The need to use so many troops to evacuate the wounded over nearly impassable terrain persuaded division command to call off the plan to drive the Japanese back and establish a command outpost there. All members of the main force were withdrawn into the 37th's perimeter by 17 February. This sortee had cost the patrol five dead and twenty-nine wounded. Its only positive result was to discover that the Japanese had brought in a large force immediately to the front of the left flank of the perimeter.[11]

One of the most colorful and effective units operating under corps command was the 1st Battalion of the Fiji Infantry Regiment. This battalion consisting of 777 enlisted men and 34 officers, commanded by Lieutenant Colonel J.B.K. Taylor of the New Zealand Army, arrived at Bougainville in late December. Taylor was wounded the first night ashore and was replaced as commander by Major Gregory Upton, who was in charge of the battalion during its long-range patrols in late December and January. The Fijian troops were well trained, proud of their uniforms and ability to march, and according to reports, loved to sing a wide variety of Fijian songs as well as the more modern American tunes. Almost immediately after their arrival, plans were under way to use their unique abilities as jungle fighters to establish a combat outpost far to the east of the mountain range, most of which was controlled by the Japanese.[12] On 28 December a reinforced company of the Fiji Battalion moved out along the Numa Numa Trail with its first objective the village of Ibu more than twenty miles north of Cape Torokina. Once there, they were to make note of enemy activity along the east coast and report these movements to corps headquarters. In addition they were to disrupt Japanese lines of communication whenever possible. The detachment would be supplied by air drops.

The Fijians had reached their objective by 2 January and established a strong defense line around the village. They found a site suitable for a landing strip eight miles from Mount Balbi and hacked down the underbrush so that the L-4 observation planes from the 37th and Americal divisions could land. One pilot, Lieutenant Charles Cross, made thirteen such flights across the high, rugged mountains before he crashed in the jungle. His body was never found. Such flights, however dangerous, facilitated the quick exchange of information and could also provide a speedy means of evacuation of any wounded. Fijian patrols were active along the east coast all during January. They made detailed reconnaissance of the coast from Asitivi Mission to Kiviri Point and engaged in a number of fire fights with small Japanese patrols. In an attack on a Japanese strongpoint at Pipipaia, forty-seven Japanese were killed without the loss of a single Fijian.

By the end of January the Japanese decided to eliminate the Ibu outpost as a part of their proposed attack plans on the perimeter. They began on 14 February with a major attack against one of the roadblocks. The Fijians received permission to abandon Ibu and retreat back to the perimeter. They fought a series of well-planned rearguard actions and reached the west coast on 19 February, where the 37th Division Reconnaissance Troop had established a covering beachhead. During the withdrawal, an estimated 120 Japanese had been killed; only one Fijian had been slightly wounded. For the number of troops involved and the information on enemy movements obtained, this action by the Fiji unit far ahead of the defensive perimeter was the most successful operation during this phase of the Bougainville campaign.[13]

Reports from all sectors held by the Americal Division indicated a buildup of Japanese forces; so corps command decided to expand the bridgehead east of the mouth of the Torokina River. General Hodge ordered Company C of 1/132, supported by artillery and tanks from the 754th Tank Battalion, to clear out all enemy defenses three hundred yards east of the bridgehead lines. Early in the morning of 29 January all available howitzers from division artillery pounded the target areas. Then at 0830 Company C moved out along the beach area and turned inland at the edge of the jungle. Almost immediately the company was struck by intense rifle, machine gun, and mortar fire. The Japanese had constructed a series of pillboxes of dry ground over an area extending at places up to four hundred yards deep. These were all well hidden by the tall grass and junglelike growth. A broad swampy area on either side precluded flank attacks, and the riflemen were forced to approach head on. Unfortunately the tank crews had buttoned up in order to escape small arms fire, and the crews could not locate the pillboxes. At that point Staff Sergeant Jesse Drowley, in charge of a reserve squad on the perimeter line, saw what was happening and rushed forward, at first simply to pull some of the wounded to safety. Then he spotted two of the forward pillboxes. He raced across open terrain to the tanks, attracted the attention of one crew, and climbed on top of the tank so he could talk to the tank commander through the hatch. From this position, he used a submachine gun with tracer bullets to direct the tanks against the pillboxes. Despite a very serious chest wound, Drowley continued with his self-appointed mission and was hit again, in the left eye. The tanks with his guidance destroyed the pillboxes and the rest of the men of Company C, emboldened by the sergeant's actions, moved in and destroyed the remaining nineteen pillboxes. After recovery from his wounds, Sergeant Drowley was decorated with the Congressional Medal of Honor, the only member of the Americal Division to be so honored.[14]

The increasing contacts by patrols of both divisions with strong Japanese patrols during February indicated that the Japanese high command might be contemplating a major attack. Such suspicions were confirmed by statements from prisoners, who related that the Japanese 6th Division was planning a major thrust in early March. This information persuaded General Griswold not to attempt a further expansion of the perimeter, particularly on the extreme right flank in the direction of the beach village of Mavavia, about three thousand yards east of the Torokina River. However, he did decide to occupy the Magine Islands lying about a mile offshore south of Mavavia. He wanted to prevent the Japanese from using the small coral islands to get a good view of activity along the Americal beach line, but even more important, he wanted to have this observation post to watch Japanese movements near Mavavia. Surprisingly, when elements of the 21st Reconnaissance Troop occupied both islands on 27 February, they found no Japanese on either. Apparently the Japanese had not appreciated the value of the islands. The reconnaissance troop quickly set up defensive positions on both and two 75-mm self-propelled guns were brought from the perimeter to lay flanking fire on the Japanese positions to the northeast.[15]

From a purely tactical viewpoint, the Japanese position confronting the perimeter was not desperate, although the Americans from the very beginning had seized the initiative. The American perimeter by March was based on a series of hills in the central part of the line and was anchored on either flank by swampy ground and the Laruma and Torokina Rivers. However, even the highest ground held by the Americans, Hills 608 and 700, were at a lower elevation than the heights held by the Japanese. To the immediate north of Hill 700 was Blue Ridge, and three thousand yards away to the southeast were Hills 1000 and 1111. These gave the Japanese excellent views of American frontline positions. They unquestionably knew the approximate number of army troops present and that the front being defended was too long to be manned in great strength or in depth. The task for General Hyakutake in planning his counterstroke would be to decide how many men would be needed to break the defenses and where it would be most profitable to strike.

General Hyakutake had been under pressure from his superiors since the initial marine landings to take definite action to clear the lodgment. After the actions that forced the Japanese from the heights around the Torokina River, Hyakutake finally decided to cease defending and go on the attack. Preparations for his offensive, code named TA, began in early January. In all, he designated over fifteen thousand men from his total strength of nearly forty thousand to take part in the operation. The major element of his force was the 6th Division, a regular peacetime unit of the Japanese army now commanded by Lieutenant General Masatane Kanda. It had been directly involved in China operations from the very beginning of the invasion in 1937 and had had a starring role in one of the great atrocities of that war, the rape of Nanking in December 1937. Prior to its arrival in Bougainville in January 1943 it had also participated in several other operations against Hankow and Changsha. It was a veteran division whose officers, particularly those of the highest rank, were anxious to drive the Americans into the sea. For the TA operation General Kanda would also have under his command the 1st and 3d Battalions of the 53d Infantry Regiment and part of the 81st Infantry Regiment from the 17th Division. In addition he brought forward an artillery group consisting of four 150-mm howitzers, two 105-mm howitzers, and a large number of 75-mm mountain guns to add their fire power to the regimental artillery in support of the infantry attack. Artillery ammunition supplied for the heavy-caliber weapons totalled three hundred rounds apiece, of which one-fifth were to be used in direct fire support, the rest for interdicting the airfields.[16] The operation as conceived by Hyakutake's staff would be a joint army-navy venture, presumably with air strikes from Rabaul against the American perimeter and airfields to be coordinated with the infantry attack.

It is very difficult to understand what motivated Japanese strategic and tactical planning not only on Bougainville but in most of the campaigns in the Central and South Pacific. Hyakutake's proposed attack on the perimeter is an excellent example of such an operation. The glib, easy explanation would be that it was simply a case where the code of *bushido* dictated a fatalistic, last-chance attempt to drive the Americans into the sea similar to the one at Guadalcanal. But the situation of Bougainville was considerably different from that at Guadalcanal. Hyakutake's troops on Bougainville held the high ground overlooking the American positions, and he and his staff should have recognized that except for strengthening the perimeter, the marine and army units had not attempted any concerted major offensive since the latter part of December. The terrain, covered with dense jungle, would have protected his bases in the north and south of the island, and he still had over forty thousand troops of the 17th Army and an additional twenty thousand sailors of the 8th Fleet in southern Bougainville with which to contain any serious American offensive.

There appear to be dual reasons for Hyakutake's planned attack. One is the pressure from his superiors to try to negate the three airfields on Bougainville operating in support of the almost continuous attacks on Rabaul. Another reason may be simply faulty intelligence information. Although difficult to believe, there is evidence that Hyakutake thought that the Americans had only one division with which to defend the perimeter. One would imagine that even without naval and air support, his patrols in the months since December would have ascertained that General Griswold had two reinforced infantry divisions in addition to service personnel. Had Hyakutake known this, perhaps he would have committed more than fifteen thousand troops to the attack. The faulty information about the number of his enemy doomed the venture to failure from the beginning and made ludicrous the idea that the Americans would be defeated by 17 March. The Japanese staff had been so confident that they had planned the unconditional surrender ceremony and had even designated the spot where General Griswold would stand.[17]

Hyakutake's problems were further intensified by the total dominance of the United States Navy in all areas of the central and northern Solomons. The various destroyer divisions made regular sweeps down the Bougainville Strait, bombarding Buka and the Shortlands. The navy PBYs, the Black Cats, operated at night in conjunction with PT boats and LCT gunboats to interdict coastwise barge traffic as well as barges ferrying Japanese troops from Choiseul. Although Admiral Takeda later boasted that he managed to run the gauntlet and transport fourteen hundred men by barge to Empress Augusta Bay, the reality was that Hyakutake could not count on moving any significant number of troops by sea.[18] The escort ships necessary for any large-scale amphibious operation were not available. They had either been sunk in late 1943 or withdrawn from the Solomons and New Britain by a fearful Japanese high command.

More devastating to the eventual success of any strong Japanese attack on the perimeter was the lack of air cover, direct reflection of the constant raids on Rabaul and the obvious lack of skilled Japanese pilots to man what aircraft was left. Air raids on the perimeter had by mid-January become only nuisance strikes, most of which were carried out at night. Few were as successful as that of the early morning of 23 January when two Japanese bombers after flying back and forth across the Americal sector let loose a string of bombs, some of which by luck landed on the division command post. They made a shambles of the office and tents of the chief of staff and the G-2 and wrecked the quarters where General Hodge and some of his staff lived. Fortunately, none of the senior officers were hurt in this raid, although damage to equipment was extensive.[19] This lucky strike simply exemplifies what could have been achieved if Hyakutake could have counted on only a small portion of those planes destroyed by AIRSOLS and the 5th Air Force in the previous months.

To understand Japanese plans to reduce the perimeter, one must also consider the context, the broader aspect of the war during the first months of 1944. The Allied High Command had not yet decided against a direct amphibious assault to take Rabaul. General MacArthur still believed that such an invasion would be necessary, notwithstanding the difficulty and the cost, and it was for this reason, and others, that the 1st Marine Division was landed on the opposite coast of New Britain at Cape Gloucester in January.

Even more important was Admiral Halsey's decision to occupy the Green Islands, located thirty-seven miles northwest of Buka and fifty-five miles east of New Ireland. The occupation would cut off the Japanese on Bougainville from supplies and reinforcements from the Rabaul area. Nissan, the largest of the islands, was reportedly only lightly defended, and its flat terrain appeared ideal for building an airstrip. On 29 January a reconnaissance force, a total of 330 men of the 30th Battalion of the 3d New Zealand Division, landed on Nissan. After a quick surveillance all that Halsey suspected was confirmed, and the overlarge scouting force was withdrawn. He then gave the order to land the 14th Brigade Group of the 3d New Zealand Division. The decision to utilize such a large force against the small garrison was based on the fear that the Japanese with over 100,000 men on the Gazelle Peninsula and New Ireland might attempt a counterattack. In fact, aside from air strikes against the convoy, the Japanese at Rabaul did nothing to halt the invasion. By the end of D day, 15 February, 5,800 New Zealanders were on shore, and within five days of mopping up had killed the 102 Japanese on the island. The seabees began work on the projected airstrips, and by 4 March the fighter strip was handling its first planes. A bomber field was ready for the first light bomber strike against Kavieng on 16 March. Within days, PT boats sortied out from Nissan against any Japanese supply ships operating to the east. With the loss of the Green Islands, the ring around Rabaul was almost complete. For General Hyakutake, the loss meant that the only direct link between Rabaul and Bougainville was by submarine. For the rest of the war the Japanese on New Ireland, New Britain, and the Solomons were isolated from one another.[20]

The air strikes against Rabaul continued unabated through January. AIRSOLS now had definite air superiority. The 13th Air Force on 12 January began to operate B-25 medium bombers from the airstrip on Stirling Island. The new Piva airfields on Bougainville gave AIRSOLS fighters and attack bombers forward bases close to Rabaul. Heavy bombers (four squadrons at a time), medium bombers (three squadrons at a time), and seven squadrons of torpedo and dive bombers struck at Rabaul on a daily basis. General Ralph Mitchell, commander of AIRSOLS, had designated the airfields first-priority targets, followed by shipping in Simpson Harbor. To protect the bombers, AIRSOLS had by the end of January more than two hundred fighter aircraft.[21] A typical strike was that of 17 January, when twenty-nine dive bombers and eighteen torpedo bombers, escorted by seventy fighters, concentrated on ships in the harbor, sinking five. On that day approximately seventy-nine Japanese fighters rose to intercept the American planes. Seventeen were shot down.

Despite such heavy plane losses, the Japanese were not yet ready to concede the air over Rabaul, although they stopped sending large numbers of ships to New Britain. Later in January, Admiral Koga sent the 2d Air Squadron, the very best planes and pilots he had available, down from Truk. The ninety-eight planes brought Admiral Kurita's force up to three hundred available aircraft once again. AIRSOLS continued pounding Rabaul's five fields and by mid-February had destroyed most of the barges in the harbor, driven away larger ships, and shot up many of the planes sent by Koga. The last significant dogfight over Rabaul occurred on 19 February, when 50 Japanese fighters intercepted an incoming attack by 145 American planes, and 23 Japanese planes were shot down.[22]

These attacks on Rabaul and targets of opportunity in the vicinity were accomplished with very few losses to Allied pilots. Unfor-

144 Bougainville

tunately the Marine Corps lost two of its leading airmen during these air battles. Major Gregory Boyington, the leading Marine Corps ace, and his wingman, Captain George Ashmun, were shot down on 3 January. Boyington was subsequently captured and spent the rest of the war in Japanese prison camps. Lieutenant Robert Hanson of VMF-215 destroyed four Japanese planes on 1 February, bringing his total to twenty-five planes before he was killed on a strafing run on Cape St. George three days later. Both Boyington and Hanson later received the Congressional Medal of Honor.[23]

While AIRSOLS was pounding Rabaul, events far to the north, at Truk, would play a most important role in the Japanese efforts to maintain a viable base there and, by extension, their ability to support Hyakutake on Bougainville. On 17-18 February Admiral Marc Mitscher's Task Force 58 sank 200,000 tons of Japanese shipping and destroyed over three hundred planes, many of which were destined for Rabaul. A follow-up attack by Admiral Spruance and a strong naval force organized around the new battleships *Iowa* and *New Jersey* bombarded the battered island and sank two destroyers. Truk's usefulness as a fleet anchorage and advance naval base was over. Soon Admiral Koga would move his headquarters to Koror in the Palau Islands. The devastating losses at Truk also sealed the fate of Rabaul. Koga reluctantly ordered all serviceable planes and their crews out of Rabaul, leaving only thirty damaged fighters and twenty-six bombers to defend the town and harbor.[24]

After this, the Allied bombing continued unabated, concentrating on the airfields and military installations. By the end of April the objective of neutralizing Rabaul had been completed without the necessity of an invasion. The hundred thousand Japanese left stranded on New Britain were never a factor during the rest of the war. They did not even receive mail from Japan after February.

General Hyakutake and his staff must have been aware that the success of their proposed TA offensive would rest solely upon the infantry without adequate air or naval support. Nevertheless, planning and preparations for the offensive went ahead in a mood of optimism. The basic plan for the field commander of the 17th Army units, Lieutenant General Masatane Kanda, was simple. Three task forces, named for their commanders, would attack strongpoints in the American perimeter. The major thrust was to be directed at 37th Infantry positions. The first force, the Iwasa Unit commanded by Major General Shun Iwasa, consisted of the 23d Infantry Regiment, the 2d Battalion of the 13th Infantry, attached engineering troops, and two batteries of light field artillery and a mortar battalion—in all, approximately 4,150 men. Its objective was Hill 700 on the right flank of the 37th Division lines almost directly in the center of the perimeter (Map 9). After taking that strategic position, the Iwasa Unit was to drive directly toward the two Piva airfields, which Hyakutake planned to capture by 10 March.

The Magata Unit, commanded by Colonel Isashi Magata, consisted of most of the 45th Infantry Regiment, with artillery, mortar battalions, and engineers attached—a total of approximately 4,300 men. Hyakutake and Kanda considered the 45th to be among the best units on Bougainville. Its objective was the low ground west of Hill 700 held by the Americal 129th Regiment. Beginning on 11 March, the Magata Unit was to break the perimeter line, then drive south and cooperate with the Iwasa Unit to take the Piva airfields. Afterward, it would operate on a broad front to capture the Torokina airstrip by 17 March.

The smallest of the forces, the Muda Unit, commanded by Colonel Toyohorei Muda, consisted of two battalions of the 13th regiment and an engineering company—a total of 1,350 men. Its objective was first to capture Hills 260 and 309 in the Americal sector and then, in conjunction with a battalion of the Iwasa Unit, capture the strategically important Hill 608 from the Americal's 182d Regiment by 10 March. Thus they would secure the left flank of the Iwasa Unit as it drove south.[25] The confidence of the Japanese senior officers can be seen in the fact that the combat troops were supplied with rations for only two weeks.

The Japanese had begun earlier in the year to improve the trails, particularly the net leading from the Mosigetta-Mawaraka area. A rough road had been completed through the jungle to the jump-off positions for the infantry. Nevertheless, the movement of over fifteen thousand troops with all their equipment proved to be a major task that would have dampened the spirits of all but the most ardent warriors. Artillery units had a particularly difficult time pulling their heavy guns through the jungle to get them into position to support the attack. Their task was made even more difficult by the daily downpour that flooded the streams, washing away many of the makeshift bridges and making some trails veritable seas of mud. American intelligence by mid-February was aware of the large-scale movement toward the perimeter and Allied planes repeatedly attacked the trails. Despite all these difficulties, the Japanese soldiers displaying their tenacity and ability to overcome the most difficult obstacles, brought up the supplies and eventually had all the guns in place for the attack. The date had originally

Map 9. JAPANESE COUNTERATTACK
9-17 March 1944

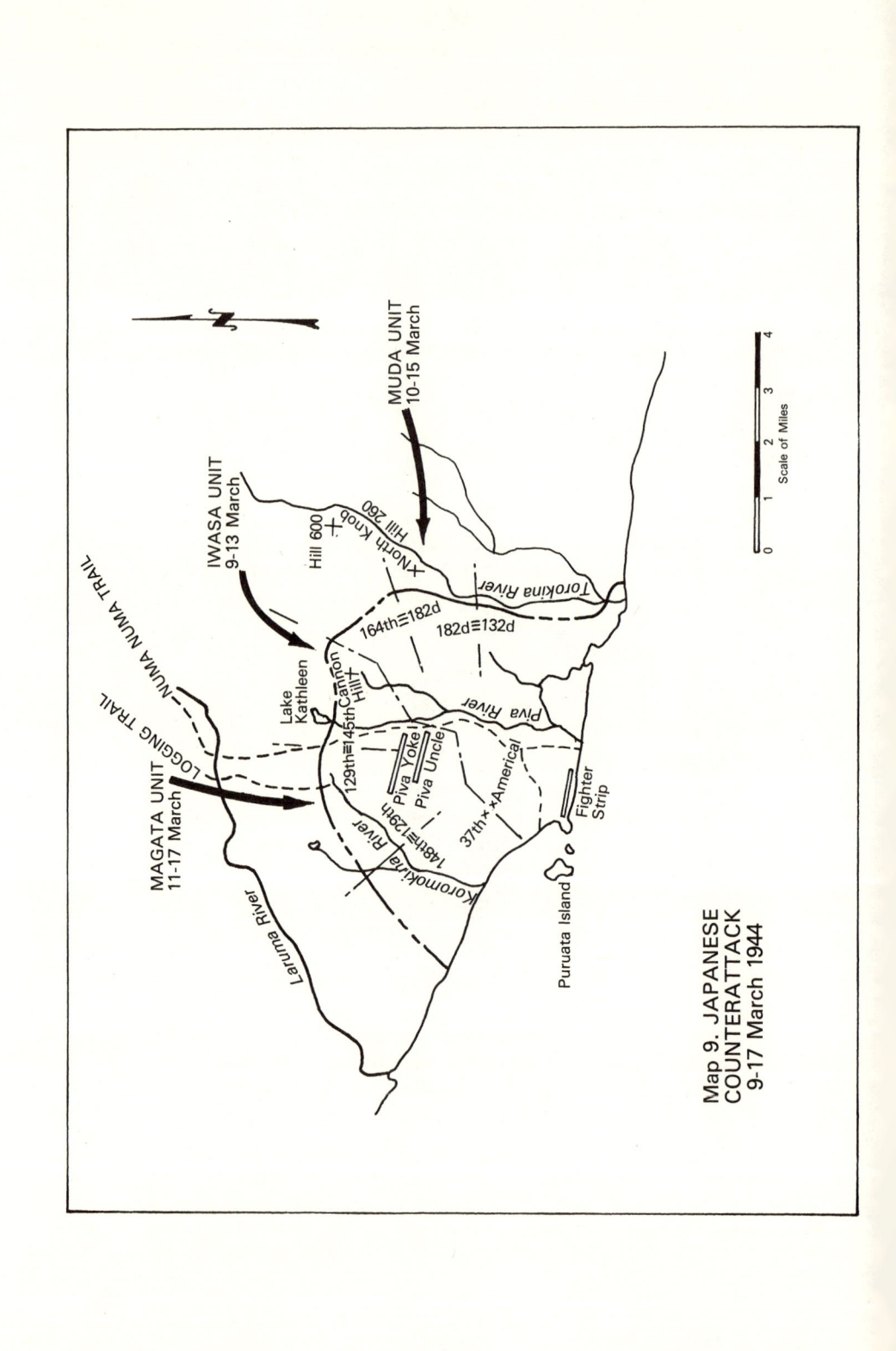

Consolidating the Perimeter 147

been set for 6 March but was postponed for two days because some supplies had not arrived. The attack was rescheduled for early morning of 8 March.

All was in readiness on the evening of 7 March, the Iwasa Unit behind Hill 1111, the Magata Unit behind Mount Nampei, the Muda Unit at Peko village on the East-West Trail, and the special artillery unit in place near Hill 600. How much the Japanese soldiers had been emboldened by the rhetoric of General Hyakutake's earlier exhortation is not known, but it obviously was intended to bolster the morale of the attackers. His message was clear:

> The time has come to manifest our knighthood with the pure brilliance of the sword. It is our duty to erase the mortification of our brothers at Guadalcanal. Attack! Assault! Destroy everything! Cut, slash and mow them down. May the color of the red emblem of our arms be deepened with the blood of the American rascals. Our cry of victory at Torokina Bay will be shouted resoundingly to our native land.
>
> We are invincible! Always attack. Security is the greatest enemy. Always be alert. Execute silently. Always be clear.[26]

Not to be outdone, General Kanda in his order of the day of 24 February exhorted his troops:

> To avenge our mortification since Guadalcanal
> Will be our duty true and supreme.
> Strike, strike, then strike again
> Until our enemy is humbled forevermore!
> Brighten with the blood of the American devils
> The color of the renowned insignia on our arms.
> The cry of our victory at Torokina Bay
> Shall resound to the shores of our beloved Nippon.
> We are invincible!
> No foe can equal our might;
> To attain our aims we must always attack
> And our enemies we must smite.
> Danger comes soonest when it is despised,
> Caution and prudence will bring no grief.
> Serve in silence and bear all pain.
> The shame of our souls will give us strength
> To preserve our nation and our glory.[27]

General Griswold, aware of the impending action, issued no such manifestos. Instead, he and his subordinates made every preparation for repulsing the attack. The men of the 37th and Americal divisions were on full alert in their foxholes and bunkers waiting for the great Japanese counterattack.

9. The Japanese Counterattack

General Hyakutake's offensive began early in the morning of 8 March with the bombardment of parts of the beachhead and the Piva airstrips. The Japanese artillery concentrated its fire on Piva Yoke instead of the forward areas of the perimeter, which would be the main initial point of attack. Even this artillery fire was delivered spasmodically and with poor coordination despite the high vantage points from which the Japanese surveyed the central segment of the American positions. American corps and division artillery countered immediately, the 37th Division guns firing on the suspected hills to the northeast and the Americal howitzers concentrating on those to the east. The 6th Field Artillery Battalion and the 129th Infantry's cannon company were so situated that they could fire directly at the gun flashes. All other guns were directed by forward observers or spotter planes. Destroyers in Empress Augusta Bay also fired counterbattery missions. By midmorning marine dive and torpedo bombers were flying neutralization missions against Hills 250 and 600. Then in the afternoon fifty-six SBDs and thirty-six TBFs, guided by artillery smokeshells, struck the main concentrations on and around hill 1111. The Japanese artillery did little damage considering the number of guns involved. One B-24 bomber at Piva Uncle and three fighters at Piva Yoke were destroyed and nineteen others damaged before the planes from the Piva strips were evacuated to New Georgia. Among aviation personnel, one man was killed and a dozen more wounded. Later shelling during the evening wounded ten others.[1] In addition, a number of tanks and one 155-mm howitzer were damaged. The barrage merely confirmed what the intelligence sections had warned. The Japanese were in force immediately to the front of the perimeter and were preparing a general attack.

Although the Americans were alerted to expect a general attack, all during 8 March the Japanese did nothing more than move troops forward and make a few probes. Their activity seemed but a continuation of what had transpired during the few previous days. The Japanese had sent out units to cut wire in front of the 145th's defenses and there had been continuous patrol contacts from 6 March onward. While the artillery duel and air attacks were going on, there were fire fights between patrols all along the perimeter. The probable reason for the delay in the main Japanese attack was that the troops were not yet in assault positions. The fierce counterbattery fire and air attacks must have caused some disruption also. Scouts reported by late morning a concentration of Japanese directly in front of Hill 700. The 37th's artillery, the cannon company, and the regiment's 4.2-inch mortars fired concentrations into the reported area approximately twelve hundred yards wide and two thousand yards deep. By the evening of 8 March the advance elements of the Japanese 23d Regiment were in place and parties of the 2d Battalion had reconnoitered Cannon Hill, a rise slightly lower than and to the west of Hill 700.[2] They were massed for the attack only three hundred yards in front of the barbed wire guarding the perimeter of Hill 700.

The key objective for two battalions of the Japanese 23d Infantry, Hill 700, has been compared to the humps on a camel's back. The hump to the left was slightly lower than the one to the right; the saddle in between running from west to east rose sharply to the peak. Because the slope of the hill on all sides was extremely steep, 65 to 75 percent, General Beightler had not imagined that the hill would be the target of the expected attack. A historian of the 145th described the difficulties in just manning the hill: "Even before the actual battle, Hill 700 was a tricky mountain ridge to master. But one trail led to the area. It traversed slopes so steep that crags and roots became safety stirrups, often saving a man from a disastrous fall. Engineers were at first perplexed by the problem of building a supply road to follow the perimeter. Until they accomplished this mission, every round of ammunition, every bit of food, every drop of water had to be carried through the jungle rains and heat to the top of the highest ridge.[3]

Hill 700 on the evening of 8 March was held by Companies E and F of 2/145 with machine guns from Company H on line. Company F was in reserve and the mortars of Company H were in position on the south slope. The line was anchored by earthen and log pillboxes with connecting trenches, backed by infantry in foxholes. Extra rations, water and ammunition had been brought up in preparation for an attack on the hill positions. Wire and some mines had also been placed in front of the most likely lanes of approach and the infantry was directly backed by a field artillery battery and a mortar company. The rest of Colonel Whitcomb's regiment held a total of two miles of front: 1/145 held the line on the low ground south of Cannon Hill, and 2/145 was in division reserve.

The men on line had become accustomed to the daily drenching rainfall, but it was particularly severe all during the night of 8-9 March. It was during this downpour that the Japanese attacked Hill 700. Soon after midnight two companies of their 2/23 attacked the north slope of the hill against the 1st Platoon of Company G, which was holding the saddle between the crest of the hill and another high point to the left named Pat's Nose. Other Japanese attacked Company E, which was holding the highest elevations of Hill 700. Both attacks were beaten off. Then at approximately 0230, General Iwasa launched his main attack. He sent 2/23 against the saddle, followed by 3/23. The historian of the 145th commented: "The enemy stormed the hill, clawing his way up the steep slope, yelling like a maniac, suidically putting everything he had into a frontal attack designed to take the highest point on the hill. . . . The 145th Infantry, defending the ridge, were somewhat taken aback by an enemy so unreasoning as to crawl up the 70-degree slope on all fours, rifles slung over their backs."[4] Despite the heavy fire from all along the 145th's forward line, the Japanese came on en masse, many of them screaming threats in English and even singing American songs, presumably in attempts to unnerve the defenders of the hill.[5]

American artillery opened up on the area immediately in front of the lines and presumably was quite effective in breaking up the follow-up attacks by 3/23. No members of this unit were known to have reached their objective.[6] Nevertheless, despite severe losses, men of 2/23 using bangalore torpedoes blasted their way through the protective wire and knocked out one of the pillboxes. Through this gap the Japanese moved onto the saddle, set up their machine guns, and began to attack adjacent strongpoints and to assault the crest. By daylight they had secured a penetration of the 145th's line seventy yards wide and fifty yards deep. They would continue to expand this perimeter until, by 1200, they had captured seven pillboxes and had brought up machine guns and mortars with which they could put McClelland Road, the only lateral supply road for the 145th, under direct fire. Supply of the forward troops then became very difficult, since the three-quarter-ton trucks and half-tracks could not use the road. All supplies had to be hand carried. Evacuation of the wounded also became difficult and dangerous. Japanese machine guns on the crest of the hill were able to cover the ridge with accurate and deadly grazing fire. They had placed other machine guns in trees on the spur of the hill about a hundred yards to the rear of the ground-emplaced weapons, which could sweep the entire front. With the exception of a few scattered trees and shallow trenches, there was little cover for troops of the 145th who moved up the steep slopes attempting to retake the lost positions. All during the day the Japanese were also extending the trenches repairing the old pillboxes, and building new ones.[7]

General Beightler soon after the beginning of the attack released 1/145 from division reserve and Colonel Whitcomb attached it to 2/145. The 117th Engineer Battalion was then moved forward and by 1145 had occupied the reserve positions vacated by 1/145. The first attempt to recapture Hill 700 was launched at noon, 9 March. Company C moved northward against the saddle in a direct frontal assault while two platoons of Company F attacked the saddle from the flanks. Company C was halted by devastating fire two-thirds of the way to its objective, and the men were forced to dig in and hold what they had gained. Meanwhile the riflemen of Company F had retaken five of the lost pillboxes, and the line, now reinforced, was solidly established by nightfall just south of the crest. Beightler had ordered two tanks forward late in the afternoon to take enemy targets under direct fire, particularly those that menaced McClelland Road, but the terrain proved too steep for them to be used effectively.[8] Despite the breakthrough, the offensive of Iwasa's force, with casualties estimated at more than five hundred dead, had been contained. The 145th had in turn lost 23 killed and 128 wounded.[9]

Perhaps the losses during the previous night persuaded the Japanese not to attempt another night attack on 9 March; instead, they used occasional machine gun and mortar fire to disrupt the fitful sleep of the Americans. The 37th Division artillery in turn placed protective and harassing fire in front of 2/145. At 0645 on 10 March, General Iwasa launched an attack at the same time the Muda Force began its assault on Hill 260 in the Americal Division sector. Iwasa hoped to broaden the wedge driven into the American lines and to reinforce his troops on the saddle. All such attacks during the morning were met with a hail of fire from all available weapons and failed to gain any advantage. General Griswold brought up more reinforcements for the 145th that morning. Meanwhile, engineers put together a bangalore torpedo seventy-two feet long by connecting sticks of dynamite like a long pipe. The object was to climb the hill and then snake the charge down the opposite side into one of the pillboxes. Unfortunately the Japanese spotted them and fired a knee mortar, hitting the torpedo and killing the engineers. Another ruse was attempted shortly after noon with the object of getting the Japanese on the saddle to surrender. A public address system was set up with speakers aimed at Hill 700, and one of the division's Japanese interpreters spoke to the defenders. He informed them of the odds against their success and told them that they could not be reinforced. If they surrendered, it would be considered honorable. To die needlessly was foolish. For the short time he spoke all was quiet, but seconds after he had finished the Japanese directed a mortar barrage on the section of the hill from whence he was broadcasting.[10]

The day ended in a qualified victory for the riflemen of the 37th Division. At 1115 an air strike by thirty-six planes and continual artillery fire had obviously had an effect on the Japanese. However, much of the afternoon of 10 March was taken up in regrouping elements of the 1st and 2d Battalions, which had been mixed during the previous attacks. A general attack on the hill was ordered at 1700 and proceeded in spite of intense mortar and artillery fire. The Japanese were driven from the crest of the hill. All but four pillboxes were taken, and except for a gap approximately forty yards wide, the original main resistance line was reestablished. The Japanese had lost heavily during these attacks, which also cost the 145th 3 dead and 121 wounded. Surprisingly, the Japanese made no serious attacks on sectors held by troops of the 129th and 148th Regiments. All during 9 and 10 March, units of these regiments had sent out patrols and there had been a number of smaller fire fights. In all these engagements the 129th had four men killed and five wounded while the 148th reported only one enlisted man wounded.[11] It was obvious that Iwasa was not going to deviate from his original plan and attack any area other than that adjacent to Hill 700 until he had secured a breakthrough in this main defense area.

At daybreak on 11 March the Japanese command ordered an attempt on a projection called Pat's Nose approximately 150 yards west of Hill 700. The approach to Hill 700 had given the Japanese attackers some protection when they initiated the attack two days before. There was no such protected route for those who tried to storm Pat's Nose. They had to advance in the open up a very steep slope against the defenses manned by Company G, backed by elements of Company B. The 37th Division's historian described this attack: "Brandishing their prized sabers, screeching 'Chusuto' (Damn them!), the Jap officers climbed up the slope and rushed forward in an admirable display of blind courage. The men screamed in reply 'Yaruzo' (Let's do it!) and then 'Yarimosu' (We will do it!). As they closed with the American doughboys, the leaders cried 'San nen Kire!' (Cut a thousand men!)."[12]

As the Japanese clawed their way up the hill they were met by point-blank fire from every available weapon. Because of the steep slope, mortar fire could not be brought in close to the defensive line, but fire from 37-mm guns located on the flank channeled the Japanese attack into the teeth of the heaviest fire, and they were cut to pieces. The rear echelons, however, kept advancing over the dead bodies of those who had been leading the charge. Despite the problems of terrain and accurate fire from the men of Company G, some of the Japanese managed to break through the barbed wire and attacked the emplacements of the 3d Platoon before they, too, were destroyed. This futile, near suicidal attack lasted for an hour. By 0800 the remnants of the attacking battalion had withdrawn, leaving behind eighty-four dead on the upper slopes of the hill.[13]

General Beightler, concerned over the inability of the 145th to reduce the Japanese positions on Hill 700, had shifted 2/148 from a reserve position to the 145th sector and moved the newly arrived 1/24 into direct reserve. Before resuming the attack on Hill 700, Beightler sent his aide-de-camp forward to get more information on the situation. He found the regimental commander, Colonel Whitcomb, suffering from extreme battle fatigue and relieved him from command, replacing him with Colonel George Freer who had been the executive officer. The 2d Battalion of the 148th reached its assembly area at 1115 and prepared for what was hoped would be the final assault on the Japanese-held positions on Hill 700. Preparatory to this attack, those positions were hit by a murderous concentration of fire from the three 105-mm howitzer battalions, guns from the 145th's cannon company, and mortar fire from all companies of the 145th. At 1330 two platoons from Company E of 2/148 moved east from Pat's Nose in an attempt to flank the saddle while a third attacked west from Hill 700. Eight men were killed before the encircling platoon reached the crest from the north. Five more men were lost before the momentum of the attack waned and 2/148 dug in on the ground it had gained.[14]

The attack against the Japanese defenses continued on 12 March with the men of Companies E and F converging on the enemy's strongpoints. Using grenades, rifles, and flame throwers, they reduced the pillboxes one by one. By 1300 the Japanese held only one pillbox.

An historian of the 145th Regiment described the fight for this last strongpoint:

> On the second day, the last held enemy pillbox was subjected to everything an infantryman has at his command. Hand grenades by the dozen were thrown at the emplacement. Still there was responding fire. Flame throwers scorched the hidden Nip into silence. The searching parties entered the charred remains of the emplacement only to hear the click of a Japanese grenade being detonated. In the far corner they made out the dim outline of a Jap, eyes bloodshot, mouth bleeding, face seared, clothing burned. His clenched fist held a grenade. Even as the men dove for cover outside the pillbox, the Jap threw the grenade at them as in a dying gesture.[15]

Despite such desperate heroics, mopping up of Hill 700 was completed by midafternoon and the 145th's line was restored to the positions held before the Iwasa attack.

Admitting defeat on 13 March, General Iwasa pulled back what was left of his shattered command to the relative safety of the Blue Ridge, approximately two miles east of the American perimeter. During the day, as the Japanese were retreating, American planes dropped 123 tons of bombs on the intermediate areas, and destroyers off shore lobbed their five-inch shells into the high ground to the north and east of the perimeter.[16] After Iwasa's retreat, the men of the 145th had the dubious honor of policing the slopes of Hill 700 and burying the corpses left behind. In an area roughly fifty yards square, corpses that could be identified were counted. This count included only those within the barbed wire lines in front of the pillboxes. As one oberver noted, the carnage was a sight to turn even the most cast-iron stomach:

> Enemy dead were strewn in piles of mutilated bodies, so badly dismembered in most cases that a physical count was impossible. Here and there was a leg or an arm or a blown-off hand, all to show for the vanished and vanquished enemy. At one point, Japanese bodies formed a human stairway over the barbed wire. Five enemy were piled one on top of the other, as each had successively approached the location to use a predecessor as a barricade and then fall on top of him as he in turn was killed.
>
> Farther out from the perimeter, where a little stream wound its way parallel to it, Japs killed by the concussion of thousands of

mortar shells lay with their heads, ostrich fashion, stuck under the least protection they could find.[17]

Braving the overwhelming stench from the decaying bodies littered all over the area, bulldozer operators scraped up the mutilated remains and covered them over in mass graves.[18]

While Iwasa's Unit was attempting to hold its gains on the saddle area of Hill 700 on 10 March, the second phase of the Japanese attack began on the right of the American lines in the Americal sector. At dawn Colonel Muda's 13th Infantry began its attack on Hill 260, held by elements of the 182d Infantry. The hill, a twin-peaked rise close to the west bank of the Torokina River approximately four miles north of its mouth, was covered with heavy vegetation. The hill itself measured only 850 yards along its north-south axis and at its widest a mere 450 yards, and it was shaped roughly like an hourglass, with the highest elevations to the north and south connected by a narrow saddle. The eastern slope of the hill was precipitous, steepest along the South Knob, where it was almost perpendicular. The South Knob, which was considered the most important part of Hill 260, had been occupied by men of 2/182 since early January, and vigorous patrolling had also been carried on regularly along the saddle and on the unoccupied North Knob. The hill was about half a mile east of the 182d's main line of resistance. Between Hill 260 and the main line of the Americal was a small stream named Eagle Creek, which provided a natural defensive barrier. There was but a single trail leading from the main perimeter to South Knob. A small bridge over the creek could take vehicular traffic. The last hundred yards to the top of South Knob was a steep stairway cut into the sides of the hill.

Possession of this portion of the hill was important for both sides. The Americans had built a platform near the top of a 150-foot banyan tree from which forward observers could see any enemy activity along the Torokina River or along the highlands to the northeast. Conversely, if the Japanese could seize the hill they could have good observation of the American-held Hills 608 and 309 and the area behind them.[19]

Colonel Muda moved the 3d Battalion of the 13th Infantry to the place of departure under cover of darkness. The thrust of his attack was not directed against the weakly held North Knob or the saddle but aimed at the South Knob, held by a reinforced platoon of Company G of the 182d and a forward observer team of the 246th Field Artillery Battalion. Despite the steep slope the Japanese under the cover of intense machine gun and mortar fire burst in among the outnumbered Americans. At 0638 regimental headquarters received word that the platoon was being attacked by a company of Japanese infantry. This information proved to be a profound understatement, for in fact Muda had committed two full companies to the preliminary attack. Except for a few men who managed to escape and take refuge in a pillbox, all the defenders were wiped out or dispersed. The Japanese took the banyan tree and quickly established a defensive perimeter on the crest of the South Knob. General Griswold, upon being apprised of the developments, ordered General Hodge to hold Hill 260 at all costs. This order surprised many of the Americal's staff since they had not expected to try to hold the hill in the face of a concerted Japanese attack.[20]

Colonel William Long, commanding the 182d, immediately responded to the order from higher headquarters by ordering two companies, E and F of the 2d Battalion, to occupy the North Knob. They did so without opposition and made contact with some of the survivors of Company G. Company E at 0845 was ordered to attack South Knob from the southwest while Company F moved south. The company began its attack at 1045 but halted after the troops had advanced a few yards into the cleared zone. The men took whatever cover was available and waited for flame throwers before trying to advance farther. At approximately 1445 the commander, Lieutenant Colonel Dexter Lowry, ordered the attack resumed; Company E split and attempted an envelopment. The northern prong of the envelopment was halted but the infantrymen of the southern prong, using grenades and flame throwers, managed to gain a lodgment within earshot of the men of Company G who were still holding out in the pillbox. Lowry ordered a further attack at 1600 but his troops were exhausted. By then more than 50 percent of Company E was out of commission, and the small contingent of effectives could gain no ground. Lowry decided to hold the ground they had previously gained and prepare to attack the next morning. At approximately 2100 the Japanese launched a bayonet attack against Company F but were driven back.[21]

The Japanese reinforced their position during the night, and early in the morning of 11 March they struck at Company E. Although this attack was beaten off, Colonel Lowry found the situation of the company had become desperate. Of the 7 officers and 143 enlisted men who had left the perimeter the day before, only 1 wounded officer and 35 enlisted men, 15 of them wounded, were still holding the slight lodgment of South Knob.[22] Company G was sent to relieve the beleaguered Company E but was halted by yet another Japanese flanking attack on Company E. General Hodge, fearful of reducing his main defense line, felt that he could send no more reserves to the hill and therefore decided to break off the action and pull Company G and what was left of Company E off South Knob. They retired, unimpeded by the Japanese, behind Eagle Creek. There they joined Company B and then proceeded to cut a new trail up to the crest of North Knob. After widening the perimeter there, Companies F and B began another two-pronged attempt to drive the Japanese off South Knob. Supported by flame throwers, men of Company B got across the saddle and on to the knob close enough for the men who had been trapped in the bunker the day before to escape. At 1900 the staff decided to pull the attackers off South Knob, believing that the day's gains could not be held given the local superiority of the Japanese. They retreated back to the more defensible positions on North Knob.[23]

The Americal assault continued on 12 March against Muda's troops who were well entrenched on South Knob. There had previously been minimal artillery support for the men of 2/182, but now that there was no American outpost on South Knob, the artillery could begin working over the area preliminary to infantry attacks. Even then, the Japanese positions were so close that the troops on North Knob had to be moved back to avoid casualties from the shell bursts striking South Knob. Difficulty in getting adequate supplies to Companies F and B up the narrow trail postponed the attack until early afternoon. Then Company B in a column of platoons with six flame throwers attempted to storm the height from the northwest. The leading platoon was halted by machine gun fire from pillboxes dug in on the west slope. Once these were spotted a concentration of mortar and machine gun fire was directed against these Japanese positions, enabling the following platoon to reach the top of the knob. There, it was pinned down by heavy fire from machine guns sited east of the observation post banyan tree. American mortar fire, together with the work of the flame thrower operators, who were covered by BAR men of the 3d Platoon, soon negated these positions. It appeared that the South Knob would soon be in American hands once more, but a combination of circumstances postponed the victory. Ammunition for the attacking platoons was running low, there had been numerous casualties, there were no more reserves, and it was already late in the day. A last attempt was made to reinforce the knob when Company A of the 132d tried to scale the height from the southwest to join Company B of the 182d on the crest. A burst of machine gun fire killed the company commander, however, and disorganized the attack so much that under the best of conditions the men could not reach the top before dark. Reluctantly, higher command decided that Company B did not have enough men to hold what they had gained and ordered it to return to its previous position on the North Knob.[24]

The Japanese on South Knob had repulsed every attempt to retake the hill, and although artillery and mortar fire had played havoc with them, they showed no signs of abandoning their positions. To some senior officers it appeared that the cost of assaulting South Knob was disporportionate to any advantage to be gained. Because there were no more troops to commit to the struggle, at least none that General Hodge wanted to use, such gains as were made by Company B had to be given up. Unless the Japanese decided to withdraw, any further attacks would probably end the same way. There seemed little point in continuing the fight for a rise a half mile beyond the main perimeter line. The Americal staff therefore asked for permission to pull off South Knob. Griswold refused the request and a new attack was ordered for the next day using two companies of 1/132.

The attack was almost a copy of that of 12 March. After a heavy artillery concentration was directed against the South Knob, Company A struck southward along the narrow saddle while Company B attacked up the southwest slope. Both ran into very heavy fire from combined weapons of the defenders and could make little headway. Surprisingly, the two companies of the 182d that had led the attack the day before had not been kept in immediate reserve but had been pulled back within the perimeter. Therefore there were no reserve troops available to help exploit the minor gains made during the afternoon. As night fell, Major Raymond Daehler, the battalion commander, reluctantly pulled his men off the knob and retreated to safer ground.[25]

General Hodge contemplated using tanks against the entrenched Japanese but gave up the idea because the tanks could not cross Eagle Creek, and even if they could, their effect would have been minimized by the steep slopes of South Knob. Hodge reluctantly decided to cease any further attempt to drive the Japanese off South Knob. He had noted that patrols had revealed no enemy activity to the northeast and therefore concluded that the Japanese had no more reserves. The three-day action against the Muda force had obviously so weakened it that it no longer posed a danger to the perimeter proper. Instead of being directly attacked, the Japanese could be contained and continually harassed by combat patrols and neutralization fire from the 246th Field Artillery Battalion and supporting mortar fire.

During the entire engagement over ten thousand 105-mm rounds struck South Knob, and even before the Japanese retired, the hill was completely denuded of vegetation. Artillerymen of the 182d's cannon company emplaced their 75-mm pack howitzers on Hill 309 and brought the knob under direct fire. One main target was the banyan observation tree, which was successfully knocked down late in the afternoon of 17 March. By that time only a screening force of Japanese remained on the hill. General Kanda had decided to move most of what was left of Muda force around to the right to support Colonel Magata in his attempt to break through the line held by the 129th Regiment in the center of the 37th Division sector. On 18 March, in a combined assault, Americal infantrymen began what was hoped to be the final attack against the reduced garrison on the knob.

General William McCulloch, who had assumed direct command of the effort, continued the assault on South Knob on 18 March by sending Company A of the 132d to advance along the saddle while Company B, divided into three prongs, once more attempted to reach the crest from the southwest. Again it appeared by midafternoon that the Japanese would be driven from their positions, but the attackers were met with withering fire from bunkers and were forced to fall back for reorganization. Company A had made only a few slight gains. The Japanese still held the knob as dusk came. The attack was resumed at 1410 on the next day. The same companies after a heavy artillery preparation followed the same lines of advance. Although both companies were again halted short of the crest by rifle and knee mortar fire, the flame thrower teams managed to destroy several pillboxes.

General McCulloch then concluded that the approaches that had been used over and over again were the ones most heavily defended, and he decided to try to take the hill by approaching from another direction. Thus on 20 March, Company B, reinforced by a platoon from Company A, circled the south end of the knob and reached the base of the trail on the east. The tired infantrymen soon discovered that the Japanese could pour an equal volume of fire in this direction, and this attack proved to be no more successful than all the others. By this time both companies of the 132d were too far below minimum strength to hope for success, and they were returned to the perimeter to be replaced by men of the 182d.

During this entire operation the bulk of the Americal Division was simply on alert while the higher command attempted to reduce South Knob with inadequate forces. Thus the attackers, without the necessary manpower, were required over and over to take ground at great cost, only to be forced to surrender it and then retrace their steps the next day. Eventually, command decided to stop the costly and futile large-scale attacks and instead send out probing combat patrols against the Japanese. The final reduction of the positions on Hill 260 was left to the artillery and supporting mortars. Finally on 28 March, three patrols from the 182d moved out from the base of the hill. Surprisingly there was no rifle fire from the Japanese. The patrols inched their way cautiously up the hill, expecting at any time to be met with withering fire from the defenders. But there was no one there; the few remaining Japanese had left during the night. At 1245 the patrol leader reported to division headquarters that Hill 260 was secure.[26] The three-week battle for this insignificant knoll had cost the Americal 98 dead and 581 wounded. The victors, like their counterparts on Hill 700, everywhere encountered dead, decaying bodies that had to be buried quickly. The infantrymen counted 560 dead Japanese on the knob.[27]

The Japanese of the 45th Infantry Regiment under the command of Colonel Magata had limited their actions to heavy patrol activity while the Iwasa Unit was attacking Hill 700. In retrospect this was a mistake since documents were taken from dead Japanese during the early phase of that engagement that detailed the entire Japanese plan of action. So Magata's thrust was expected. However, the terrain fronting the 129th Regiment, which was holding the center of the 37th Division line, was much more favorable for the Japanese than that encountered by either the Iwasa or Muda forces. The land was relatively flat, although cut by many gullies. The 129th's line, defended by two battalions, extended over two miles, curving slightly from just east of the Numa Numa Trail southwest to the right flank of the 148th Regiment. Several tributaries of the Korokina River flowed south through the defense area, the most important being Taylor Creek, located a thousand yards west of the Numa Numa Trail, and Cox Creek, approximately half a mile west of Taylor Creek. The Japanese had easy access to the 37th's lines, first via the Numa Numa Trail and then following the lowlands and gullies adjacent to the creeks.

Colonel John Frederick, the regimental commander of the 129th, had recognized the potential vulnerability of this position and had organized a defense in depth during the two months prior to the attack. The position, much stronger than that of the 148th guarding Hill 700, was anchored by a large number of mutually supporting earthen and log pillboxes and protected by a double apron of barbed wire, in front of which antipersonnel mines had been laid. Machine guns had been sited to provide interlocking fire and additional barbed wire had been placed to channel potential attackers into the main machine gun fire lanes. The 129th's cannon company of 75-mm pack howitzers, and its mortar sections had been augmented by 37-mm and 40-mm antitank guns, which could fire cannisters in flat-trajectory direct fire. Thus although Colonel Magata's men did not have to climb up steep cliffs to get at the American positions, they would find the 129th's defenses near impregnable to relatively lightly supported infantry attacks, no matter how fanatically delivered.[28]

On the right of the line, 2/129 would bear the brunt of the Japanese attacks. Its commander, Lieutenant Colonel Preston Hundley, had three rifle companies on line. Company F, on the left, defended the area around Cox Creek; the Logging Trail and Taylor Creek were in Company G's sector, and on the right, Company E held the section near the Numa Numa Trail. On 11 March the contact between Japanese and American patrols had increased, as had the amount of incoming mortar fire. American supporting artillery fired intermittently into the areas where the Japanese were located. Colonel Frederick at 1600 ordered all his outposts back into the main perimeter and division artillery fired a ten-minute concentration along the 2d Battalion front. At dusk a heavy fire fight broke out as the Japanese opened up with machine guns and mortars on Company G's area. During the exchange of fire, which lasted until 1920, men in the pillboxes did not fire their machine guns, since they did not want to reveal their positions. The firing died down to only a few exchanges during the night, generally directed at Japanese infiltrators, who were attempting to cut through the barbed wire.

At dawn of 12 March, Magata delivered the first of his major attacks with two battalions in column, the 1st and 45th, centered on a hundred-yard front straddling the Logging Trail, the sector held by Company G. Although the attacking Japanese suffered very heavy casualties from machine gun and BAR fire, they penetrated the first line of defense by sheer weight of numbers. Moving up the streambed running into the sector they captured one pillbox after another until they held a total of seven. Colonel Frederick moved up his reserve battalion, 1/129, to support hard-pressed Company G, and in concert with mortars and fire from the antitank platoons, he counterattacked, retaking one pillbox by midmorning. Early in the afternoon an attack by Company C, 1/129, recaptured another pillbox and a subsequent Japanese counterattack was beaten off. By the close of the day the Japanese still held five pillboxes and thus had a minor lodgment within the American lines, but all attempts to expand it had been contained. During the night of 12-13 March, artillery and mortars pounded the concentration areas of the Japanese. Searchlights from the antiaircraft regiment were used to try to illuminate the Japanese positions, but because of the many draws and depressions, it was not possible to use them directly. Instead, the searchlight crews aimed the beams against the low overhanging clouds, "and thus by reflection, illuminated the entire sector with a soft, reflecting light very much the same as moonlight." The results were very gratifying. Scores of automatic weapons zeroed in on the Japanese, "mowing them down as though by a giant scythe."[29]

Colonel Frederick had requested on 12 March that his position be reinforced by Sherman tanks of the 754th Tank Battalion, which was held in corps reserve. This request had been refused. After another attack by the Japanese at 0400 on 13 March, which gained another pillbox, General Griswold agreed to send the 1st Platoon of Company C, tank battalion, forward, with the stipulation that they be used only to augment the infantry as they took back the lost pillboxes. Four tanks supported a midmorning assault. Despite the difficulty the tankers had in depressing the 75-mm guns to fire into the declivities where many Japanese had taken cover, two pillboxes were recaptured. Another tank-infantry attack began at 1315 but was halted since the tanks were low on fuel and ammunition. They were replaced by tanks of the 2d Platoon, which assisted the infantrymen of the 129th in destroying all the other pillboxes held by the Japanese and restoring the front line roughly to the positions held before the Japanese attack of the previous day.[30]

Corps had ordered the reconnaissance troop forward to occupy the right sector of the threatened area, and the 131st Engineer Regiment took over the extreme left. Thus on 14 March the American defenses were stronger than they had been before the initial enemy attack. That the Japanese had been seriously mauled in the previous assaults was borne out by their relative quiescence the next day. On 14 March there was only intermittent small-arms and mortar fire from the Japanese as Colonel Magata shifted some of his troops to more favorable positions. Infantrymen of 2/129 moved forward under cover of tanks and repaired the wire, and others worked feverishly to repair and strengthen emplacements damaged in driving the Japanese back. This work was done without drawing much enemy fire.

At 0400 on 15 March, the Japanese launched a heavy local attack against the right of Company F. By dawn they had captured one pillbox and penetrated approximately a hundred yards into the perimeter, where they were checked. A coordinated counterattack by Companies F and C in conjunction with a thirty-six-plane strike against intermediate Japanese positions, retook the pillbox. By then, however, the Japanese within the salient had dug in, many of them among the roots of banyan trees. The aide-de-camp, General Charles Craig, forward to observe the fighting, requested tanks. It required two attacks by the riflemen, supported by a platoon of Shermans, before the line was restored. The men of company F that evening counted 190 dead Japanese within the sector. By contrast, the action that day had cost the 129th 10 dead and 53 wounded.[31]

The Japanese repeated the attack the next morning at 0400 on the high ground east of Cox Creek with a larger force of elements from three battalions. They penetrated approximately seventy-five yards before their momentum was halted. Company B, supported by a platoon of tanks from Company A of the 754th Tank Battalion, counterattacked and restored the original line by midmorning. Shortly after noon the tanks moved beyond the wire and shelled the draws and ravines in front of Company F until their ammunition was exhausted. Once again the Japanese had paid heavily for no gain, 194 dead and 1 prisoner taken. The American losses were less than the previous day—only 2 dead and 63 wounded.[32]

Generals Hyakutake and Kanda, having failed to carry out their initial plan, withdrew the bulk of their forces from Hills 700 and 260 and shifted them westward in preparation for one final attempt to break through to the Piva airfields. There was a five-day break in the major action while the Japanese transferred the 13th and 23d Regiments to reinforce what was left of Colonel Magata's 45th Regiment. Meanwhile, they maintained patrols, which sometimes got into fire fights with American patrols. A number of Japanese were taken prisoner during these patrol actions. From time to time the Japanese would lob mortar shells into the 129th's sector.

During this lull in the fighting, the tired American riflemen and engineers were busy strengthening the defenses. Pillboxes were rebuilt, tactical wire reestablished, illuminating devices installed, communications improved, and the many Japanese dead buried. Information gained from prisoners and reconnaissance led General Beightler to conclude that the Japanese would launch a major assault on 23 March. It was estimated that General Kanda had approximately 4,850 men at his disposal to renew the attack on the 129th's front.[33]

The preliminary assault began late in the evening of 23 March when the Japanese moved up a large draw in the Cox Creek area. The night was very dark and they took advantage of the darkness and the natural cover to strike directly toward the 2d Battalion command post. In a frenzied attack they knocked out three pillboxes and penetrated that portion of the line held by Company F, despite murderous fire from the battalion's mortars and machine guns. With dawn it became apparent that about a hundred Japanese soldiers had seized a low ridge only twenty-five yards from the command post.

The salient held by the Japanese was so narrow that artillery or air strikes could not be used. Therefore a combined tank-infantry attack was planned. General Beightler ordered two companies from the 148th Infantry, whose front was quiet, to back up the 2d Battalion. Two platoons of the antitank company, and one platoon of Company K, 129th, in conjunction with a platoon of tanks from the 754th Tank Battalion, prepared at 0725 to counterattack. Using grenades and following on preparatory fire by the Shermans' 75-mm guns, the infantrymen stormed the Japanese positions and within twenty minutes had reoccupied much of the territory lost during the night. A further attack by the 1st and 3d Platoons of Company K with tank support was begun at midmorning. The Japanese, dug in, contested every yard of ground. The attacking riflemen used smoke grenades to indicate targets for the tank gunners, who then used their big guns to blast pillboxes, banyan roots, or whatever afforded the hapless Japanese some shelter. The Shermans' .50-caliber machine guns supported the advancing infantry squads, who literally rooted out the Japanese from the banyan trees. By noon the enemy within its narrow salient had been annihilated.[34]

Elsewhere along the 129th front the Japanese were attempting to concentrate forces earlier that morning. Observers from Company C spotted them and directed mortar fire on them, breaking up a potential attack. The division's artillery also fired on suspected Japanese positions and, as soon as the line in the area of Company F had been restored, began a systematic probing fire on the gullies and ravines along the front. But for the Japanese, the worst was yet to come. General Beightler early in the afternoon received approval from General Griswold of his plan to destroy the last major Japanese forces dug in in front of the 129th. Corps artillery's 155-mm guns and all artillery from the Americal not directly engaged were placed under the general direction of General Leo Kreber, commander of the 37th Division artillery. These guns and the 37th's own artillery—seven battalions in all—began a concentrated fire on the very narrow sector where the bulk of the surviving Japanese were dug in. For twenty-five minutes this heavy and medium artillery in combination with the bulk of the 37th's mortars fired over four thousand shells, the heaviest artillery concentration yet seen in the Pacific war.[35] An infantryman of the 129th recalled:

All these big guns opened fire into this area about five hundred yards in front of us, and I remember what they called a million-dollar barrage and it's something you never forget—the big guns shooting over your head. It was very frightening because you wondered whether one of these shells would not go far enough. It was all jungle out in front of us and when they got done it was all cleared out. They had knocked everything down. A lot of Japs were killed by this. . . . I can remember the day after the big attack the bulldozers came in and dug these huge trenches and we had to go out and take the Japanese and drag them into these. Because of the warm weather they began to smell pretty bad. Many, many killed![36]

Even before the artillery barrage the Japanese commanders had realized the failure of their plans. General Hyakutake had so informed his superior, General Imamura, and had received permission to withdraw. Hyakutake moved the 6th Cavalry and portions of the 4th South Seas Garrison unit north to cover the retreat. Harried by two battalions from XIV Corps reserve and the Fijians, what was left of the Japanese 6th Division began an orderly retreat on 27 March, leaving behind in the 129th sector a vast amount of materiel. Included in the captured equipment were nine 75-mm mountain guns, three 37-mm guns, five 90-mm mortars, two 20-mm antiaircraft guns, ninety light and fifty-one heavy machine guns, fifty-two grenade launchers, hundreds of rifles, and even seventy-three officer sabers.[37]

More that that, they left behind thousands of dead. An accurate figure will never be known, but a body count revealed 2,489 killed in the area from their deepest penetration to a short distance beyond the tactical wire. It is probable that many more were killed and buried farther out. Patrols reported the stench of dead bodies far beyond the immediate front line. A reasonable estimate, although probably not completely accurate, placed the total Japanese casualties during the three-week operation on all fronts at more than 5,500 dead and 3,000 wounded.[38] Later Major General Kanzuo Tanikawa, former staff officer of the Japanese 8th Area Army, in recapitulating its operations, admitted that the 6th Division had lost 2,398 killed and 3,060 wounded in the March operations. Other units directly under General Kandas's control had lost another 3,000 killed and 4,000 wounded. These rough figures tend to confirm American estimates of the near total destruction of Kanda's forces.[39] The XIV Corps had lost 263 dead.

In retrospect what can be said of the failure of this last major Japanese attack in the Solomons? It failed for many reasons. Perhaps the most important was the incompetence of Generals Hyakutake and Kanda. They launched the assault without adequate knowledge of the ground strength of their enemy and knowing very well that the Americans controlled the air. They depended upon the loyalty, bravery, and fanatical devotion of the Japanese soldier. Although these doomed infantrymen bravely attempted to carry out the tasks assigned them, their commanders expected too much. Even before the final assaults began, the majority of the Japanese were sick. An examination of prisoners of war and Japanese bodies showed that 90 percent of 6th Division troops were suffering from malnutrition, malaria, dysentery, beri-beri, or skin diseases. Captured documents and prisoner interrogations described the deplorable conditions under which they had lived. According to the 37th Division Personnel Narrative, "It is apparent that [the Japanese soldier's] food supply supplemented by roots, herbs and certain vines would have lasted only until 1 April. In an attempt to bolster the combat morale of his command General Kanda, Commanding General, 6th Division, promised his men the luxuries of fine foods, once the Allied perimeter with its large ration dumps was captured. With this short-lived incentive the Japanese forces were thrown, very much against their will, into battle."[40]

The Japanese senior commanders not only had underestimated the total nmbers of men manning the American perimeter but obviously had not learned the power of American massed artillery, which eventually caused so much havoc. Conversely, they overestimated what their own artillery could achieve. They never massed their artillery on a single point or area in support of their assaulting troops. Rather, they allowed for single gunfire on a variety of targets, mainly the airfields. Many of their larger-caliber guns were destroyed by American counterbattery fire, leaving the Japanese commanders only the Japanese infantryman to secure Hyakutake's goals. In all sectors the attacks by these ill-fed, sick, but loyal troops were successful in taking initial objectives and establishing bridgeheads in the American lines, largely because of local superiority in numbers. When a battalion of infantry concentrates on a narrow front of seventy-five to a hundred yards, it becomes a mass of humanity, difficult to stop even though it presents an ideal target for automatic weapons. Despite their near fanaticism, however, the Japanese could not hold their initial gains against the superior fire power of the 37th and Americal divisions.

A further reason for the failure of Japanese attacks was the inflexibility of the plans. It was only after the Iwasa and Muda forces had been defeated that the bulk of the surviving 6th Division was concentrated against the 129th. Until then, there were three uncoordinated, piecemeal attacks. On a lower tactical level, the Japanese junior officers did not evince much originality. To paraphrase the Duke of

Wellington, the Japanese came on in the same old way and were killed in the same old way. Forty-five years later a rifleman of the 129th still wondered at the way the Japanese attacked a defensive line.

> The Japanese were very strange. I remember a fight; it may have been after the big battle. We were told that they were coming. There was a little hill outside of the perimeter and a man would come over this hill and the men in my platoon would just take aim and shoot him. And the next would come over the same way and we'd shoot him. And then the next would come over the same place instead of spreading out. We got the impression that they were either doped up or drunk. They never seemed to think, "The man ahead got killed there, I'll go on this side." So our guys would just sit there and shoot them and yell, "Got another one, got another one."[41]

Hyakutake's defeat did not end the Bougainville compaign, but the badly battered 6th Division had to be reconstituted before it could once again prove a threat to the Allied perimeter. General Beightler expressed the feelings of many in stating that the beating administered to the 6th Division was a partial repayment for its role in the rape of Nanking in 1937. Nevertheless, Hyakutake's 17th Army was still a formidable force, and in the following months the men of XIV Corps would find it costly to enlarge the perimeter to more commanding ground on the north and east. Although the Japanese planned another concentrated assault on Allied positions, they would never again launch a major attack. For all practical purposes, the battle for the Solomons was over, Rabaul was negated, and the Allied war effort became concentrated upon the Marianas, the Carolines, and the Philippines. Bougainville became a backwater, but men would nevertheless continue to die in its steaming jungles.

10. The 93d Division Affair

The Japanese were in full retreat by 28 March. The Magata force, with an estimated strength of over fifteen hundred men, utilized the Numa Numa Trail and withdrew toward the northern part of Bougainville. The remnants of the Iwasa and Muda forces, covered by reinforcements from the 4th South Seas Garrison unit and the 6th Cavalry Regiment, moved quickly along a number of trails to the relative safety of southern Bougainville.[1]

The enemy's disengagement brought on a change in the tactics of XIV Corps. Instead of standing on the defensive, all American frontline units now took the offensive. General Griwold had no intention, however, of attempting any far-reaching offensive to eliminate the Japanese presence. He realized that Bougainville was no longer important. Rabaul had been neutralized, the Japanese navy had been withdrawn from the Solomons, and the Japanese air force in the South Pacific was practically nonexistent. Therefore General Hyakutake's remaining forces, cut off from outside aid, could do very little harm if adequately contained in their strongholds in the north and south. Griswold had already issued orders to Beightler and Hodge on 23 March that outlined the limited objective of XIV Corps. In his instructions he made clear that he wanted the 37th and Americal divisions, reinforced by elements of the 93d, to "take immediate action to harass and deny the enemy's line of supply in southern Bougainville." He further ordered his divisional commanders "at the earliest practical moment to coordinate those actions with a limited offensive against the west flank and rear of the hostile forces in the front, cutting their lines of communication in northern and western Bougainville and destroying the maximim number of enemy and his materiel."[2] The two weeks following Hyakutake's decision to call off his offensive witnessed very aggressive patrols by elements of both divisions complying with General Griswold's instructions.

In the 37th Division sector it was not until 1 April that the last pocket of Japanese resistance was eliminated in front of the 129th when elements of the 148th moved up to Hill 205 and drove away a small number of Japanese still dug in there. General Beightler and his staff had already made plans to expand the outpost line of the 37th northward in the area between the Marabie and Laruma rivers. On 2 April, Company I of 3/148 and elements of the newly arrived 2/25 moved out from Hill 205 up the Numa Numa Trail and crossed the Laruma River in the face of considerable automatic weapons fire. They established a bridgehead on the west bank and had advanced almost half a mile from it before nightfall. Reinforced the next day by the Fiji 1st Battalion and a chemical mortar platoon, the infantrymen moved farther north against intermittent Japanese fire. By 7 April they had advanced as far as the forks of the Laruma River. Later other patrols moved into the region south of the village of Lesiapaia located approximately five miles from the forks of the Laruma. A series of trail blocks were set up along the Numa Numa and many secondary trails. Other 37th Division patrols ranged as far up the west coast of Bougainville as Cape Moltke without encountering any Japanese.[3]

There would be considerably more contact with the Japanese in the Americal sectors. On 29 March a patrol of the 132d operating in the vicinity of Hill 501 ran into a block by an estimated battalion. The patrol called in artillery fire just before breaking contact at dusk; the next day the men found thirty bodies in the area of the concentration. Meanwhile, patrols of the 164th pushed north and northeast toward the hills that had given shelter to the enemy artillery during the Japanese offensive. On 1 April, General Robert McClure became commander of the Americal Division, General Hodge moving on to command XXIV Corps. On that same day the 164th, operating north of Hill 250, ran into a force of Japanese estimated at more than a hundred men. Devastating artillery fire forced the Japanese to abandon their positions and move directly toward the Americal patrol. After a brief fire fight the Japanese broke and ran, leaving fourteen dead behind. By the evening of the next day, strong outposts had been established on Hill 250 and the steeper neighboring Hill 600, and advance patrols of the 164th began searching all the trails leading northwest to Hills 1000 and 1111. The larger-caliber guns left behind by the retreating Japanese were located and destroyed.[4]

The heaviest action in the Americal sector was in the south along the shores of Empress Augusta Bay. Here the 132d on 5 April launched a preliminary attack ultimately directed at capturing the small coastal village of Mavavia. A concerted attack two days later destroyed twenty Japanese pillboxes. The Japanese defenders, perhaps still suffering from the aftershock of the fighting in March, offered little resistance. Possibly the harassing fire from destroyers standing offshore and from 155-mm guns of XIV Corps, although causing little physical damage, had the desired psychological effect. On 8 April a tank-infantry attack eliminated most of the pillboxes west of the village. The following afternoon Company C of the 2d Battalion occupied the destroyed village; the Japanese defenders simply melted away. Meanwhile other 132d patrols had been busy in the jungle around Hills 500 and 501, attempting to locate as many of the Japanese defenses as possible.

General McClure had decided to extend his outpost line eastward to secure the heights just west of the Saua River comprising Hills 155, 165, 501, and 500. The major role in this task would fall to the 132d. However, the regiment was augmented by the newly arrived black battalion, 1/25, and the 3d Battalion of the Fiji Infantry as well as the 247th Field Artillery in direct support. The 132d's cannon company, with four 75-mm howitzers, was also in place on the Magine Islands. These guns could also support the other black battalion, 1/24, in its activities near the mouth of the Mavavia River.[5]

The Fiji battalion began the attack on 13 April by moving southeast to secure positions east of Hill 65 from which they could protect the left flank of 3/132. The next day that attacking battalion had reached its jump-off point approximately seven hundred yards west of Hill 65. The attack on the first objective, Hill 165, began on the morning of 15 April. Progress was difficult because of the many small gullies in the intervening area and the jungle growth. The nearly incessant rains had turned many areas into mudholes through which the riflemen had to struggle. It was not until early afternoon that they reached the base of the hill, but there was no resistance and the hill was soon occupied. Security on Hill 165 was turned over to Company A of the 25th Infantry while 3/132 pressed on to take Hill 155. Sections of the black infantry company then moved to this rise, relieving 3/132 for an attack on Hills 500 and 501 the next morning.

The Japanese contested the north base of Hill 500 during the morning of 16 April, and 3/132 was pulled back briefly to enable the artillery to work over the hill. The riflemen, following close on the barrage, secured Hill 500 by noon. Once again they were halted by the Japanese, who counterattacked along the south slopes. All during the following day the Japanese blocked further advance despite heavy artillery and mortar fire. The firing, which continued intermittently during the night, eventually had good effect; by 18 April the Japanese defenders had moved off Hill 501. This last of the hill objectives was also manned by men of 1/25, while 3/132 garrisoned the area south of the hill. The Fiji troops immediately began extensive patrolling between this hill line and the Saua River and within two days reported that the entire area was free of Japanese.[6] By the end of April, units of XIV Corps had established a strong outpost line far beyond the main perimeter and strong daily patrols were scouring even farther in all directions. Contact with the Japanese during the summer was minimal.

Bougainville had been selected by the highest echelons of command for an experiment utilizing black troops in combat. Elements of the 93d Division and the 24th Regiment would be fed slowly into action to see how well they performed. Events connected with the expansion of the outpost line would have far-reaching implications for the employment of black troops in other areas of the Pacific war. In order to understand the successes and failure of the black units involved in this experiment, one must understand something of the background to their deployment in the South Pacific.

The most salient fact to note is that the army of World War II was segregated, and despite the need for manpower, many of the most important men in government and the armed forces did not wish to tap the resources of the black community. There were many reasons for this reluctance. The most obvious was the frank, overt racism of some in decision-making positions, many of whom were from southern states. These men were generally convinced of the inferiority of black people and believed they could learn only the simple tasks. Many senior commanders, despite the historical record of service and heroism of black soldiers from the beginnings of the nation, questioned the bravery and patriotism of black soldiers. Others who did not share such racist views were nevertheless opposed to utilizing black soldiers to their fullest potential because they recognized the many difficulties in trying to provide adequate training and equal opportunity for blacks within an army that was still for all practical purposes segregated. Therefore, recruitment of blacks into the army was slow. By the end of 1943, despite political pressure from liberal congressmen and the black community, there were only 150,000 blacks in combat-designated units. There had been a considerable number of racial incidents in various camps throughout the United

States, and most black units, notwithstanding their designations, were used primarily for transport, service, or labor.

One of the major questions for all black units was related to command personnel. At the beginning of the war there were few black officers, and even with the rapid expansion of the officer corps during the first two years after Pearl Harbor, few black officers had the training or experience to assume the command of company-sized units. Because of this shortage, as well as the conventional wisdom that blacks were not capable of command, most of the senior officers of black units were white. The resultant imbalance often created hostility not only between enlisted personnel and officers but between the lower and more senior officer ranks. This had a deleterious effect on training, as did the general apathy in higher headquarters about the specific reason for training black combat divisions. A number of observers reported low morale among black units, including the 93d Division. Once the 93d learned that it was scheduled for overseas duty, the morale of the men and efficiency of its components increased markedly.

It was most obvious during the first two years of the war that no theater commander wanted black units. In 1942 General Marshall concurred with the recommendation that no black troops be sent to the United Kingdom. Although this position was later modified, it clearly indicated the dominant attitude toward using black troops in the theater of war designated by Washington as the most important. For some time blacks were not sent to the Caribbean either, because commanders feared that since American blacks had a higher standard of living, they could cause problems with the less-fortunate black populations of the islands. In the Southwest Pacific, Australian politicians, whose own government had an all-white policy, were pressuring General MacArthur to refuse to accept black American troops and to send back any who had already been dispatched. To his credit, he adamantly refused to be swayed by their arguments.[7] Even the Belgian government in the fall of 1942 complained to Washington because a black quartermaster company had been sent to the Congo.[8]

Despite the negative reaction to the employment of black troops, pressure was mounting in the United States to utilize more black units in combat zones. Chief among those pressuring the armed forces was Congressman Hamilton Fish of New York, who recalled how well black troops under his command had performed during World War I. The black press and many distinguished black professionals were also very vocal in protesting the obviously discriminatory practices of the armed forces.

Reacting to this pressure, Secretary of War Henry L. Stimson, although he himself had definite reservations about using blacks in combat, and General Marshall began to urge the Central Pacific command to take black combat units. In early 1943 General Delos Emmons in Hawaii expressed his disagreement with a plan to send the 93d Division to help garrison the islands, thus freeing a white division for direct combat. Nevertheless, he was ordered to make preliminary plans for the utilization of the division in Hawaii. The general consensus in Washington during the summer of 1943 was that troops of the 93d be kept as far away from combat as possible.

This attitude began to change later in the year, and a tentative proposal was put forward to General Harmon to find some use for the division in the South Pacific. Higher command came to believe that the 93d, after additional jungle training, might be used on Bougainville. Harmon had already expressed his negative feelings about having any significant number of black troops under his command, even though he had not been scheduled to receive another division before mid-1944. Now, realizing that his superiors wanted someplace to put the 93d Division, he relented and suggested that the 93d could be used to relieve first-line white troops for rest and rehabilitation. Despite the negative reaction of General Emmons, the War Department had decided to send the 93d to Hawaii and on 23 December had ordered it to proceed to the port of embarkation in San Francisco.[9] With General Harmon's reluctant acceptance of the posting of a black division to the South Pacific, the orders were changed on 2 January 1944, directing the 93d to New Georgia.

By all accounts the 93d was the better of the two black infantry divisions despite a number of admitted deficiencies. The 93d had been activated in May 1942 with a main strength of two regular infantry regiments, the 25th and 368th. It was expanded to full size by the draft and acted in part as a training division to provide cadres for the later-activated 92d Division. Its training cycle proceeded in much the same way as that of all-white divisions activated at the same time. Its training base at Fort Huachuca in Arizona was hardly the ideal spot for teaching jungle warfare, but this choice did not reflect discrimination; many divisions trained in one type of environment, only to find themselves operating in combat in exactly the opposite terrain, geography, and weather. Reports on the training of the 93d were in the main good. Both General Leslie McNair and General Joseph McNarny in separate reports in the summer and fall of 1942 expressed satisfaction with the division. General McNarny noted that "the 93rd Division appeared to be in fine shape and General Hall doing an excellent job."[10] These observations seemed confirmed by the division's performance during the Texas and Louisiana maneuvers from April to June 1943. Thus, despite General Harmon's reservations, he was getting a division that according to all reports was as good as any division that had not yet seen action.

Despite the focus on the 93d Division and the question of its deployment, it was not the first to be sent into combat. A black infantry regiment was already active in the South Pacific. This was the 24th Infantry, a regular army unit, which had been sent to Efate in New Caledonia in April 1942. From its arrival it had provided the major defense for the Efate perimeter and a potential offensive striking force under the command of Colonel Hamilton Thorn. Once the threat of imminent invasion was laid to rest by American success on Guadalcanal, the men of the 24th were assigned to service functions: they loaded and unloaded ships, built roads, provided details for malaria control, and performed quartermaster and ordnance services. The 2d Battalion was detached to Guadalcanal between 1 March and 6 August to provide basic work details on the island, and the rest of the regiment moved to Guadalcanal in August. The 3d Battalion was then sent to Munda to operate ration dumps and provide pools for a myriad of labor tasks. Most of the troops of the 24th would be engaged in this type of work throughout the rest of the war.

The one exception was to be 1/24. Its commander, Lieutenant Colonel John L. Thomas, received orders to prepare his command to be a part of XIV Corps, only recently put in control of Bougainville operations. The battalion landed on 30 January 1944 at Empress Augusta Bay and was assigned to a backup role as part of corps reserve. Moreover, though the main focus in Bougainville and Washington would be on the black infantry units, a black artillery unit, the 2d Battalion, 54th Coast Artillery, had been posted from Espiritu Santo. It arrived in Bougainville six days after 1/24 and became a part of XIV Corps artillery.

General Griswold on 29 February, perhaps in compliance with instructions from Washington to use black troops in combat only after adequate preparation, detached 1/24 from corps reserve and attached it to the 37th Division. Here the troops were to help prepare the frontline positions and were assigned the west half of the 129th's reserve line. General Beightler on 11 March was given direct control of the battalion, and he reoriented it to the 148th's sector, where one company was placed directly on line between two battalions of the

176 Bougainville

148th. That evening in helping to repulse a Japanese attack the unit lost its first two men. The next day the first combat patrol of the 24th encountered a small number of Japanese and acquitted itself well.[11]

When this minor action was reported in the American press, it brought an immediate reaction from the War Department.[12] Against the recommendations of many senior officers, the secretary authorized a "national policy" of using black units in combat. Now those concerned at the highest levels did not want negative publicity caused by committing unprepared units. General Marshall on 18 March in an "eyes only" message to General Harmon reiterated that elements of the 93d Division should be used only after those units had been adequately prepared. Four days later Marshall asked for full particulars on the way the 24th had been used and wanted complete details on further plans for the battalion. General Harmon assured Marshall that no dangerous operations were planned for either 1/24 or the elements of the 93d then loading for Bougainville. They would be attached to veteran units and used initially for combat patrolling or for mopping-up operations.[13] It is obvious that Washington was aware of the glare of publicity that would focus on these black combat units and that not only the black press but many who had opposed their commitment on racial grounds would look carefully at all aspects of the use of black troops. No other units of comparable size deployed in the Pacific theater were ever subjected to such scrutiny even before they saw any significant action.

While all these communications concerning the use of black soldiers were flashing back and forth across the Pacific, the 93d Division was on its way to the South Pacific. The decision had already been made not to commit the entire division to a combat role. Two of its regiments, the 368th and 369th, were to be used as occupation troops on islands already captured. The 368th did not even land at Guadalcanal but was sent immediately to garrison Banika Island in the Russells. The 369th, after a brief stopover, was posted to New Georgia to relieve units of the 43d Division for deployment elsewhere. Only the 25th Regiment, the 593d Field Artillery Battalion, and a medical and an engineer battalion were scheduled for Bougainville. They off-loaded in Guadalcanal on 17 February and within ten days were undergoing training in scouting and patrolling in a jungle setting. After three weeks of such training the combat team boarded transports for Bougainville and arrived at Empress Augusta Bay on 29 March.[14]

General Griswold by this time had placed 1/24 under control of the Americal Division. These were the troops that relieved men of the

182d on Hill 260. After uneventful patrol activity, the battalion then moved to relieve units of the 132d controlling the beach areas between the Torokina and Mavavia Rivers. Here the patrolling became much more dangerous. On 19 April a patrol of nineteen men encountered a large body of Japanese across the Mavavia and were forced to retreat. The patrol leader and three men became trapped on the other side of the stream. They were rescued later in the afternoon by a counterattack with tanks from the 754th Tank Battalion. On 24 April the battalion, supported by two platoons of tanks, attacked the Japanese positions and by nightfall had cleared the enemy from more than a thousand yards of beach. The advance continued until halted by the swampy areas adjacent to the Moi River. Then 1/24 was replaced in that area by 2/132 and moved back into a supporting position. Later the battalion would actively patrol to the north and east as far as the Reini River. Through no fault of the officers and men of 1/24, their frontline action was limited, and the unit was relieved and sent to the Russell Islands on 25 June. Eleven of its men had been killed in action, two later died of wounds, and thirteen were wounded. It had accounted for an estimated forty-seven Japanese dead. General Griswold considered its combat performance, however limited, to have been good.[15]

General Griswold, true to his promise to General Marshall, assigned the newly arrived 25th Regiment to relatively quiet duty. His operations memorandum of 30 March stated: "The 25th RCT will receive intensive training and patrolling in jungle operations. The 1Bn/25th will then take over the sector now occupied by 1Bn/132 Inf. placed under control of C.O. 132nd Inf. Relief to be effected when new area 1/132 is ready. 2nd Bn/25th Infantry will take over sector occupied by 1/182nd Inf. and placed under operational control of C.O. 182nd. 3rd Bn/25th Inf. remain in present position under Op. Control of C.O. 164th Infantry."[16] On this same day officer observers and two ammunition and pioneer platoons of the 25th accompanied the 132d on patrols toward Hill 500. By mid-April men of 1/25 were being used as backup troops in the 132d's assault on Hills 165, 500, and 501. The first men of the regiment were killed when a party of 1/25 escorting a wounded man on a litter was ambushed by a Japanese patrol. Four men were killed in the engagement although the wounded man was conveyed to safety.[17]

Very shortly after landing, 2/25 was detached from the Americal and assigned to the 148th Infantry of the 37th Division. The battalion along with 3/148 and two companies of the Fiji regiment were formed into a task force whose assignment of 2 April was to pursue the Japanese withdrawing northward along the Laruma River. The mission of 2/25 was to cross the Laruma, then move east and secure a trail junction near the mouth of Jaba River. In order to do this men and equipment had to be lowered by rope down a sixty-foot bluff against some fire from a few Japanese defending the river crossing. Early in the afternoon of the following day a small patrol led by the regimental intelligence officer crossed the river and discovered a machine gun nest and a number of pillboxes. Reinforcements from Company F were sent across and, with considerable difficulty, silenced the machine gun. Private Wade Fogge won the division's first Bronze Star during this engagement by knocking out three enemy pillboxes with his rocket launcher. Company F had five wounded and estimated that twenty Japanese had been killed in this engagement. By 5 April the 2d had completed its mission and was returned to command control under the Americal's 182d.[18]

In the tasks assigned them, the officers and men of the 25th had at all times performed ably, if not heroically. This performance was fully in keeping with the expectations of those responsible for sending the regiment to Bougainville. Generals Griswold and Beightler had not recklessly thrown untried black troops into the most dangerous areas but had eased them into combat situations accompanied by seasoned troops. The 3d Battalion, however, as of 5 April, had not participated in any combat patrols with the 164th Regiment to which it had been attached. That evening it received orders to commit Company K on its first mission, one that would modify the good opinion that had been formed of the combat potential of the black units and, by extension, would have ramifications far beyond those of the usual company-level fire fight.

The task assigned Captain James Curran, the white officer commanding Company K, and his black platoon leaders seemed relatively simple. Accompanied by a machine gun platoon, Company K was to move eastward from Hill 250 approximately two miles and by nightfall of 6 April set up a trail block. Curran would also have with him Captain William Crutcher and three enlisted men from the 593d Field Artillery Battalion, who would act as observers in case artillery support was needed, and an officer and enlisted man from a photographic unit to take pictures of the operation for release to the press. Sergeant Ralph Brodin of the intelligence section, 164th Infantry, was also assigned as a combination aide and guide.

The company moved out in line at 0645 on 6 April with the 1st Platoon in the lead and the 3d Platoon providing rear guard and machine gun sections in between the three platoons. All went well until the company discovered an old Japanese hospital area approximately a quarter of a mile from its objective. The company halted in a dense jungle area as the 1st Platoon sent out patrols to check the supposedly abandoned huts. Soon one of these patrols began firing toward the left front and the patrol leader reported killing two of the enemy. The company commander decided to investigate and went forward, only to be fired upon. Two men of the patrol were wounded. Captain Curran then ordered the two other platoons forward to flank the 1st Platoon.

So far everything had been done by the book, and the company was in good position to respond to any enemy activity. Then, without orders, some men of the 1st and 2d Platoons opened fire, and they were joined by the 1st Machine Gun Section firing at both left and right flanks. Curran ordered a cease fire, which was passed on by the patrol leaders, and the unauthorized fire halted briefly. But soon it was resumed, and some men began to panic. Thus when Curran ordered the flank platoons to close up on the center, the 1st Platoon was caught in friendly cross fire, apparently being attacked from the flanks and rear. Sporadic fire was also coming from the Japanese in front. Curran then ordered the 1st Platoon to withdraw, only increasing the confusion; some of the men, including the platoon sergeant of the 1st, had already dropped their packs and disappeared.

Curran reported his situation to battalion headquarters and was ordered to retire three or four hundred yards and re-form his company. This he was able to do only with great difficulty; the men, most of whom were obviously very frightened, continued to fire and then fall back. In places instead of forming a single line, men were lying two or three deep, the rear soldiers firing over the heads of those in front. Men of the 1st Platoon were reluctant to move off the trail and provide flank cover while the other platoons retired. Soon there was chaos. Sergeant Brodin, the only experienced infantryman, tried to calm the situation by walking up and down telling the men there was nothing to worry about. At the same time Curran was desperately trying to stop the indiscriminate firing. Their efforts were to no avail. Without adequate leadership at the platoon level, the troops fired in all directions at any bush that was believed to conceal an enemy. Upon being informed of the situation, battalion ordered Curran to fall back to Hill 250 to reorganize.

The first men of Company K reached friendly lines late in the afternoon. These included the missing platoon sergeant and the company first sergeant, who observers noted, was old and fat. He was carried across the Torokina River. Under questioning, these men reported that they had encountered a large body of the enemy, perhaps an entire regiment, concealed in the jungle, but none of them had actually seen any Japanese. When all the troops finally reached Hill 250 it was discovered that the thirty-minute fire fight had claimed the lives of Lieutenant Oscar Davenport, the weapons platoon leader, and nine enlisted men. Twenty men had been wounded. The company had left its dead behind, along with a machine gun, mortar, radio, and mortar ammunition. More telling than anything else, they had tossed away two BARs, eighteen M-1s, and three carbines during the panic. Later, as the entire incident was pieced together, the consensus was that there had been no more than a squad of Japanese in the hospital area and that most of the casualties had been caused by the indiscriminate firing of the men of Company K.[19]

The problems of the Company K patrol were not yet finished. A patrol from Company L was sent out the next day to recover the dead but ran into enemy opposition short of the hospital area, and after losing one man in the fire fight, retreated without recovering the bodies. On 8 April, therefore, Lieutenant Abner Jackson, leader of Company K's 1st Platoon, led a carrying party of forty men to the site. Nine bodies were found, but the men of Company L refused to handle them despite threats of disciplinary action. Only when troops from Company K were brought up could three bodies and some equipment be carried back. Not until the following day did another carrying party led by the battalion commander bring back the other bodies and the rest of the abandoned equipment.

The ordeal of Company K had ended. The episode had displayed the lack of experience that was endemic in the 25th. The panic and indiscriminate firing at an imaginary enemy were certainly not to be condoned, let alone approved, but in the context of the Pacific war, this was not the first or only time that there had been a similar occurrence. White army and marine units had been known to overestimate an enemy, shoot at friendly troops, or panic during their first contact with the enemy. Although battalion and division headquarters could not have been pleased with the actions of Company K, they recognized that its performance could be attributed in a large degree to inexperience, and ultimately it was forgotten if not forgiven. On 11 and 13 April, men from the same company were involved in further patrol activity in conjunction with the 164th, and they acquitted themselves very well.

General Griswold appointed a committee to investigate the actions of Company K on 14 April, and it took testimony from almost every man involved. This investigation formed the basis for Griswold's report of 10 May to General Harmon. He concluded that (1) the 25th had had little jungle training and was not prepared to deal with the problems encountered; the men were willing to learn, but they were generally able to retain less than white troops; (2) morale of officers, particularly whites, was low, in contrast to high morale of enlisted personnel; (3) junior "colored" officers made minimal attempts to carry out instructions and as a rule did not have control of the enlisted men; (4) initiative was generally lacking among platoon commanders and lower grades; (5) the 25th Infantry, though supposedly better trained than 1/24th, had not shown any such superiority.[20] This report, with corroborating evidence, was passed on to higher headquarters and by the end of May had reached Washington.

Meanwhile, on 8 April units of the 25th were ordered to back up the 132d, which was to assault the hill lines adjacent to the Torokina River. They were to relieve those Americal units as soon as the hills had been taken. By 25 April battalions of the 25th were all in outpost positions. Five days later control of the 25th and all its attached units passed to a provisional brigade under the command of General Leonard Boyd, the assistant divisional commander of the 93d Division. Units of the brigade continued to patrol beyond the outpost line in cooperation with troops from the Americal. The 93d Division reconnaissance troop did yeoman duty protecting the engineer battalions constructing roads. On 20 May all units of the 25th on line were relieved and were ordered to move into staging areas in the rear.

The 2d Battalion left Bougainville for the Green Islands on 24 May, followed by 3/25 on 11 June and 1/25 on 20 June.[21] The brigade was dissolved, and on 15 June the 93d Division came under control of the Southwest Pacific area command. Ten days later 1/24 left for the Russell Islands. These movements left the reconnaissance troop and the 49th Coast Artillery Battalion as the only black troops on Bougainville. The reconnaissance troop continued to perform well, taking part in the battle for Horseshoe Ridge on the East-West Trail in early July. After seven months it, too, was ordered off the island to join the rest of the 25th Regiment. The 49th Coast Artillery was well integrated into the artillery defenses. It had performed very well during the main Japanese counterattack in March, men of the unit winning six bronze stars, two air medals, and a commendation from General Kreber, commanding corps artillery. Ultimately the unit was attached to the 135th Field Artillery and placed in positions far outside the main perimeter to provide fire support to the 37th and Americal divisions in the Laruma Valley. The 49th continued on in Bougainville until ordered to Finshafen in February 1945.[22]

With such good general service by most of the black units, it could

182 Bougainville

be expected perhaps that the fiasco of Company K could be chalked up to inexperience. Such was not to be. Rumors began to circulate almost immediately, and with each retelling, the actions of the black soldiers became worse and the number involved escalated. Within months, this one company had been inflated to a regiment and ultimately a division. Perhaps this was the culmination of wishful thinking on the part of white officers and men who so wanted to believe in the innate superiority of whites that they would accept without question stories of the cowardice of an entire division. The malicious stories continued long after the war. Even General Marshall, who should have known better, related in an interview in July 1949 that the men of the 93d Division "wouldn't fight—couldn't get them out of the caves to fight."[23] It would have done little good to point out to General Marshall that Company K was operating not from caves but in dense jungle.

The most cogent defense offered for the action of this one company came from the commanding officer of the 25th Regiment, Colonel Everett Yon:

> Had this organization been given prior instruction and been accompanied by an experienced platoon of the 164th Infantry in its initial action, the results would have been far different. The force encountered was small but equipped with machine guns. The majority of our casualties were inflicted by other men of the company. This has resulted in many instances in jungle warfare when troops were committed without proper seasoning. Early in May a company of the 182d Infantry, a veteran of two years of jungle warfare, encountered an inferior force of the enemy east of the Saua River, became disorganized and returned to the perimeter of the 3d battalion, 25th Infantry on Hill 65 after darkness. The above facts are not offered in condonation of the failure of Company "K" to carry out its mission, but they were contributing causes.[24]

Many senior officials in Washington, however, who had only reluctantly approved their use in combat, were more than willing to condemn all black troops on the basis of this one incident. The information on 1/24 and the 25th was sent to General Marshall, who forwarded copies to Undersecretary John J. McCloy. He, in turn, in his covering letter to Secretary Stimson, pointed out that one small incident should not be used to prove the case against black soldiers, alluding to the success of the 99th Air Squadron in Europe. Stimson was dubious of such optimistic arguments and noted that he did not believe black units could become really effective unless the officers were white. Given the early arguments that the requisite number of white officers to fully staff more black divisions were not available, these doubts by the secretary of the army and its chief of staff were enough to stifle any significant future combat role for black troops. The officers and men of Company K when they set out on their mission on 6 April could have had no idea of the crucial role they would play in high-level policy decisions regarding the deployment of black combat units.

11. The Final Phase

Actions elsewhere in the South and Southwest Pacific theaters during the spring of 1944 would relegate the Bougainville operations to tertiary importance. The occupation of the Green Islands in February, followed by the seizure of Emirau in the St. Matthias Group on 20 March, completed the isolation of Rabaul, which had meanwhile been systematically pounded into impotence. Operations undertaken by the 1st Marine Division at Cape Gloucester and by the army's 40th Division at Arawe further contained the Japanese on New Britain. Elsewhere, General MacArthur's forces on 29 February began the operation to seize the Admiralty Islands, whose Seeadler Harbor gave Admiral Halsey's ships one of the better anchorages in the South Pacific. MacArthur had received permission from the Joint Chiefs to leapfrog past the Huon Peninsula to seize Hollandia and Aitape on the northwest coast of New Guinea. This brilliant manuever resulted by the end of April in the encirclement of an entire Japanese army, rendering it useless for further operations. Thus the focus of Allied forces in the Pacific areas had shifted. No longer in a defensive mode, the Central Pacific and Southwest Pacific commands were looking ahead to the invasion of the Marianas and the Philippines.

Illustrating very well this change of emphasis was the altered role of Admiral Halsey. In April he was informed that he would relinquish command of the South Pacific area and take most units of the 3d Fleet north to Hawaii. There, for the rest of the war he would interchange command with Admiral Spruance of the increasingly powerful big Blue Water Fleet, which by mid-1944 could proceed relatively unopposed anywhere in the vast Pacific. The change in command was a part of a general restructuring that on 15 June assigned General MacArthur control of the bulk of all Allied forces then operating in the South Pacific. Admiral Halsey's successor, Vice Admiral John H. Neston on Noumea, would command only a fraction of the military units available to his predecessor. General Griswold's XIV Corps was to be removed from Bougainville as soon as practicable to be used in the invasion of the Philippines.

The task of General Griswold's forces, which would continue to operate on Bougainville until later in the year, remained the same as before the Japanese offensive in March. The perimeter had to be strengthened and manned at all times since Griswold fully expected the Japanese to launch another major offensive. The enemy had to be kept off balance by continual patrolling and by establishing strongpoints at strategic locations far removed from the main defense lines. Senior American officers never seriously considered offensive operations designed to capture the entire island, believing that they would be a needless waste of men and equipment. Constant air, land, and sea observation could keep track of the main Japanese forces in the north and south. As long as they remained quiescent they were no threat to the perimeter, and certainly any action by General Hyakutake could have absolutely no bearing on the war's outcome. The Americans decided to allow the Japanese space since they could now do little harm.

The living conditions of the Japanese soldiers, never good under the best of circumstances, became increasingly desperate. Added to the dangers that forward troops always faced, such as contact with large American combat patrols, was the growing specter of starvation. Sealed off from regular supplies from New Ireland or New Britain, Hyakutake's army had to depend entirely on its own labors to acquire food. The normal rice ration of 750 grams of rice for each soldier was cut in April 1944 to 250 grams, and beginning in September there was no rice ration.[1] A large portion of the available army and naval personnel had to be put to work growing food. Allied pilots took delight in dropping napalm on these garden plots whenever possible. The native workers who had been impressed into service were the first to defect, but soon many soldiers also just walked away from their units, taking the chance of surviving in the jungle on what could be gathered. After the failure of the March attack, morale in most units became deplorably low. There were instances, normally unimagined in the Japanese army, of open insubordination and even mutiny. Although General Hyakutake dreamed of a midsummer offensive, it became obvious that no operations as large as that smashed in March could be undertaken for months, if ever. General Hyakutake gradually lost the respect of his junior officers, who blamed him and the older officers for their repeated defeats. This situation became so bad that a number of them were relieved of their commands in February 1945. Perhaps as a result of this challenge to his authority, Hyakutake in April 1945 suffered a stroke, which paralyzed his left side. General Kanda succeeded him in command of the 17th Army, and he was replaced as divisional commander by Lieutenant General Tsutomu Akinage, who had been the army's chief of staff. Perhaps to the dismay of the junior officers, Kanda continued the cautious defensive policies of his predecessor. From a rational, realistic point of view, he could do nothing else.[2]

Thus, almost as if by agreement, both sides adopted a defensive posture that minimized the conflict in the no-man's-land between them. Inside the American perimeter the work of making life easier for the more than sixty thousand troops continued. The road network was improved, more semipermanent buildings were erected, movie theaters were built, and athletic fields were constructed. Boxing matches were arranged, and baseball and softball games were encouraged. Such activities must have seemed puzzling to the Japanese observers, who nevertheless did little to interfere with the games. Presumably a number of Japanese, perhaps remembering their own enjoyment of baseball before the war, watched with a tinge of jealousy. Certainly one such was observed in the 37th Division area. A former infantryman recalled the incident:

> A large baseball field had been cut from the jungle on Bougainville not far from the Piva fighter strip. After things had settled down after the 2nd Battle of Bougainville, and the perimeter stabilized, someone noticed a raggedy-assed Jap way out in the shadows of the jungle off right field watching a game. Field glasses later verified this first supposition. He came back for other games and was soon a rather regular fan—cautious but regular. There was no easy way to get to him and no officers of the "gung-ho" variety were informed. Besides, the 37th GI's figured "He can't be all bad;" besides, he somehow managed to root for 37th teams, showing his approval of hits and runs for the home team! He was somehow indicative of the rapport developed all along the perimeter by summer 1944.[3]

Division rest camps had been built where some frontline soldiers, on the recommendation of doctors, could have a week off from their normal duties. Those GIs who could took advantage of the warm water behind the reef and swam without fear of stonefish or sharks. One infantryman, however, viewed the ocean as an enemy; he would rush up to the waves, strike them with his fists, and curse them for standing between himself and home.[4] Radios were installed in dayrooms in unit areas and tuned to an island radio station at corps headquarters called the Mosquito Network. It brought news of the outside world and current hit tunes from the States to the rear-echelon troops. Several large movie theaters were carved out of the forest areas. At one such theater, which was surrounded by tall trees in the 37th Division sector, an amusing event confirmed the close proximity of the now-quiescent Japanese. An observer recalled:

> One night some captured Japanese film of the sinking of the USS *Lexington*, an aircraft carrier, was being shown along with the regular Hollywood movie at the 37th Division theater, possibly at "Loewe's Bougainville." As the Jap planes laid bomb after bomb and torpedo after torpedo into the listing *Lexington*, there suddenly came shouts of "Banzai! Banzai!" from the tangled but huge branches of a banyan tree on a near side of the rows of seats. A Jap had hidden himself to watch the movie but was overcome with patriotism at the sight of his comrades in the airforce sending an enemy ship to the bottom! He was pulled from the tree with no trouble and entered the POW compound, perhaps the last victim of the carrier *Lexington!*[5]

Even some major USO shows reached Bougainville. In August Randolph Scott led a group of entertainers, and a few weeks later Bob Hope with his entourage, including Jerry Colonna and Frances Langford, put on shows for both the 37th and Americal divisions; Jack Benny's troupe arrived soon afterward. Other less well known performers, including opera singers, entertained thousands of XIV Corps personnel. In addition, large divisional bands gave regular concerts, and enterprising amateur actors in both divisions put on skits, most them broad satires in which very little was immune from attack.[6] Nothing could be done about the heat, rain, and insects and little about the worst evil of all—boredom. Still, conditions were far better than those endured by the marine assault troops who landed on Bougainville the previous November.

Life was even relatively easy for the men manning the main defensive positions. For the first time in months they could pitch tents and sleep above ground, abandoning the dugouts as living quarters. To keep the men from becoming too relaxed or too idle divisional headquarters began a rigorous program of combat training. Later in the fall this program was also intended to prepare them for further, more active combat operations. Both divisions were involved in these mock combat situations. In early July the 37th Division began amphibious training, including everything from practice in combat loading to debarkation exercises and amphibious landings. After a week of such training for each regiment the infantrymen began a series of combat problems, using live ammunition and explosives to attack fortified positions. They began with platoon problems, followed by battalion attack operations in which tanks, artillery, and air strikes were used against the imaginary enemy. The Americal used the area around Hill 250 for its full-scale regimental training. After moving into position, an infantry battalion would attack up the Torokina River toward the hill as direct support units fired live ammunition into the target. Combat observers were present during each training exercise to note and later correct any obvious errors. At the same time the cannon companies were familiarizing themselves with their new weapon, the M-7, self-propelled 105-mm howitzer, which had replaced the smaller 75-mm pack howitzers.[7]

For many front line troops, however, there was no play acting; the real war continued as patrols from both divisions moved farther and farther into Japanese-held territory, mainly to keep the enemy off balance. The 164th and 182d Infantry of the Americal were very active with long-range missions in the Reini-Tekessi region. From 1 May to 28 June, patrol after patrol from the 164th probed deep into the interior. During this long period only one contact was made. One American was killed and one wounded while the Japanese left behind twelve dead. After the 182d took over the responsibility of patrolling this region, the Japanese abandoned their hill positions and retreated eastward along the East-West Trail, and despite several contacts with the enemy, there was no significant action until the regiment was in turn relieved by the 164th. On 28 September a patrol from Company E attacked an estimated forty Japanese in the vicinity of Tavanatu village, killing eighteen before the survivors fled. No further action of any significance occurred in this sector until 17 November, when the reconnaissance platoon discovered a number of enemy soldiers in a small village. The subsequent attack on the village destroyed the entire garrison of twenty-three men. This was the last contact with the Japanese until 24 November, when the 164th was relieved by elements of the 3d Australian Division. The American toll for all actions in the Reini-Tekessi operations was seven men killed and fourteen wounded.[8]

The major area of conflict during the summer and early fall was in the upper Laruma River region. Here the 37th Division had established some trail blocks and had sent out aggressive combat patrols during April, May, and June. These patrols were made more difficult by the terrain, a series of ridges and sharp peaks separated by deep ravines, whose steepness made many areas almost impassable unless trails were used. Yet there were few of these native trails in the extreme upper river areas. All the hills were covered with rain forest and heavy undergrowth. The battalion of the 37th that operated in the Laruma area had its own light artillery and mortar sections and was backed by the 155-mm guns of corps artillery. On 15 July the zone of divisional responsibility was changed, and the Americal Division took over more of the central sector of the perimeter. Two days later 2/164 had relieved all elements of the 37th. Its mission was the same as that of the 37th, namely, to maintain trail blocks closing hostile routes of approach, to place harassing fire on known Japanese positions, and to destroy as many of the enemy as practicable. In addition, reconnaissance of the Karina-Igiaru-Magerikopal areas was to be undertaken.[9]

On 20 July, Company E of the 2d Battalion attacked an organized Japanese position directly in front of the battalion's main defenses and drove the enemy from the hill. The battalion observation post was then established on the now-renamed Nip Hill. Patrols determined the existence of a strong Japanese position on a ridge near the village of Igiaru. A reinforced platoon of the 2d battalion attacked this strongpoint on 28 July but was beaten off, and two men were killed. Subsequent attempts on 2 and 3 August also failed to dislodge the Japanese. For the next three days the opponents contented themselves with exchanges of grenades and mortar fire. Then on 7 August the Japanese, in company-size strength assaulted the 3d battalion's position but were thrown back. That evening they attempted to infiltrate the Americal position but were repulsed with heavy losses. The next day patrols discovered thirty Japanese dead in front of the battalion defenses. The battalion maintained constant mortar and machine gun fire into known enemy positions as the Japanese retreated farther eastward.

The 2d Battalion relieved the 3d in the forward areas and discovered that the Japanese were strengthening some of their positions, particularly in the vicinity of the village of Sisivie. Fire fights between American patrols and the enemy became a daily occurrence, and the enemy sites were pounded by mortar and artillery fire. On 22 August aircraft operating from the Piva airstrips dropped eight tons of bombs on the Sisivie fortifications. A week later a patrol of the 1st Battalion worked through the village of Karina, and reached the top of Nip Hill from the north. The following day a platoon-sized enemy force attacked the battalion's dug-in positions. It was repulsed, and three Japanese were killed. The occupation of the top of Nip Hill made the Japanese roadblock positions, the launch points of their previous attacks, untenable, and they withdrew in the direction of Igiaru.[10]

On 2 September the 182d relieved the 164th in the upper Laruma region and continued the aggressive patrolling and intermittent shelling of the enemy-held areas. The Japanese ambushed a small patrol on 24 September and managed to wound the commanding officer and kill eight enlisted men. The regimental commander then ordered an attack on the strong Japanese positions, committing a full company in an attempt to dislodge the enemy. This attack was not successful, and it drew a counterattack during the evening of 27 September by an estimated eighty Japanese. The battle for the hill position lasted all night and cost the Americans four dead and fifteen wounded. Higher headquarters then decided to commit the entire regiment to clear out the Japanese in a wide area of the upper Laruma. On 29 September the 1st and 3d battalions blocked all approaches to the target from the east, south, and west. The 2d Battalion then made a wide sweep east and west and completed the encirclement of the Japanese on 2 October. All the Japanese positions in the target area were destroyed after three days of hard fighting, and 105 men were killed. During the following week attempts to extend American control over Piateripaia village were unsuccessful, although the village and surrounding areas were very heavily shelled by corps artillery. The village was eventually captured by the 132d which had relieved the 182d during the first two weeks of October. From Piateripaia and Sisivie, elements of the regiment continued patrolling throughout October with diminishing contacts. The other two regiments of the Americal would also make few contacts whenever they operated in the forward areas of the Upper Laruma, and during November and early December there were no important enemy contacts. Therefore when the 132d was relieved by the 29th Infantry Brigade of the Australian army on 10 December, the forward blocking line in this region had been stabilized because the Japanese had largely conceded their previous strongpoints to the Americans.[11]

While these relatively unimportant, albeit very dangerous, small-scale operations were going on, events elsewhere would drastically alter the Bougainville operation. By August, marine and army units operating in the Central Pacific had seized Saipan, Tinian, and Guam in the Marianas, and Admiral Spruance's 5th Fleet had all but destroyed Japanese naval air power at the "Turkey Shoot." General MacArthur's attention was directed far to the north of New Guinea and the Solomons as he prepared to invade the Philippines; that invasion was tentatively set for January 1945. When MacArthur received favorable reports from Admiral Halsey after his raid in the Palaus and eastern Philippines, however, the date for the invasion of Leyte was moved up to mid-October. MacArthur needed as many divisions as possible, including XIV Corps, to take part in the landings.

The decision had been made by mid-July to remove XIV Corps as soon as possible and replace it with the Australian II Corps consisting of the 3d Division (7th, 15th, and 29th brigades) and the 11th and 23d brigades. The corps commander was Lieutenant General Sir Stanley Savige, an experienced veteran of North Africa, Greece, Syria, and New Guinea. The commander of the 3d Division was Major General William Bridgeford, a senior staff officer who had not commanded a large formation in the field before, though most of the brigade commanders had seen much action, mostly in New Guinea. The Australian II Corps, with more then thirty thousand men, appeared to be adequate to the task of continuing General Griswold's concept of keeping the Japanese under surveillance and defending the perimeter against any counterattack that might threaten the airfields.[12] Later the Australian commanders would complain of the lack of shipping, particularly of barges, but these were in short supply and MacArthur's headquarters in mid-1944 could not see any need to part with scarce shipping and equipment for what they saw as a policing responsibility in a by-then unimportant area. In New Guinea too, MacArthur had been content to defend the airfields and to let the Japanese "wither on the vine."

General Sir Thomas Blamey, commander of the Australian army, disagreed with this policy. He wanted to seek out and destroy the enemy wherever he could. As long as Blamey had command over only Australian troops early in the New Guinea operation, his ideas prevailed and they were adopted by the American commanders in 1942 and early 1943. With the success of MacArthur's bypassing strategy, however, it became counterproductive to attempt to destroy every Japanese garrison in the territory seized. Since most of the positions in New Guinea taken from the Japanese after 1942 had been secured primarily for airfields, it appeared logical merely to establish a defensive perimeter, man this with sufficient troops to drive back any Japanese attack, and bypass the bulk of the enemy, leaving them to their own resources in the jungle. The success of such operations was a determining factor in the strategic planning for the Cape Torokina

192   Bougainville

landings in November 1943. If MacArthur's concepts had worked so well in New Guinea and later on Bougainville, why would the Australians desire any drastic alteration? To answer this question one must look at the command relationships in the Southwest Pacific theater.

Even General MacArthur's most ardent defenders would agree that at times he was very difficult to work with; he was opinionated and often took inordinate personal credit for what others had achieved. Soon after his arrival in Australia in early 1942, he envisioned Americans in the primary role in the offensives that would lead to the recapture of the Philippines and ultimately the defeat of Japan. With inadequate equipment and poor logistical support, the Australians had fought well in denying Port Moresby to the Japanese and would later bear the brunt of the fighting along the Kokoda Trail and in capturing Buna and Gona, the first major success for the Allies in New Guinea. Nevertheless, they were increasingly underutilized and their commanders all but ignored as the American forces were built up in the theater. All but one of the key positions in MacArthur's command were held by Americans. Only after considerable Australian protests was General Blamey named commander of all Allied ground forces. Very soon he discovered that this was largely a titular position. MacArthur and his chief of staff, Major General Richard Sutherland, made the basic strategic decisions, and Lieutenant General Walter Kruger, commander of the American 6th Army, certainly did not take orders from Blamey. For all practical purposes Blamey, although treated with courtesy, was ignored as far as possible and in reality commanded only the Australians.[13]

After the Leyte invasion MacArthur's headquarters in the Philippines was generally out of touch with the Australian contingent, which still made up one-third of the paper strength of his force. The greater part of the Australian army was consigned to what MacArthur considered a rearguard garrison role first in New Guinea and then later on New Britain and Bougainville. Therefore the Australians were always chronically short of heavy equipment and shipping.[14] To a proud army the neglect evinced by MacArthur and the lack of credit for what the Australians had achieved had to be humiliating. General Blamey and other senior officers were also angry at being left out of the major decisions concerning overall strategy in the Southwest Pacific. Therefore while MacArthur's attention was elsewhere and Blamey had a relatively free hand, he decided to revert to the more aggressive tactics the Australians had employed in the war in New Guinea.

Once the Philippine invasion began, MacArthur became more

and more concerned with that complex, large-scale campaign and paid less attention to controlling what his Australian subordinates were doing in New Guinea and Bougainville. Thus, after American units were relieved by Australians, not only tactical command passed to their leaders, but strategic objectives on a limited scale were also determined by General Blamey and his subordinates. By the fall of 1944, American strategists, although disagreeing with the Australians, were willing to allow them to have their head as long as what they did and their demands for supply did not threaten the more important offensives in the north.

In defending his strategy to the Australian government in May 1945, General Blamey was very candid concerning the Solomons. Three courses of action had been open to him, he said. The first was to continue the American policy of pure defense; the second was to mount an all-out offensive with full-scale air and naval support; the third was to be more agressive in patrolling deep into enemy-held territory, destroying garden areas and bases with the purpose of starving and eventually totally destroying the Japanese garrisons. He chose the third alternative, rejecting the American policy because he believed that such a passive defense policy would destroy morale, create discontent, and decrease resistance to sickness. Blamey never explained how he arrived at these conclusions. It is doubtful that he checked with the ordinary foot soldier, who one suspects was much like his American counterpart. If given the choice between a relatively comfortable sedentary life in the rear areas or aggressive patrolling in a hot, humid jungle with the very definite risk of being killed, it is likely that most would choose the former, even if it took the edge off combat efficiency. The second choice, according to Blamey, could not be considered because air and naval units were not available and the Australian ground forces were inadequate to the task. Blamey and Savige had embraced the third alternative even before their troops reached Bougainville.[15] By the close of 1944, however, aggressive patrolling had become an active offensive policy directed at clearing the Japanese from central Bougainville and driving them into enclaves in the northern and southern parts of the island.

Advance elements of the Australian 3d Division Headquarters arrived at Empress Augusta Bay on 6 October to prepare for the arrival of rest of the division. The first unit to arrive was the 7th Brigade, which by mid-November had relieved the 129th and 145th Regiments of the 37th Division on the northern flank of the perimeter. On 22 November, General Savige assumed command of all island operations from General Griswold. Between 24 November and 12 December all

194 Bougainville

American frontline units were replaced by Australians; the 29th Brigade relieved the sector of the 182d, the 11th took over from the 148th, and 2/8 Commando[16] occupied the northeast bulge of the perimeter, previously held by the 164th. Integration of the Australian units proceeded so rapidly that by Thanksgiving most American troops were in bivouac within the perimeter awaiting transport from Bougainville. The first units, part of the 37th Division, left on 13 December. Three days later the bulk of the division was aboard transports heading for Lae in New Guinea. The division later had a brief stopover at Seeadler in Manus before joining four other divisions of General Kruger's 6th Army in its assault on Lingayen Gulf in Luzon. The Americal Division had to wait longer for its relief from Bougainville. During December its regiments were engaged in training exercises, particularly amphibious operations. Then the first of a total of thirteen transports arrived at Empress Augusta Bay on 8 January. Soon the men of the Americal were on their way northward to join X Corps of General Robert Eichelberger's 8th Army with the specific task of pacifying northwest Leyte. Thus, except for a few service troops, all American units were gone from Bougainville by 1 February 1945.[17] The Australians now had full control of the perimeter, and General Savige could continue the operations against the Japanese without any fears of American criticism. Those criticisms would come later, when the Australian parliament began to question the wisdom of Blamey's strategy.

The first activity by the Australians after their arrival was on the extreme left flank of the perimeter. Here the various units of the 37th Division had sent a parol each week toward Kuraio Mission, twenty miles away; 2d/8th Commando continued this patrol activity for the next five weeks until it was relieved by the 11th Brigade on 12 December. During this entire period the patrols met the enemy only once, encountering two unarmed Japanese, in all probability deserters. When they refused to surrender, the patrol shot them. A few times the Australians used barges to scout farther up the coast. Not surprisingly, they found their maps to be woefully inaccurate. In all these northward ventures, the few signs of Japanese confirmed what American intelligence had believed: the majority of the Japanese were in the south, having conceded much of northern Bougainville to the invaders.[18]

Most of the contacts with the Japanese during the summer of 1944 had been along the Numa Numa Trail around Piaterapaia and westward along the Choho Ridge to Sisivie. This area continued to be dangerous for patrols. Northeast of Piateripaia was George Hill, which had been ocupied by units of the Americal Division, but fifty yards beyond was Little George Hill, and this was held by the Japanese. The unwritten truce that had existed during the summer and fall was broken by men of the Australian 9th Battalion. On 25 November a platoon made a surprise attack on Little George under cover of smoke bombs and killed twenty of the startled defenders while losing two killed and six wounded. Brigade command next decided to drive the Japanese from the higher elevations of Arty Hill, so called because of the many rounds fired into it during the previous months. Arty Hill was located approximately two hundred yards northeast of Little George Hill. On 13 December, ten Australian air force planes attacked the enemy position on Pearl Ridge, which dominated the left flank of the Australians' northward advance. Then on 18 December a full company of the 9th Battalion attacked Arty Hill after bomb-carrying Corsairs and a battery of artillery worked over the enemy position. The Australians attacked up the slope from the southeast. Their major problem until just before the crest was the loose soil, which made climbing the steep slope difficult. After an hour of close infighting, the position was taken. Twenty-five Japanese were killed and twenty recently dug graves were also discovered.[19]

General Savige understood that the main Japanese force, the 6th Division, was located in southern Bougainville and therefore decided to concentrate the bulk of the 3d Division on the south flank with the objective of capturing Mosigetta and Mawareka. First he needed to know the size and location of Japanese forces south of the Jaba River. He gave this assignment to the 29th Brigade, which had completed the relief of the Americal's 182d Regiment on 10 December. From 13 December onward, patrols of varying size were sent out along the narrow beach trail called the Jaba Road. These crossed the Jaba and one element was transported well south of the river by barges. There were a few clashes with small numbers of Japanese, but the penetration deep into Japanese territory was accomplished with minimal losses to both sides. By 20 December the Australians had three companies operating south of the Jaba and were preparing to attack an estimated two battalions of the Japanese 13th Regiment located near Mosina. Thus, even before Savige had issued his general instructions on 23 December, the Australians had, much to the surprise of the Japanese, launched a series of strong probes into areas that had generally been quiet while XIV Corps manned the perimeter.

General Savige's instructions of 23 December to subordinate commanders clearly enunciated the immediate goals as envisioned by his staff, which would lead to the ultimate destruction of the Japanese in southern Bougainville. The campaign was to consist of three simultaneous offensives. In the north the Japanese would be forced back into the narrow Bonis Peninsula, where they would be destroyed. In the central highlands the enemy would be pushed off the high ground near Pearl Ridge. That area would then be used as a base for aggressive patrolling to a minimum depth of four thousand yards, thus threatening the important line of communication for the Japanese along the east coast. The major area of operations would be in the south, against the main concentration of Japanese army and naval troops.

Inasmuch as General Savige had only twelve infantry battalions available to carry out these goals, the instructions of 23 December were optimistic in the extreme. There had been a considerable debate between MacArthur's intelligence head, Major General Charles Willoughby, and the Australians over the number of Japanese on Bougainville, the Americans claiming a smaller number than Blamey's staff believed were present. Even if the lower American estimates were accepted, the Australian forces would still have been only on an approximate parity with the Japanese. The true figures, as ascertained after the surrender, gave Hyakutake an advantage in numbers of approximately 1.5 to 1. Why, then, did Savige believe he could succeed in ultimately carrying out his plans?

Allied intelligence of the conditions of the Japanese troops was remarkably good. The Australians were aware that the total casualties suffered by the Japanese during the American period amounted to over eight thousand dead. During this same period estimates placed the numbers of Japanese who died of illness at almost ten thousand. For months following their abortive attack on the perimeter in March, the Japanese were dying from illness at the rate of three thousand a month. As the Australian historian Gavin Long noted, "The neglect by the Japanese officers of their own men seems to have been little less callous than their neglect of their prisoners of war."[20] The Japanese, cut off from regular supplies of food, had begun large-scale agriculture in order to provide enough food to sustain the troops. They were raising a wide variety of vegetables in garden plots many acres in size, most of them in the southeast. This effort, however necessary, required a large contingent of workers, which Hyakutake had to draw from his regular force.

Savige began his offensive in the central sector early in the morning of 30 December when the 25th Battalion, after a preliminary air strike, advanced against the Japanese, estimated at ninety men, who held the strategic Pearl Ridge. Company D was halted on the right by heavy fire from the enemy entrenched on the far side of a crater and was forced by late afternoon to dig in. In the center, Company B had reached its objective by 1500 and was ordered to wait until the following day before resuming the assault. During the night the Japanese made a number of attempts to drive back the Australians but with no success. Resuming the attack early on 31 December, the right-flank companies approached their objectives by different routes and had captured the strategic height by 1630. Later it was discovered that the Japanese had over five hundred men defending Pearl Ridge. Its capture by a battalion of Australians who suffered relatively few casualties clearly indicated the loss of morale and fighting spirit of the Japanese frontline troops. From the ridge the Australians could view the sea on both sides of the thirty-mile-wide island and could begin planning for negation of the enemy to the east. Supplying the troops in that central area required more than three thousand native carriers; so it became imperative to build jeep trails beyond the escarpment. In a major engineering feat, the Australians installed a three thousand-foot-long cable partway up the ridge and used it to pull a bulldozer to the top. Thus the long-range patrols operating from Pearl Ridge during the following weeks were guaranteed adequate supplies even though fewer natives were used.[21]

On 31 December, General Savige ordered General J.R. Stevenson, the 11th Brigade commander, to begin operations as soon as possible directed toward controlling the northwest coast of Bougainville after destroying the enemy garrisons south of Soraken Point (Map 10). The 31st/51st Battalion, which had already been patrolling beyond Kuraio Mission, was assigned this task. The main body was to proceed along the coast, while long-range patrols operated on the right flank in the jungle and hills to flush out any Japanese and drive them toward the coast. By 16 January one Australian company had reached Rukussia village twenty-five miles up the coast from the mission. During the next three days there were skirmishes with the Japanese as the company moved farther north. A platoon left the main track, cut through the foothills, and after crossing the Genga River led an attack on the village of Kunamatoro before returning to report that all evidence pointed to a stiff Japanese defense along the Genga. This information proved accurate.

The enemy was dug in on the curved, wooded Tsimba Ridge, which commanded the open space across which the Australians had to advance. All direct attacks for the next few days against these defenses proved fruitless. A platoon did cross the river on 25 January a third of a mile east of the ridge, whence it was hoped they could attack the Japanese entrenchments. The Japanese sought to wipe out this

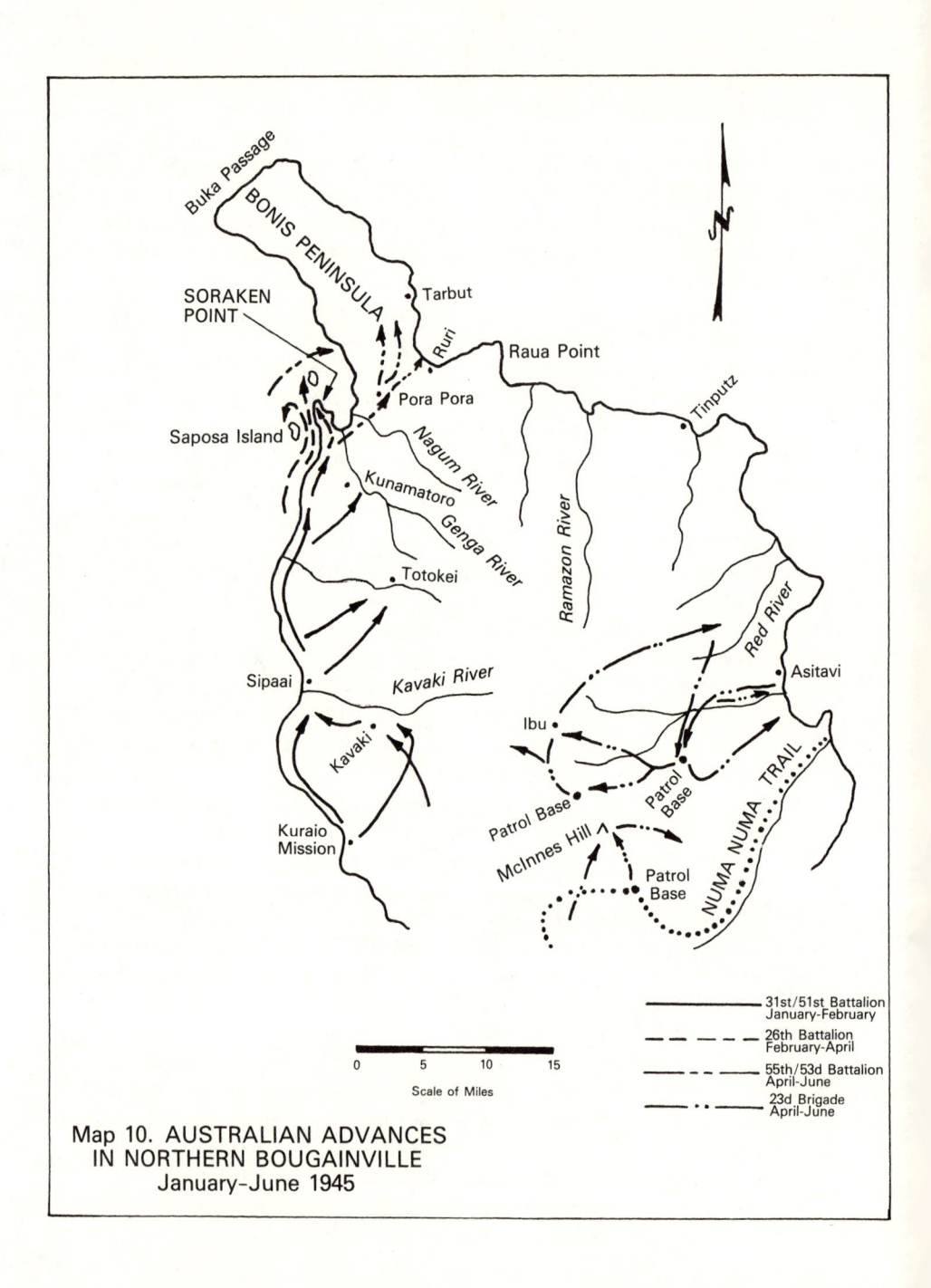

Map 10. AUSTRALIAN ADVANCES IN NORTHERN BOUGAINVILLE
January–June 1945

bridgehead without success. Requests from the Australian company commander for tank support were denied by General Savige, who inexplicably wanted to save them to "surprise" the Japanese in the south when he opened his main offensive. The Australian infantry therefore had to take the ridge with minimal artillery and mortar support. It was not until 6 February that the main defenses were taken, and three days later the last pocket of Japanese resistance was overcome along the western edge. More than sixty Japanese were killed and four field guns, three antitank guns, and nine machine guns were captured.[22]

Within two days of the capture of Tsimba Ridge, patrols had cleared the north bank of the river, and the main force could press forward toward Soraken. One company had branched off on 4 February to clear the region around Kunamatoro, after which it was scheduled to swing back to join the drive on Soraken. For the next two weeks the unit would fight a series of small actions before finally driving the Japanese from their ridge defenses on 22 February. By this time the main party had made a series of encircling maneuvers, cutting the Japanese escape routes. Two Australian platoons reached the coast north of the Gillman River and forced the Japanese to abandon their positions south of the river. The 26th Battalion which relieved the 31st on 22 February, continued the pressure on the Soraken sector. On the night of 12 March the Australians landed a reinforced company along the southern border of Soraken plantation and harassed the Japanese enemy until 20 March, when they withdrew. By 26 March an attack on the center of the Japanese line, coordinated with an amphibious landing, drove the Japanese from the peninsula and forced them to fall back north of Pora Pora village and ultimately to the narrow neck of the Bonis Peninsula. Landing parties had also secured Taiof and Soposa islands just off the Soraken Peninsula. At the same time guerrilla forces were operating in the Numa Numa area and farther north in the Teoparino region, reporting on troop movements and wherever possible setting ambushes for the hapless Japanese who felt themselves safe in territory that they believed they still dominated.[23]

The work of the native guerrillas in the central and southern parts of Bougainville has been largely ignored even by the Australian government. Originally, during the early years of Japanese occupation, the guerrillas were organized for defense by the coast watchers, who for three years provided Allied headquarters with extremely valuable information on ship and troop movements.[24] Led by a few Europeans, by late 1944 the native irregulars inaugurated a reign of terror among

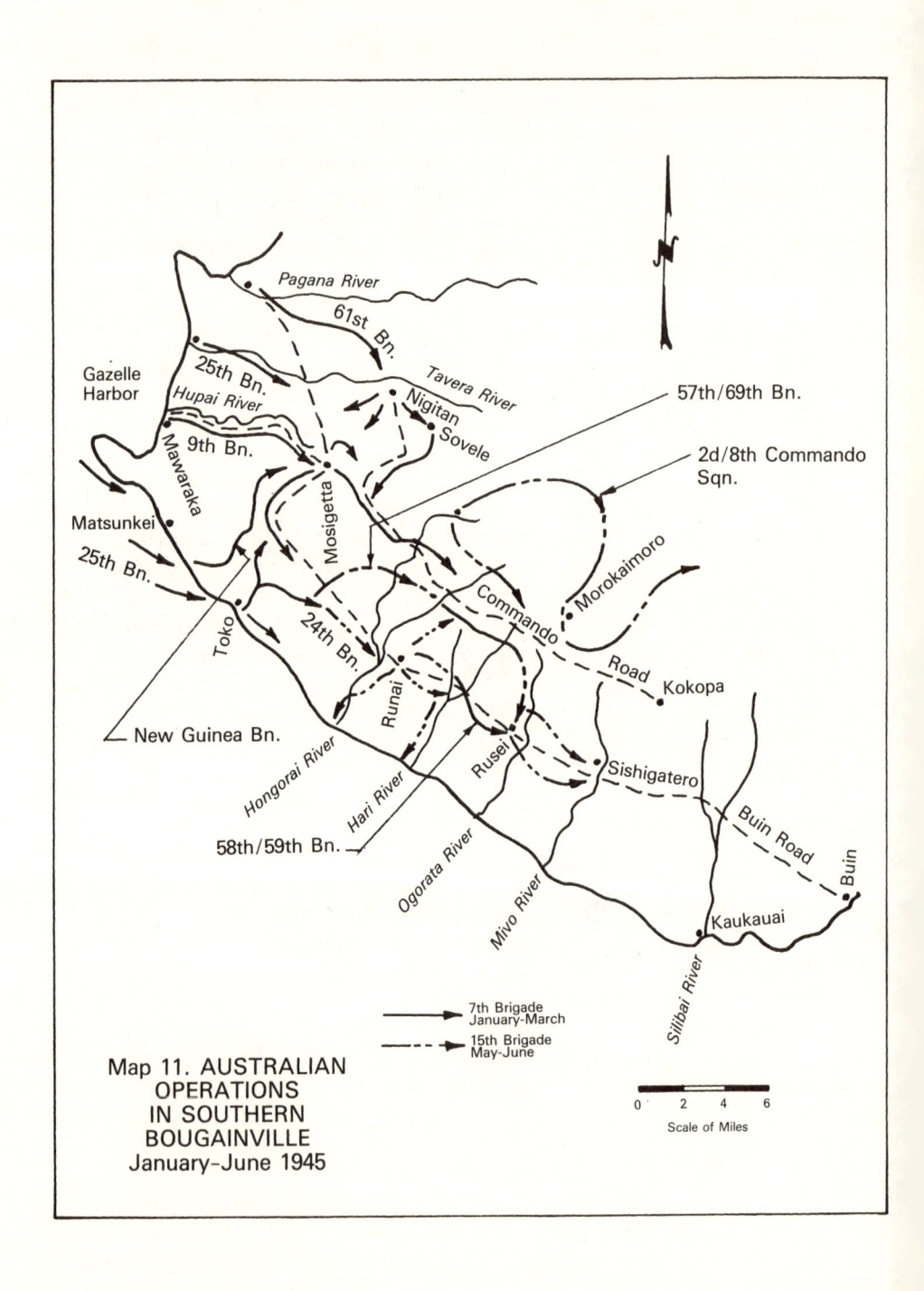

Map 11. AUSTRALIAN OPERATIONS IN SOUTHERN BOUGAINVILLE January-June 1945

the Japanese. The Bougainville natives, commanded at first by Lieutenant P.E. Mason and later by Captain C.W. Seton and armed with captured weapons, controlled much of the hilly forested country in the area from Maridan village eastward to Kieta. This force, operating with the aid of air drops, became so powerful that by August 1945 its leaders were planning a direct assault on the east-coast base of Kieta, where the Japanese still had perhaps as many as one thousand men. It was estimated that in the eight months that the native force operated in conjunction with the main Australian advance, always within enemy territory, they had killed more than two thousand Japanese soldiers.[25]

On 28 December, Brigadier R.F. Monaghan, commanding the 29th Brigade, received orders to begin the offensive against the main force of the Japanese in southern Bougainville (Map 11). A part of the 15th Battalion moved along the coast trail, and another section was landed from barges south of the Tavera River. Within two days all Japanese had been cleared from the vicinity of the coast south to the Adele River. At the same time men of the 47th Battalion had advanced up the Jaba River to its confluence with the Pagana. This action resulted in a number of fire fights with small Japanese units, which generally retreated without causing the Australians any casualties. The first major objective of the coastal advance was the village of Mawaraka located south of the Hupai River. By 9 January a bulldozer had cut a good trail along the coast from Tavera to the Adele River, thus expediting the movement of troops and supply. The next day units of the 29th Brigade had crossed the Hupai, where they met considerable opposition from Japanese holed up in earthen and log pillboxes. The Australians brought up four antitank and two field guns to fire point-blank into the fortifications. At a cost of eight killed and thirty-one wounded, the 47th Battalion had gained control of the territory adjacent to the lower Hupai by 10 January. The Australians proceeded slowly south toward Mawareka, expecting the Japanese to expend considerable effort to defend this key to the Gazelle Peninsula. General Kanda, however, had decided not to contest the Australian advance in this sector, and on 17 January an Australian patrol entered the village without opposition. A patrol on 19 January took Makotowa, one and a half miles upriver, while another from the New Guinea Battalion was landed by sea to probe Motupena Point. Thus by the end of January the Australians had advanced over twelve miles along the coast and controlled a large area extending more than six miles inland.[26]

General Savige had accurately concluded that the main Japanese force, the 13th Regiment, would not be able to offer much determined resistance north of the Puriata River approximately ten miles south of his advance units. He decided to push his forces southward as quickly as possible along trails through Mosigetta and beyond while his commando units operating in the bush approximately five miles inland moved to secure crossings over the river. The advance was challenged in a desultory fashion by separate Japanese units attacking from ambush. They did not hold up the forward movement but did inflict a few casualties on the Australians, who used fire power to dislodge the enemy from its positions. Failing this, they would make wide sweeping moves through the jungle to get behind a position and then work their way back toward the Japanese. Corsairs of the New Zealand air force struck ahead of the advancing Australians, whose way south was checked more by swamps and thick undergrowth than by Japanese resistance. By 9 February the Australians had broken out of the undergrowth into fairly open territory. Two days later the advance troops of the 25th Battalion entered Mosigetta, which had been abandoned on orders from General Kanda. The Japanese of the 13th Regiment then retired south of the Puriata River. Only small Japanese rear guards opposed the further advance southward. Once again the Australians used barges to land troops behind enemy lines to take Toko village, and the 25th Battalion moved into the interior toward Barara, which, despite the foul weather, was taken by 20 February. It had rained steadily for over a week, mud was knee-deep, and trains of six or seven jeeps had to be pulled forward by tractors.[27]

Toko now became the main supply base; landing craft brought needed supplies and unloaded despite the heavy surf. After April the road was improved, and the Australians began using the beach at Motupena Point, where there was calmer water, and then bringing supplies south by truck. Tanks were brought forward to Toko on 17 March in preparation for what Savige expected to be a major battle as the Australians moved south of the Hongorai in the direction of one of the main Japanese garden areas. Earlier the Australians had gouged out of the undergrowth at Mawaraka an airstrip that could handle the light Auster aircraft, whose patrolling gave the ground troops extra intelligence of Japanese strongpoints ahead.

By early March leading elements of the 25th Battalion had crossed the Puriata and established a perimeter two hundred yards south along the Buin Road. On 5 March a few Japanese were driven off a small knoll close to the roadway. It was named after Private C.R. Slater, who was wounded in the action. Moving along the Buin Road, one company was almost trapped on 13 March as it advanced on Hiru Hiru village. Falling back, the Australians dug in along a line from Slater's

Knoll across the Buin Road. Here they sustained a number of attacks from a considerable force, which at one time was firing on the Australians from three sides. Reinforced by other elements of the 25th Battalion, the company counterattacked, and by 19 March had driven the Japanese from an extensive system of pillboxes near the junction of the road to Hatai village. This action, which concluded on 22 March, had been conducted in areas of deep undergrowth and the advancing infantry was plagued by continual rainfall. Eight Australians had been killed and nineteen wounded. Nevertheless, they had apparently cleared the way to attack across the Hongorai and the garden area to the east, and an estimated fifty Japanese had been killed in this operation.[28]

On 18 March an Australian patrol had killed eight Japanese and captured a document indicating that General Kanda planned a large-scale counteroffensive against the 25th Battalion sector, which was deployed along the Buin Road, anchored by Slater's Knoll. Awaiting this attack, the 25th Battalion improved its defenses, particularly on the knoll, and later brought four tanks across the Puriata River to back up the defense. Thus, the forward echelons were well prepared when about a hundred Japanese charged a rear section of the defense line during the evening of 27 March. After two unsuccessful attempts to break through, they retreated back toward the river. In the meanwhile other Japanese had dug in along the Buin Road between battalion headquarters on the knoll and the forward companies. Farther north another Japanese attack hit the 9th Battalion but it was stopped by concentrated machine gun fire. The next morning the Australians discovered forty-two dead Japanese. They knew that these two strikes were only preliminary because a prisoner, a sergeant of the Japanese 13th Regiment, reported that a full-scale offensive would soon be launched with his entire regiment taking part.

This major Japanese attack began on 30 March at 0700, directed at one Australian company to the south of the knoll, which successfully beat off four attacks by Japanese with fixed bayonets, who screamed epithets and charged directly at the Australians' fixed positions. By midafternoon there were only sixteen unwounded Australians within their perimeter, and the survivors then pulled back to join the main defense lines. The Japanese pressed their attack against the Australians on 31 March and forced the evacuation of other portions of the defensive line, but ultimately, they paid a price. The Australian machine guns played havoc with the Japanese frontal assaults. The tanks in the early afternoon entered the action with a combined infantry-tank attack that drove the Japanese off; the abandoned positions were reoccupied. The next day two companies established a strong perimeter half a mile south of Slater's Knoll and prepared for a resumption of the Japanese attacks. The Japanese commanders did not launch any new assaults immediately. Rather, over the next three days, they reorganized their battered units, sent out patrols, and cut the communications lines of the Australians.

Then in the early morning of 5 April, Lieutenant Colonel Kawano, commanding the 23d Japanese Regiment, led a renewed attack against the strongest part of the Australian perimeter, Slater's Knoll. At 0500 the Japanese assaulted the north side, and a few minutes later a larger force struck from the southwest. Although there were fewer than 150 men on the knoll, they had sighted their Bren and Vickers guns in on every possible avenue of approach. In addition the artillery had registered in on the potential target areas the previous day. The Japanese, abandoning any idea of subtlety, simply attacked the knoll in waves reminiscent of the action against the Americans a year earlier, although on a smaller scale. The results of the banzai charges were also the same. The Japanese dead were piled up in heaps in front of the wire. There was no breakthrough; the nearest any Japanese came was within a few feet of the rifle pits. The main battle for the knoll was over by 0620. Farther south a series of smaller attacks were directed against the two companies that had moved in to support the 25th Battalion troops on the knoll. These too failed. By 1300 tanks from this southerly position had linked up with the troops on the knoll and were aiding in flushing out the last of the Japanese troops, who had vainly sought cover in the underbrush in the immediate vicinity.[29]

General Kanda's offensive was a disaster. Interrogation of captured prisoners showed that he had employed a total of approximately 2,400 mostly fresh troops. Between 28 March and 5 April at least 620 had been killed and perhaps 1,000 more wounded. If one considers the loss rate from sickness and desertion, two entire regiments, the 13th and 23d, had been all but destroyed. The official Australian historian echoed earlier American observers when he noted of the Japanese that their "staff work was confused, their artillery fire inaccurate, the practice of invariably cutting signal wires before their attacks robbed them of surprise, and the habit of making repeated charges against strong positions and often from the same direction led to crippling losses."[30] Indeed, the entire series of attacks by the Japanese is as inexplicable as the Australian's desire to conquer all the island. Even had they succeeded on Slater's Knoll, they would only have delayed the Australian advance. General Kanda did not have the force available to alter the military situation. It would have been far more profitable for him to eliminate banzai charges and to use the men to harass the Australians, making them pay for each yard of territory in casualties suffered.

Eventually that is what Kanda decided to do, while his men busied themselves in constructing the main defensive position, which ran from Buin to Taurikoiru, Tsurutai to Tonlei Bay. He brought in more troops by abandoning the Shortland and Fauro islands, and soldiers scattered throughout Bougainville were moved back and concentrated in the Erventa area. This concentration was completed by July 1945.[31]

Kanda not only had the problem of defending against increasing Australian pressure in all areas of Bougainville; he also had to deal with the lowered morale of his own troops. A Japanese appreciation written after the war succinctly noted that "the fighting spirit of our men dropped considerably due to the lack of anti-tank equipment," and "due to violent bombings of our strategic points and quarters, the natives that were serving as runners and scouts began turning against us. They began marking our installations, making them easy targets for enemy bombers."[32] Kanda's orders were not to contest the Australian advance to the Hongorai River but to harass the advance whenever possible.

After the Japanese counteroffensive, General Savige decided not to move ahead immediately, partly because of the difficulty of bringing supplies forward. Much of the terrain over which the engineers were cutting wider trails was low-lying, swampy ground. Trees had to be cut, and logs laid down to provide a firm base for untracked vehicles. Even the main arteries in this area, the Buin Road and the Commando Road, two and a half miles northeast of it, had to be corduroyed before they could bear heavy traffic, and many creeks and rivers had to be bridged. All of this effort was made more difficult by the continual rains. Many of the frontline troops needed to rest and recuperate from the strenuous efforts of the past two months. Malaria and jungle rot spared the Australian infantrymen no more than they did the Americans. Savige also had to reorganize his advance units, the 15th Brigade which had jungle fighting experience in New Guinea replaced the 7th. The Australian's armor was in sad condition also; many of the tanks were in a state of almost complete disrepair. This situation would not be corrected until early May, when an additional squadron of the 2/4 Armored Regiment, with its Matilda tanks, arrived.

Thus almost as if by agreement, Australian and Japanese troops made very little contact for two weeks following the banzai attacks of the first week of April. Then Savige and Bridgeford decided to move south once again in a concerted effort. The plan was for the 15th Brigade to attack forward, with the 29th guarding the lines of communication. The leading element in the Australian advance was the 24th Battalion while the 58th/59th protected the flanks and the 57th/60th moved along the Commando Road. Backing this movement was an extra regiment of artillery and four 155-mm guns, which were displaced far forward to give extra fire power if needed. Savige also had the advantage of increased air support, since there were now four instead of the two original New Zealand squadrons based on the island.

On 26 April the 24th Battalion began to advance toward the Hongorai River along the Buin Road, and the 57th/60th paralleled its movement along the Commando Road. The 24th moved behind a creeping barrage, encountering little opposition, and within two days the Australians had advanced almost three miles, a third of the way to the Hongorai. They met more opposition along the Commando Road, where the 57th/60th lost a number of men to Japanese ambushes. As the Australians neared the river, it became obvious that although morale might not be as high as before, Japanese soldiers were not prepared to surrender. The Australians, using loudspeakers, tried to convince them of the futility of further resistance, but these attempts failed miserably; in fact, Japanese resistance stiffened. The Japanese brought up field guns and concealed them along the trails to take the Australian infantry under direct fire, but the Australian tanks advancing in front of the infantry negated their effectiveness. The ultimate outcome was that a number of Japanese field guns were knocked out of action since their placement did not usually allow for easy extrication. The Japanese also placed a number of mines on and adjacent to the trails in hopes of destroying the tanks. Although these tactics did not halt the Australians, they did cause a number of casualties. The 24th Battalion in its move to the Hongorai suffered twenty-five killed and ninety-five wounded. Many of these casualties occurred between 7 and 9 May, when more than a hundred Japanese, supported by artillery, attempted to overrun the forward positions. More than half the attackers were killed in this abortive assault, the most serious Japanese loss since Slater's Knoll.[33]

After reaching the Hongorai, the Australians regrouped and sent out long-range patrols to ascertain the strength and location of the main Japanese elements before resuming the advance to the Hari River. It was estimated that over fifteen hundred Japanese with a number of field guns blocked the route south. Beginning on 15 May and continuing to 22 May, the four Corsair squadrons of the New Zealand air force attacked Japanese positions adjacent to the Buin and Commando roads. On 17 May the 57th/60th Battalion crossed the upper Hongorai. By 27 May three companies, supported by airstrikes, had reached the junction of the Oso River. Meanwhile the 58th/59th Battalion, supported by tanks and aircraft, attacked the strong Japanese positions adjacent to Buin Road, particularly a high point near the village of Uso called Egan's Ridge.

After nine days of bombardment the Japanese abandoned this strongpoint. Their forces west of the Jaro River were broken into smaller units retreating southward. The 58th/59th continued to advance through the underbrush, discovering hastily abandoned Japanese positions. They were held up briefly at the Peperu River on 6 June but all elements resumed the southward movement on 11 June with three companies of the 57th/60th thrusting wide to the south on the far side of the Ogarta River to cut the Buin Road near Rusei village. At the same time the 58th/59th made an outflanking move to the north, cutting the Buin Road a few miles east of the Hari. The maneuvers as planned by Savige were successful in the extreme, and by 20 June the brigade had cleared the territory up to Garrett's Trail which connected the village of Kingori on the Mobiai River with Rusei village to the south. A further flanking attack by a company of the 57th/60th advanced the Australian position to a track, which they called Killen's Track, and thence to the Mivo River on 24 June.[34]

Meanwhile in the extreme northern portion of Bougainville the Japanese had retreated to the Bonis Peninsula, and the approximately eighteen hundred troops there had established strong defensive positions across the narrowest part of the island. The bulk of these troops were naval forces formed by blending together a number of labor units into four small battalions. Their initial contacts with Australian patrols showed clearly that their morale was good and they would tenaciously resist any attempt to take their dug-in positions, anchored on the many small knolls, some of which were fifty feet or more high.

The Australian 11th Brigade was worn out. It had been on line for more than three weeks, and the constant patrolling in the hot, humid climate had taken its toll. Many companies were down to less than half strength. Therefore it seemed sensible to avoid direct assaults on the enemy positions and instead make a flanking movement by sea, landing a company over the reefs at the Porton Plantation, where there were thought to be only about a hundred Japanese. This unit would then drive eastward and link up with the main force driving north from the Buoi Plantation.

In the early morning hours of 8 June, six landing craft discharged 190 men of the 26th Battalion unopposed, but the Japanese reacted very soon, pinning down the Australians in a very narrow perimeter. The company had unwittingly landed in the midst of a strong Japanese position, and by midmorning it became obvious that the enemy had at least twelve automatic weapons and were pressing their attack from the north and east. Later in the day more Japanese reinforcements arrived, and there was fighting at very close quarters. The Australian battalion commander decided on 9 June to withdraw the company that evening before it was wiped out by the Japanese. All during the morning the Japanese attacked the perimeter in waves, only to be cut down by combined rifle and machine gun fire, augmented by an artillery battery that laid its rounds within a few yards of the perimeter. Three barges dashed in to shore at 1630 and took the wounded aboard first and then the rest of the company. One barge with approximately fifty men aboard got safely away, but the other two were overloaded and could not back off the beach. Finally at approximately 2230 one of the barges drifted off. The other, however, with sixty men on board, remained stuck fast and to make the situation worse was holed and taking water. The steel sides of the vessel offered protection from small-arms fire, but the Japanese threw a phosphorous grenade on board, which started a fire. A number of men rushed forward and were swept overboard. The Japanese kept up a continuous fire on the trapped craft. The following day aircraft helped the thirty-eight men still alive on the barge by strafing the Japanese positions at regular intervals. Then in midafternoon another landing craft attempted the run in to shore, but Japanese fire damaged its steering mechanism. That evening a Japanese soldier swam out to the craft, clambered aboard, killed two men, and wounded others. Soon afterward an antitank gun fired two rounds into the stricken barge, blowing off its stern. The ordeal of the trapped men finally ended when assault boats in the early morning of 11 June moved in to the beach while the Japanese were distracted by very accurate concentrated artillery fire from all the guns of two batteries. After two hours all the living had been evacuated, thus ending the abortive attempt to flank the Japanese defenses in which 23 Australians had died and 106 had been wounded.[35] Although the Japanese losses were probably greater, the defeat of the landing attempt bolstered the morale of the Japanese naval unit defenders while dissuading the Australians from a further attempt at dislodging the Japanese in the immediate future.

By the end of June in the major area of operations, southern Bougainville, the main Japanese forces were confined to an area only about fifteen by thirty miles, in the east into a narrow section inland from Numa Numa, and in the north in the Bonis-Buka area. It was estimated at that time that the Japanese army had dwindled to approximately fourteen thousand men and the navy to about three thousand men. Over eight thousand were in the Buin area, now only thirty miles from the advancing Australians.[36] By July, General Kanda had concentrated the bulk of his forces in the Erventa area and along the line Buin-Tsurikoiru-Tsurutai.[37] The Australians moving toward the Mivo River ran into even more densely forested and swampy areas, which made any rapid advance impossible. The lack of sufficient landing craft forestalled any possible plans to land troops farther down the coast. Thus, Savige's only alternative was to have his men continue to advance along the two trails southward, while keeping pressure on the Japanese in other sectors by aggressive patrolling. The final push toward Buin would be spearheaded by the 29th Brigade, which had replaced the veteran 15th by 3 July. Patrols that probed the Mivo River fords encountered heavy Japanese fire, indicating that they intended to stand and fight along the Mivo line.

The weary Australian infantrymen got relief of sorts on 3 July when the rain that had been a daily nuisance turned into a downpour and continued without any signs of abating. Although patrols contined to operate, the main offensive scheduled to begin on that day was postponed for a week. On 10 July it was still raining hard, and even small patrols could not get across the Mivo. Rain had flooded the divisional area, and the Buin and Commando roads were seas of mud. Corps headquarters postponed the main attack until 24 July. It became obvious before that date that this also was too optimistic. It was still raining; eight inches of rain fell in the thirty-six hours of 17-18 July. Almost all the bridges along the supply line were washed out, all the rivers were flooded, and the advance elements of the wet, miserable infantry had to be supplied by air. Nature had done what the Japanese could not do. D day for the main offensive was postponed until sometime near the end of August.[38]

The heavy rains continued through the first week of August. With their slackening came an increase in patrol activity. On 3 August a deep patrol surprised a group of Japanese, killing six; the next day another patrol killed nineteen. The Japanese struck back on 7 August in an ambush on an engineering party, killing six, and on 14 August they sprang a trap on an Australian patrol by pretending to want to surrender. The same kind of daily, deadly contacts were made in the eastern part of the island while the guerrilla forces there prepared to assault Kieta. Then corps headquarters was informed of the dropping

210 Bougainville

of the Hiroshima bomb and two days later of the second atomic bomb and the Russian invasion of Manchuria. General Savige on 11 August ordered all forward battalions to withdraw their long-range and combat patrols while remaining on the alert. For all practical purposes this decision brought an end to the fighting. During their six months of combat, the Australians had lost 516 dead and 1,572 wounded.[39]

The decision to halt hostilities could only have been as welcome to the victors as to the defeated. On 15 August four New Zealand aircraft, whose underwings were painted with Japanese characters indicating that Japan had surrendered, flew over the Japanese-held areas and dropped more than 200,000 leaflets relaying the news of Japan's capitulation. The first contact with a senior Japanese officer was on 18 August when a Major Otsu crossed the Mivo and was taken to Toko for interrogation. General Savige wanted to move quickly to secure the official Japanese surrender, and he sent a message to General Kanda to have him assemble his troops in four distinct areas, while he himself traveled by barge, flying the white flag, to a designated spot off Moila Point. Savige proposed that the Australian and Japanese parties would then board an Australian warship and there sign the surrender documents.

General Kanda responded by sending an officer with the message that he had not been instructed by his superiors at Rabaul to surrender. The confusion concerning surrender was clarified in part after the war by an officer in the 8th Area Army:

> About 10 August 1945, Melbourne Australia and other sources repeatedly broadcast to the effect that the Japanese Government had decided to surrender. But on the 11th we received the following orders from the Minister of War: "For the defense of our national structure, we shall never surrender even if it means total annihilation." This strengthened our determination to fight to the last. Thereafter, we continued to hear these enemy broadcasts, but until we heard the Imperial edict about noon of the 15th announcing the end of the war, everyone had hoped for a conditional suspension of hostilities.[40]

On 21 August, General Savige received a message from Vice Admiral Baron Tomoshige Samejima informing him that the Australian commander could negotiate with him but until that time all Australian ships had to stay out of Shortland Bay. Finally, after the surrender ceremony had been completed at Rabaul, Samejima, Kanda, and three other officers proceeded by sea to Torokina, where they were escorted to General Savige's headquarters. There, in front of General Savige, six senior Australian officers, an air commodore of the New Zealand air force, and an American marine lieutenant colonel, they signed the surrender documents after handing over their swords. The bloody, long-drawn-out battle for Bougainville was officially over. A final ironic touch was added to the scene when Samejima indicated that they wanted to perform a bowing ceremony in honor of the Australian and American dead. Forming ranks, they removed their hats and bowed in silence for a minute.[41]

All that was left was to concentrate the Japanese on Fauro Island and near Torokina, and by mid-October this had been done. The exact number surrendering is in dispute, Japanese sources giving 14,381 army troops, while the Australians claimed 15,041 army personnel and 6,049 naval personnel.[42] What is certain is that for the Japanese, Bougainville was a killing ground, particularly during the Australian phase of the operation. It appears logical to accept the Australian figures announced in 1946 after many interrogations and recalculations as reasonably accurate. If so, then there were over sixty-five thousand Japanese on the island when the 3d Marine Division landed. Only twenty-one thousand remained at the time of the surrender. Of those who were killed outright or who died of wounds or disease, more than eighteen thousand perished during the Australian period.[43]

It was a terrible toll for an island whose possession after March 1944 was of no consequence in bringing the war to a close. The Australian phase of the near-two-year conflict on Bougainville was characterized by daily acts of bravery under some of the worst physical conditions encountered by troops anywhere during the war. That the Australian soldiers performed so well when they had to know that what they were doing was in the larger sphere unnecessary and unappreciated at home says much for the courage and the discipline of the ordinary Australian infantryman.

Glossary

Aichi D4Y (Judy). Japanese navy dive bomber.
Aichi 99-1 (Val). Japanese navy dive bomber.
AIRSOLS. Air Solomons, composite air group operating during Solomons campaigns comprsing elements of U.S. Army Air Force and U.S. naval and marine air units, supplemented by Australian and New Zealand aircraft.
AKA. Attack cargo ship.
APA. Attack transport.
APD. Destroyer-transport (high speed).
BAR. Browning automatic rifle.
B-24 (Liberator). Heavy, four-engine, long-range, land-based bomber, built by Consolidated Aircraft and used by both Fifth and Thirteenth Air Forces.
B-25 (Mitchell). Medium, two-engine, land-based bomber, built by North American Aircraft. Staple bomber of Fifth Air Force.
COMINCPAC. Commander in chief, Pacific (Nimitz).
COMSOPAC. Commander, South Pacific.
Corps. A command organization normally comprising two or more divisions and attached support units.
Division. Triangular division after 1942 containing three regiments. Size varied with type. Marine divisions (unreinforced) normally had approximately nineteen thousand men, and army infantry divisions (unreinforced) had approximately fifteen thousand.
DUKW. Amphibious truck (Duck).
F4U (Corsair). Gull-wing fighter, fastest navy plane, built by Chance-Vought Aircraft and used extensively by marines for ground support.
F6F (Hellcat). Standard, carrier-based navy fighter from 1943 to 1945, built by Grumman Aircraft. With Corsairs, it gave U.S. forces superiority over Japanese planes.
IMAC. I Marine Amphibious Corps.
LCI. Landing craft, infantry.
LCM. Landing craft, mechanized.

Glossary

LCP. Landing craft, personnel. Addition of (R) means rocket carrying capability.

LCR. Landing craft, reconnaissance.

L-4 (Cub). Light, single-engine observation plane. Built by Piper Aircraft.

LST. Landing ship, tank.

Mitsubishi A6M (Zero). Standard Japanese army and navy first-line fighter.

Nakajima 97-2 (Kate). Standard Japanese navy high-level and torpedo bomber.

0-1 Line. Phase line indicating a target line to be reached in a given time.

P-38 (Lightning). Twin-engine fighter, the "fork tailed devil." Standard long-range fighter for Fifth Air Force. Built by Lockheed Aircraft.

P-39 (Aircobra). Early, heavily armed fighter, not suited to high-altitude fighting, built by Bell Aircraft and used extensively in New Guinea and Guadalcanal campaign in close support.

P-40 (Tomahawk, Warhawk). Early fighter, a sturdy low-level plane, built by Curtis Aircraft and used extensively in China and by Australian and New Zealand Air Forces.

PBY (Catalina). Standard, dependable, long-range patrol aircraft, built by Consolidated Aircraft and used extensively throughout the war by all service branches.

PT Boat. Motor torpedo boat.

SBD (Dauntless). Standard, carrier-based navy dive bomber during first years of the war, built by Douglas Aircraft.

SB2C (Helldiver). Standard, carrier-based navy dive bomber after 1943, built by Curtis Aircraft.

TBD (Devastator). Standard, carrier-based navy torpedo bomber during first year of the war, built by Douglas Aircraft

TBF (Avenger). Standard carrier-based navy torpedo bomber, built by Grumman Aircraft. Replaced TBD after 1942.

VMF. Marine fighter squadron.

Notes

1. Japanese Advances and Retreats

1. The monumental work dealing with Pearl Harbor is Gordon W. Prange, *At Dawn We Slept* (New York: Penguin, 1982).
2. The most detailed account of the Philippine campaign is Louis Morton, *The Fall of the Philippines* (Washington, D.C.: Department of the Army, 1953).
3. Paul S. Dull, *The Imperial Japanese Navy (1941-1945)* (Annapolis: Naval Institute Press, 1978), 106.
4. Ibid.
5. Samuel Eliot Morison, *History of United States Naval Operations in World War II*, vol. 4: *Coral Sea, Midway, and Submarine Actions* (Boston: Little, Brown, 1949), 11–18.
6. Ronald H. Spector, *Eagle against the Sun* (New York: Free Press, 1985), 214-17.
7. John Miller, Jr., *United States Army in World War II, The War in the Pacific, Cartwheel: The Reduction of Rabaul* (Washington, D.C.: Office of Chief of Military History, 1959), 2-3.
8. Robert Sherrod, *History of Marine Corps Aviation in World War II* (Washington, D.C.: Combat Forces Press, 1952), 72-73.
9. The battle of Midway is covered in detail in Gordon W. Prange, *Miracle at Midway* (New York: Penguin, 1983).
10. Morison, *Coral Sea, Midway, and Submarine Actions*, 258-63.
11. Spector, *Eagle against the Sun*, 193-95.
12. Samuel Eliot Morison, *History of United States Naval Operations in World War II*, vol. 5: *The Struggle for Guadalcanal* (Boston: Little, Brown, 1949), 87-95, 104-7.
13. Samuel Griffith II, *The Battle for Guadalcanal* (Annapolis: Nautical & Aviation, 1963), 112-22.
14. Morison, *The Struggle for Guadalcanal*, pp. 191-93; Burke Davis, *Marine! The Life of Chesty Puller* (New York: Bantam Books, 1962), 136-48.

15. Morison, *The Struggle for Guadalcanal*, 147-71, 199-224.
16. Ibid., 244-53.
17. Ibid., 270-85.
18. Griffith, *Battle for Guadalcanal*, 244.
19. Ibid.
20. Ibid., 245.
21. Henry I. Shaw, Jr., and Douglas T. Kane, *History of U.S. Marine Corps Operations in World War II*, vol. 2: *Isolation of Rabaul* (Washington, D.C.: Historical Branch, U.S. Marine Corps, 1963), 27.
22. Ibid., 169.
23. Ibid., 172; Gavin Long, *Australia in the War of 1939-1945, vol. 7: The Final Campaigns* (Canberra: Australian War Memorial, 1963), 102.
24. J.M.S. Ross, *The Assault on Rabaul* (Wellington, N.Z.: New Zealand Department of Internal Affairs, War Histories Branch, 1949), 4.
25. John N. Rentz, *Marines in the Central Solomons* (Washington, D.C.: Historical Branch, U.S. Marine Corps, 1952), 20.

2. Allied Planning

1. Spector, *Eagle against the Sun*, 185-86.
2. Miller, *Cartwheel*, 5.
3. Ibid., 12–14.
4. E.B. Potter, *Bull Halsey* (Annapolis: Naval Institute Press, 1985), 238-39.
5. Spector, *Eagle against the Sun*, 226.
6. Frank O. Hough and John Crown, *The Campaign on New Britain* (Washington, D.C.: Historical Branch, U.S. Marine Corps, 1952).
7. Sherrod, *History of Marine Corps Aviation*, 145.
8. Miller, *Cartwheel*, 69.
9. Details of the New Georgia campaign are taken from Rentz, *Marines in the Central Solomons*, 17-126; Shaw and Kane, *Isolation of Rabaul*, 41-163; Miller, *Cartwheel*, 67-188; and Eric Hammel, *Munda Trail* (New York: Orion, 1989).
10. Samuel Eliot Morison, *History of United States Naval Operations in World War II*, vol. 6: *Breaking the Bismarck's Barrier* (Boston: Little, Brown, 1950), 180-197.
11. Miller, *Cartwheel*, 124-26.
12. Ibid., 164.
13. Ibid., 187.
14. Potter, *Bull Halsey*, 252-53.
15. Miller, *Cartwheel*, 186.
16. "The Target," Enclosure with Report, Commander, 3d Amphibious Force, to Commander in Chief, U.S. Pacific Fleet, 3 Dec. 1943, Marine Corps Historical Archives, Washington, D.C., File A1-1.
17. Ibid., p. 4.
18. Miller, *Cartwheel*, 228.
19. "The Target," 7-9.
20. The list of maps is in Annex A to Admiral Halsey, Operations Order #1, 12 Oct. 1943, Marine Corps Historical Archives, File A3-1.

216 Notes to Pages 36-54

21. IMAC Reconnaissance Report of Empress Augusta Bay area, 10 Oct. 1943, Bougainville Area Operations File, Marine Corps Historical Archives, File A3-3.
22. Enclosure J with Admiral Halsey, Operations Order #1.
23. Ibid.
24. Admiral Halsey, Operations Plan #16, 12 Oct. 1943, Marine Corps Historical Archives, File B1-1.5.
25. "Planning," Enclosure with Report, Commander, 3d Amphibious Force, 5.

3. The Treasuries and Choiseul

1. Unless noted, materials in this section are developed from 8th New Zealand Brigade, Operations Report, 30 Nov. 1943, Marine Corps Historical Archives, File A7.5-1; 34th Division Historical Committee, *The Story of the 34th* (Wellington, N.Z.: A.H. & A.W. Reed, 1947); John N. Rentz, *Bougainville and the Northern Solomons* (Washington, D.C.: Historical Branch, U.S. Marine Corps, 1952); and Shaw and Kane, *Isolation of Rabaul*.
2. 3d Division Histories Committee, *Pacific Service*, (Wellington, N.Z.: A.H. & A.W. Reed, 1947), 95.
3. Shaw and Kane, *Isolation of Rabual*, 189-90.
4. 34th Division, *Story of the 34th*, 73.
5. Shaw and Kane, *Isolation of Rabual*, 192.
6. 34th Division, *Story of the 34th*, 75-78.
7. Shaw and Kane, *Isolation of Rabaul*, 193.
8. Ibid., 194.
9. Lt. Gen. Victor H. Krulak, interview by author, San Diego, Calif., 23 Nov. 1987, transcript, 9.
10. Letter, Gen. Krulak to Headquarters, Marine Corps, 17 Oct. 1960, cited in Shaw and Kane, *Isolation of Rabaul*, 195.
11. Ibid., 195.
12. Krulak, interview by author, 3.
13. Ibid., 5.
14. Gerald P. Averill, *Mustang* (Novato, Calif.: Presidio Press, 1987), 77-78.
15. Lt. Gen. Victor H. Krulak, interview by Benis Frank, 1973, Oral History Transcript, Marine Corps Historical Archives, 81.
16. Annex A, Lt. Col. Krulak, Report on Operations, 29 Nov. 1943, Marine Corps Historical Archives, File A7-1, 1.
17. Krulak, interview by author, 1.
18. Shaw and Kane, *Isolation of Rabual*, 197.
19. Averill, *Mustang*, 76.
20. Ibid., 78-84.
21. Annex A, 1.
22. Shaw and Kane, *Isolation of Rabaul*, 199.
23. Annex A, 1-2.
24. Shaw and Kane, *Isolation of Rabaul*, 200.
25. Krulak, interview by author, 7.
26. Annex A, 2.

27. Averill, *Mustang*, 87-89.
28. Robert J. Donovan, *PT 109* (New York: McGraw-Hill, 1961), 228-29.
29. Averill, *Mustang*, 90.
30. Donovan, *PT 109*, 231.
31. Ibid., 224-34.
32. Averill, *Mustang*, 91.
33. Shaw and Kane, *Isolation of Rabaul*, 204.
34. Ibid., 204, 205.
35. Krulak, interview by author, 7.
36. Ibid., 8.

4. Establishing the Beachhead

1. George C. Kenney, *General Kenney Reports: A Personal History of the Pacific War* (New York: Duell, Sloan, and Pearce), 313-18.
2. Shaw and Kane, *Isolation of Rabaul*, 186.
3. Morison, *Breaking the Bismarck's Barrier*, 292-93.
4. Miller, *Cartwheel*, 242-43.
5. Shaw and Kane, *Isolation of Rabaul*, 205-6.
6. Captain Wilcie O'Bannon, interview by author, Maricopa, Calif., 4 Nov. 1988, transcript, 4.
7. Miller, *Cartwheel*, 244.
8. Morison, *Breaking the Bismarck's Barrier*, 298-99.
9. "Seizure and Occupation of Northern Empress Augusta Bay," Report, Marine Corps Historical Archives, File A1-1, 6.
10. Ibid.
11. O'Bannon interview, 2.
12. Gen. Alfred Noble, interview by Maj. L.E. Tatem, 1973, Oral History Transcript, Marine Corps Historical Archives, 86.
13. Shaw and Kane, *Isolation of Rabaul*, 210.
14. Miller, *Cartwheel*, 248.
15. John A. Monks, Jr., *A Ribbon and a Star* (New York: Henry Holt, 1945), 40.
16. Brig. Gen. Fred D. Beans, interview by Maj. Thomas Donnelly, 1976, Oral History Transcript, Marine Corps Historical Archives, 7.
17. Monks, *Ribbon and a Star*, 8.
18. Shaw and Kane, *Isolation of Rabaul*, 214.
19. Ibid., 211.
20. Three very accurate sketches of the defenses of Cape Torokina are to be found in Marine Corps Historical Archives, File C2-2.
21. Brig. Gen. Frederick P. Henderson, interview by Benis Frank, 1976, Oral History Transcript, Marine Corps Historical Archives, 1:84.
22. Ibid.
23. "Seizure and Occupation," 16.
24. Monks, *Ribbon and a Star*, 2-3.
25. "Operations of the Third Marines Reinforced in the Bougainville Campaign, 1 November-25 December 1943," Marine Corps Historical Archives, File A10-1; Shaw and Kane, *Isolation of Rabaul*, 213.

26. Robert A. Aurthur and Kenneth Cohlmia, *The Third Marine Division* (Washington, D.C.: Infantry Journal Press, 1948), 63.
27. Ibid., 371.
28. Shaw and Kane, *Isolation of Rabaul*, 214.
29. Ibid., 219.
30. Sergeant Eugene Edwards, interview by author, Avery, Calif., Sept. 1988, 1.
31. Navy Department, transcript, *Building the Navy's Bases in World War II*, vol. 2 (Washington, D.C.: Government Printing Office, 1947), 268.
32. Monks, *Ribbon and a Star*, 43-44.
33. Ibid., 40.
34. Ibid., 34.

5. Naval Actions

1. Morison, *Breaking the Bismarck's Barrier*, 24.
2. "Interrogation of Vice Admiral Shigeru Fukudome, 9-12 December 1945," in Naval Analysis Division, *United States Strategic Bombing Survey [Pacific]*, vol. 2 (Washington, D.C.: Government Printing Office, 1946), 514.
3. "Interrogation of Vice Admiral Sentaro Omori, 16 November 1945," Ibid., 337.
4. Ibid., 338.
5. Ibid., 337.
6. Recollections of this action are to be found in Adm. Merrill and Capt. Burke's After Action Reports in the Naval Archives, Washington, D.C. The best narrative of the battle is to be found in Morison, *Breaking the Bismarck's Barrier*, pp. 305-22. Admiral Omori's account in addition to an interesting chart is in his "Interrogation," 337-40.
7. "Interrogation of Omori," 340.
8. Ibid.
9. Ibid.
10. Ibid., 338.
11. Morison, *Breaking the Bismarck's Barrier*, 319-20.
12. Ibid., 320.
13. Ibid., 321.
14. Report, Commander, 3d Amphibious Force, 9.
15. "Interrogation of Fukudome," 515.
16. Potter, *Halsey*, 282.
17. Report, Commander, 3d Amphibious Force, 10, 12.
18. Potter, *Halsey*, 283.
19. Morison, *Breaking the Bismarck's Barrier*, 323-24.
20. Ibid., 325.
21. James H. Belote and William Belote, *Titans of the Seas* (New York: Harper & Row, 1975), 228.
22. Ibid., 229.
23. Dull, *Imperial Japanese Navy*, 303.
24. Ibid., 303-4.
25. Morison, *Breaking the Bismarck's Barrier*, p. 327; Belote and Belote, *Titans*, 230.

26. Ibid., 329.
27. Kenney, *General Kenney Reports*, 323.
28. Morison, *Breaking the Bismarck's Barrier*, 329-30.
29. Sherrod, *History of Marine Corps Aviation*, 186.
30. Morison, *Breaking the Bismarck's Barrier*, 331.
31. Belote and Belote, *Titans*, 232.
32. Morison, *Breaking the Bismarck's Barrier*, 332.
33. Belote and Belote, *Titans*, 235.
34. Ross, *The Assault on Rabaul*, 6-8.
35. "Interrogation of Fukudome," 516.
36. Morison, *Breaking the Bismarck's Barrier*, 355.
37. Belote and Belote, *Titans*, 235.
38. Dull, *Imperial Japanese Navy*, 306.

6. Expanding the Perimeter

1. Arthur and Cohlmia, *The Third Marine Division*, 65.
2. O'Bannon, interview by author, 3.
3. Ibid., 7.
4. "Seizure and Occupation of Northern Empress Augusta Bay," 12.
5. Ibid., 10-11.
6. The number of Japanese landed is still in question. Shaw and Kane, *Isolation of Rabaul*, 220, state that Japanese records indicate 850 men; Miller, *Cartwheel*, 259, places the number at 475. This latter figure agrees with the report, "Operations of the Third Marines Reinforced in the Bougainville Campaign," p. IV.
7. Shaw and Kane, *Isolation of Rabaul*, 233.
8. Arthur and Cohlmia, *The Third Marine Division*, 66; Shaw and Kane, *Isolation of Rabaul*, 233.
9. Shaw and Kane, *Isolation of Rabaul*, 235.
10. "Seizure and Occupation of Northern Empress Augusta Bay," 13; Miller, *Cartwheel*, 260.
11. Shaw and Kane, *Isolation of Rabaul*, 247.
12. Ibid., 237-38; Arthur and Cohlmia, *The Third Marine Division*, 67.
13. Arthur and Cohlmia, *The Third Marine Division*, 368.
14. Shaw and Kane, *Isolation of Rabaul*, 239-40.
15. Memo, Regimental Commander, 21st Marines, to Commanding General, 3d Marine Division, on Operations on Bougainville, 31 Jan. 1944, Marine Corps Historical Archives, File A17-1, 2.
16. Ibid., 4.
17. Ibid., 3.
18. Monks, *Ribbon and a Star*, 150.
19. Shaw and Kane, *Isolation of Rabaul*, 256.
20. Monks, *Ribbon and a Star*, 192ff.
21. "Operations of the Third Marines," p. X.
22. Monks, *Ribbon and a Star*, 199.
23. Ibid., 203.
24. Shaw and Kane, *Isolation of Rabaul* 263.
25. Ibid., 264.

Notes to Pages 111-131

26. Monks, *Ribbon and a Star*, 213.
27. "Operations of the Third Marines," p. X.
28. Shaw and Kane, *Isolation of Rabaul*, 264.
29. "Operations of the Third Marines," p. XI.
30. Shaw and Kane, *Isolation of Rabaul*, 266.
31. 1st Marine Parachute Battalion, Unit Report, Koiari Raid, 30 Nov. 1943, Bougainville Operations, File A7-1, Marine Corps Historical Archives.
32. Ibid.; Shaw and Kane, *Isolation of Rabaul*, 270-72.
33. Shaw and Kane, *Isolation of Rabaul*, 274-75.
34. Colonel Fraser West, interview by author, Ione, Calif., 5 Dec. 1988, transcript, 4.
35. Shaw and Kane, *Isolation of Rabaul*, 275.
36. Ibid., 276.
37. Arthur and Cohlmia, *The Third Marine Division*, 78.
38. Sherrod, *History of Marine Corps Aviation*, 191-92.
39. Shaw and Kane, *Isolation of Rabaul*, 279.
40. Report of Operations of 21st Marines on Bougainville, 31 Jan. 1944, Marine Corps Historical Archives, File A17-1, 6.

7. The Rear Areas

1. Shaw and Kane, *Isolation of Rabaul*, 276.
2. Monks, *Ribbon and a Star*, 121-22.
3. Henry Berry, *Semper Fi, Mac* (New York: Arbor House, 1982), 162.
4. Shaw and Kane, *Isolation of Rabaul*, 289.
5. Berry, *Semper Fi*, 159.
6. Edwards interview, 4.
7. West interview, 2.
8. Ibid.
9. "Empress Augusta Bay Campaign on Bougainville Island," Enclosure A, Marine Corps Historical Archives, File A21-1, 2-3.
10. Ibid., 6.
11. Ibid., 4.
12. Shaw and Kane, *Isolation of Rabaul*, 252.
13. Edwards interview, p. 1; Shaw and Kane, *Isolation of Rabaul*, 292.
14. Karl C. Dod, *The Corps of Engineers: The War against Japan* (Washington, D.C.: Government Printing Office, 1966), 255.
15. Ibid., 526.
16. Ibid., 546.
17. Brother Howard Ellis, interview by author, San Francisco, Calif., 26 Feb. 1989, transcript, 1.
18. Navy Department, *Building the Navy's Bases*, 270.
19. Sherrod, *History of Marine Corps Aviation*, 195.
20. Navy Department, *Building the Navy's Bases*, 272.
21. Ibid.
22. Ibid., 273.

8. Consolidating the Perimeter

1. Memorandum, Lt. Gen. M.F. Harmon to Adm. Halsey, 5 Nov. 1943, Marine Corps Historical Archives, File E1-1.
2. Operations Report, Bougainville, Americal Division, 19 December 1943–30 April 1944, National Archives, Suitland, Md. File 300-0.3, sec. II, 1-2.
3. Miller, *Cartwheel*, 355.
4. Francis D. Cronin, *Under the Southern Cross: The Saga of the Americal Division* (Washington, D.C.: Combat Forces Press, 1951), 135.
5. Ibid., 132-33.
6. Regimental Staff, *The 129th Infantry in World War II* (Washington, D.C.: Infantry Journal Press, 1947), 36-37.
7. Miller, *Cartwheel*, 355.
8. Operations Report, Bougainville, Americal Division, sec. II, 2.
9. Ibid.
10. Cronin, *Under the Southern Cross*, 135.
11. Regimental Staff, *The 129th Infantry*, 40-41.
12. Miller, *Cartwheel*, 269.
13. Cronin, *Under the Southern Cross*, 139-41.
14. Ibid., 136-37.
15. Ibid., 142.
16. Miller, *Cartwheel*, 356.
17. Morison, *Breaking the Bismarck's Barrier*, 427-28.
18. Ibid., 427.
19. Cronin, *Under the Southern Cross*, 134.
20. 3d Division Histories Committee, *Pacific Service*, 109-23; Morison, *Breaking the Bismarck's Barrier*, 412-19.
21. Sherrod, *History of Marine Corps Aviation*, 198.
22. Ibid., 199-200.
23. Ibid., 200; Gregory Boyington, *Baa, Baa Black Sheep* (New York: Bantam, 1979), 219-23.
24. Morison, *Breaking the Bismarck's Barrier*, 403.
25. Intelligence Annex, 28 Dec. 1943 to 29 April 1944, to Operations Report, Bougainville, Americal Division, 13-14; Miller, *Cartwheel*, 356.
26. After Action Report, Drafts, Bougainville Campaign, 37th Infantry Division, 1 November 1943 to March 1944, National Archives, File 337-0.3, 219-20.
27. Regimental Staff, *The 129th Infantry*, 47.

9. The Japanese Counterattack

1. Sherrod, *History of Marine Corps Aviation*, 208.
2. Miller, *Cartwheel*, 359.
3. Sgt. E.R. Beinberg, 145th Infantry Regiment, "History of Bougainville, 19 November 1943-16 March 1944," National Archives, File 337-INF (145) 0.1, 1.
4. Ibid., 2.
5. Ibid., 3.
6. Operations, Personnel Narrative, Bougainville, part VI: Bougainville—37th Division, 8 Nov. 1943-30 April 1944, National Archives, File 337-0.3, 15.

7. "History of 145th Infantry Regiment—37th Division," National Archives, File 337-INF (145) 0.1, 50.
8. Operations, Personnel Narrative, 28.
9. Ibid., 29.
10. Beinberg, "History," 5-6.
11. Operations, Personnel Narrative, 29-30.
12. Stanley Frankel, *History of 37th Division in World War II* (Washington, D.C.: Infantry Journal Press, 1948), 147-48.
13. Beinberg, "History," 6.
14. Miller, *Cartwheel*, 364.
15. Beinberg, "History," 6.
16. Sherrod, *History of Marine Corps Aviation*, 209.
17. Beinberg, "History," 8.
18. Frankel, *History of 37th*, 155.
19. Cronin, *Under the Southern Cross*, 152-53; Miller, *Cartwheel*, 365.
20. Miller, *Cartwheel*, 366.
21. Operations Report, Bougainville, Americal Division, 4.
22. Operations Report, Hill 260, Bougainville, 2d Battalion, 182d Infantry Regiment, Americal Division, 10-11 March 1944, National Archives, File 300-INF (182) 7-0.3, 3.
23. Ibid., 4-5.
24. Operations Report, Bougainville, Americal Division, 4.
25. Cronin, *Under the Southern Cross*, 157.
26. Ibid., pp. 160-64; Operations Report, Bougainville, Americal Division, 5-6.
27. Miller, *Cartwheel*, 372.
28. Ibid.
29. After Action Report, Drafts, 225.
30. Ibid., 226; Miller, *Cartwheel*, 374.
31. Operations, Personnel Narrative, 38.
32. Ibid., 40.
33. Regimental Staff, *The 129th Infantry*, 53.
34. Ibid., 55-59.
35. After Action Report, Drafts, 230.
36. Ellis interview, 3.
37. Regimental Staff, *The 129th Infantry*, 61.
38. Ibid., p. 61; Miller, *Cartwheel*, 377.
39. First Demobilization Bureau, Southeast Area Operations Record, part IV: Eighth Area Army Operations, July 1949, Imperial War Museum Archives, London, File AL 5216, 111.
40. Operations, Personnel Narrative, 20.
41. Ellis interview, 4.

10. The 93d Division Affair

1. Operations, Personnel Narrative, 18.
2. Orders, Higher Headquarters, 93d Infantry Division, 23 Dec. 1943-18 Sept. 1945, National Archives, File 393-3.9.1.

Notes to Pages 170-194   223

3. Operations, Personnel Narrative, 48-54; Cronin, *Under the Southern Cross*, 192-94.
4. Cronin, *Under the Southern Cross*, 169-71.
5. Operations Report, Bougainville, Americal Division, p. 6; Cronin, *Under the Southern Cross*, 175-76.
6. Operations Report, Bougainville, Americal Division, 7.
7. Ulysses Lee, *United States Army in World War II: The Employment of Negro Troops* (Washington, D.C.: Government Printing Office, 1966), 431-32.
8. Ibid., 237.
9. Orders, Higher Headquarters.
10. Lee, *Employment of Negro Troops*, 490.
11. Ibid., 497-98.
12. *New York Times*, 17 March 1944.
13. Lee, *Employment of Negro Troops*, 499.
14. Troop Movements, 93d Infantry Division, 31 Jan. 1944-10 April 1945, National Archives, File 393-3.21.
15. Lee, *Employment of Negro Troops*, 504.
16. Ninety-third Infantry Division, Operations Memorandum #9, 30 March 1944, National Archives, File 393-3.9.1.
17. Lee, *Employment of Negro Troops*, 505.
18. Ibid.
19. Ibid., 506-9.
20. Ibid., 513-14.
21. Troop Movements, 93d Infantry Division.
22. Lee, *Employment of Negro Troops*, 515.
23. Marshall quoted ibid., 512n.
24. Yon quoted Ibid., 516.

11. The Final Phase

1. Morison, *Breaking the Bismarck's Barrier*, 431.
2. Long, *The Final Campaigns*, 150.
3. Letter, Frank F. Mathias to author, 5 March 1990.
4. Frank F. Mathias, *G.I. Jive: An Army Bandsman in World War II* (Lexington, Ky.: Univ. Press of Kentucky, 1982), 95-96.
5. Mathias to author, 5 March 1990.
6. Frankel, *History of 37th Division*, pp. 190-91; Cronin, *Under the Southern Cross*, 214-15.
7. Frankel, *History of 37th Division*, pp. 136-37; Regimental Staff, 129th Infantry, 63.
8. Annex #8, Operations Report, Bougainville, Americal Division, 1.
9. Annex #6, Ibid., 1.
10. Ibid., 2-3.
11. Ibid., 6-10.
12. Long, *The Final Campaigns*, 217.
13. John Hetherington, *Blamey* (Melbourne: F.W. Cheshire, 1954), 143-46.
14. Long, *The Final Campaigns*, 598.
15. Ibid., 67.
16. Australian regimental and battalion designations during World War II

often combined unit numbers instead of assigning a new number when two older organizations were combined.

17. Cronin, *Under the Southern Cross*, 216-17; Regimental Staff, *129th Infantry*, 66-67.

18. Unless otherwise noted, descriptions of the Australian campaigns in 1944–45 are taken from Long, *The Final Campaigns*, 90-240.

19. Ibid., 109-10.
20. Ibid., 103.
21. Ibid., 116-18.
22. Ibid., 124-25.
23. Ibid., 174-75.
24. Eric Feldt, *The Coastwatchers* (Melbourne: Oxford University Press, 1946), 123-47, 160-67.
25. Long, *The Final Campaigns*, 164.
26. Ibid., 132-33.
27. Ibid., 152.
28. Ibid., 155.
29. Ibid., 161-62.
30. Ibid., 164.
31. Interrogation Report, Shoji Ohta and Shiro Hara, 8th Area Army, Bougainville, Imperial War Museum Archives, London, File AL 5023.
32. "Jap Situation, Bougainville," Intelligence Monograph No. 35, Imperial War Museum Archives, File AL 5017.
33. Long, *The Final Campaigns*, 184.
34. Ibid., 219-20.
35. Ibid., 212-15.
36. Ibid., 217.
37. Interrogation Report, Ohta and Hara.
38. Long, *The Final Campaigns*, 221-23.
39. Ibid., 237.
40. "Jap Situation, Bougainville."
41. Long, *The Final Campaigns*, 558.
42. Ibid., 502-3, 555.
43. Ibid., 237.

Bibliography

Primary Sources

Transcripts of Interviews by Author

Edwards, Sgt. Eugene, Avery, Calif., Sept. 1988.
Ellis, Brother Howard, San Francisco, Calif., 26 Feb. 1989.
Krulak, Lt. Gen. Victor, USMC, San Diego, Calif., Nov. 1987.
O'Bannon, Capt. Wilcie, USMC, Mariposa, Calif., Nov. 1988.
West, Col. Fraser, USMC, Ione, Calif., 5 Dec. 1988.

Marine Corps Historical Archives, Washington, D.C.

Oral History Transcripts

Beans, Brig. Gen. Fred D. Interview by Maj. Thomas Donnelly, 1976.
Henderson, Brig. Gen. Frederick P. Interview by Benis Frank, 1976. Vol. 1.
Krulak, Lt. General Victor H. Interview by Benis Frank, 1973.
Noble, Gen. Alfred Noble. Interview by Maj. L.E. Tatem, 1973.
Shapley, Lt. Gen. Alan. Inverview by Maj. Thomas Donnelly, 1976

Other Documents

Annex A, Lt. Col. Krulak, Report on Operations, 29 Nov. 1943, File A7-1.
Cape Torokina Defenses, File C2-2.
8th New Zealand Brigade, Operations Report, 30 Nov. 1943, File A7.5-1.
"Empress Augusta Bay Campaign on Bougainville Island," File A21-1.
1st Marine Parachute Battalion, Unit Report, Koiari Raid, 30 Nov. 1943, Bougainville Operations, File A7-1.
Halsey, Admiral. Operations Order #1, 12 Oct. 1943, File A3-1.
Halsey, Admiral. Operations Plan #16, 12 Oct. 1943, File B1-1.5.
IMAC Reconnaissance Report of Empress Augusta Bay area, 10 Oct. 1943, Bougainville Area Operations, File A3-3.
Memorandum, Lt. Gen. M.F. Harmon to Adm. Halsey, 5 Nov. 1943, File E1-1.

226   Bibliography

Memorandum, Regimental Commander, 21st Marines, to Commanding General, 3d Marine Division, 31 Jan. 1944, File A17-1.
"Operations of the Third Marines Reinforced in the Bougainville Campaign, 1 November-25 December 1943," File A10-1.
Report, Commander, 3d Amphibious Force to Commander in Chief, U.S. Pacific Fleet, 3 Dec. 1943, File A1-1.
Report of Operations of 21st Marines on Bougainville, 31 Jan. 1944, A17-1.
"Seizure and Occupation of Northern Empress Augusta Bay," Report, File A1-1.

National Archives, Suitland, Md.

After Action Report, Drafts, Bougainville Campaign, 37th Infantry Division, 1 Nov. 1943 to March 1944, File 337-0.3.
Beinberg, Sgt. E.R., 145th Infantry Regiment. "History of Bougainville, 19 November 1943-16 March 1944." File 337-INF 0.1.
"History of 148th Infantry Regiment—37th Division," File 337-INF (148) 0.1.
93d Infantry Division, Operations Memorandum #9, 30 March 1944, File 393-3.9.1.
Operations, Personnel Narrative, Bougainville, part VI: Bougainville—37th Division, 8 Nov. 1943-30 April 1944, File 337-0.3.
Operations Report, Bougainville, Americal Division, 19 Dec. 1943-30 April 1944, File 300-0.3.
Operations Report, Hill 260, Bougainville, 2d Battalion, 182d Infantry Regiment, Americal Division, 10-11 March 1944, File 300-INF (182) 7-0.3.
Orders, Higher Headquarters, 93d Infantry Division, 23 Dec. 1943-18 Sept. 1945, File 393-3.9.1.
Troop Movements, 93d Infantry Division, 31 Jan. 1944-10 April 1945, File 393-3.21.

Imperial War Museum Archives, London:

First Demobilization Bureau, Southeast Area Operations Record, part 4: Eighth Area Army Operations, July 1949, File AL 5216.
Intelligence Monograph No. 35, "Jap Situation, Bougainville, File AL 5017.
Interrogation Report, Shoji Ohta and Shiro Hara, 8th Area Army, File 5023.

Published Works

Aurthur, Robert A., and Kenneth Cohlmia. *The Third Marine Division.* Washington, D.C.: Infantry Journal Press, 1948.
Averill, Gerald P. *Mustang.* Novato, Calif.: Presidio Press, 1987.
Belote, James H., and William Belote. *Titans of the Seas.* New York: Harper & Row, 1975.
Berry, Henry. *Semper Fi, Mac.* New York: Arbor House, 1982.
Boyington, Gregory. *Baa, Baa Black Sheep.* New York: Bantam, 1979.
Cronin, Francis D. *Under the Southern Cross: The Saga of the Americal Division.* Washington, D.C.: Combat Forces Press, 1951.
Davis, Burke. *Marine! The Life of Chesty Puller.* New York: Bantam, 1962.
Dod, Karl C. *The Corps of Engineers: The War against Japan.* Washington, D.C.: Government Printing Office, 1966.

Donovan, Robert J. *PT 109*. New York: McGraw-Hill, 1961.
Dull, Paul S. *The Imperial Japanese Navy (1941-1945)*. Annapolis: Naval Institute Press, 1978.
Feldt, Eric. *The Coastwatchers*. Melbourne: Oxford University Press, 1946.
Frankel, Stanley. *History of 37th Division in World War II*. Washington, D.C.: Infantry Journal Press, 1948.
Griffith, Samuel. *The Battle for Guadalcanal*. Annapolis: Nautical & Aviation, 1963.
Hammel, Eric. *Munda Trail*. New York: Orion, 1989.
Hetherington, John. *Blamey*. Melbourne: F.W. Cheshire, 1954.
Hough, Frank O., and John Crown. *The Campaign on New Britain*. Washington, D.C.: Historical Branch, U.S. Marine Corps, 1952.
Kenney, George C. *General Kenney Reports: A Personal History of the Pacific War*. New York: Duell, Sloan, and Pearce, 1949.
Lee, Ulysses. *United States Army in World War II: The Employment of Negro Troops*. Washington, D.C.: Government Printing Office, 1966.
Long, Gavin. *Australia in the War of 1939-1945*, vol. 7: *The Final Campaigns*. Canberra: Griffin Press, 1963.
Mathias, Frank F. *G.I. Jive: An Army Bandsman in World War II*. Lexington, Ky.: Univ. Press of Kentucky, 1982.
Miller, John, Jr., *United States Army in World War II, the War in the Pacific, Cartwheel: The Reduction of Rabaul*. Washington, D.C.: Office of Chief of Military History, 1959.
Monks, John A., Jr. *A Ribbon and a Star*. New York: Henry Holt, 1945.
Morison, Samuel Eliot. *History of United States Naval Operations in World War II*, vol. 4: *Coral Sea, Midway, and Submarine Actions;* vol. 5: *The Struggle for Guadalcanal;* vol. 6: *Breaking the Bismarck's Barrier*. Boston: Little, Brown, 1949, 1950.
Morton, Louis. *The Fall of the Philippines*. Washington, D.C.: Department of the Army, 1953.
Naval Analysis Division. *United States Strategic Bombing Survey [Pacific]*. Vol. 2. Washington, D.C.: Government Printing Office, 1946.
Navy Department. *Building the Navy's Bases in World War II*. Washington, D.C.: Government Printing Office, 1947. Vol. 2
Potter, E.B. *Bull Halsey*. Annapolis: Naval Institute Press, 1985.
Prange, Gordon W. *At Dawn We Slept*. New York: Penguin, 1982.
———. *Miracle at Midway*. New York: Penguin, 1983.
Regimental Staff. *The 129th Infantry in World War II*. Washington, D.C.: Infantry Journal Press, 1947.
Rentz, John N. *Bougainville and the Northern Solomons*. Washington, D.C.: Historical Branch, U.S. Marine Corps, 1948.
———. *Marines in the Central Solomons*. Washington, D.C.: Historical Branch, U.S. Marine Corps, 1952.
Ross, J.M.S. *The Assault on Rabaul*. Wellington, N.Z.: New Zealand Department of Internal Affairs, War Histories Branch, 1949.
Shaw, Henry I., Jr., and Douglas T. Kane. *History of U.S. Marine Corps Operations in World War II*, vol. 2: *Isolation of Rabaul*. Washington, D.C.: Historical Branch, U.S. Marine Corps, 1963.
Sherrod, Robert. *History of Marine Corps Aviation in World War II*. Washington, D.C.: Combat Forces Press, 1952.

Spector, Ronald H. *Eagle against the Sun*. New York: Free Press, 1985.
3d Division Histories Committee. *Pacific Service*. Wellington, N.Z.: A.H. & A.W. Reed, 1947.
34th Division Historical Committee. *The Story of the 34th*. Wellington, N.Z.: A.H. & A.W. Reed, 1947.

Index

ABDA command, 10
Abe, Vice Adm. Hiroaki, 18
Ainsworth, Rear Adm. Walden, 27-29
Air Solomons (AIRSOL), 3
Air So Pac, 12
Akinage, Lt. Gen. Tsutomu, 186
Allied air attacks, 2, 3, 9-10, 12, 67-68, 86-88, 89-91, 118, 130, 143-44, 145, 153, 155, 202, 206, 207, 211
Allied aircraft:
  Auster, 212; B-24, 61, 64, 86, 87, 89, 149; B-25, 61; L-4, 133-34, 138; F4U, 65, 84, 129, 130, 202, 207; F6F, 84, 87, 89; P-38, 61, 65, 84, 89, 90; P-39, 11, 130; P-40, 11, 65, 68, 84; PBY, 64, 141; SB2C, 90; SBD, 90, 129, 130, 149; TBF, 52, 87, 130
Allied air force units:
  AIRSOLS, 31, 34, 37, 61, 62, 68, 84, 86, 130, 142, 143, 144
  Australian Air, 195
  5th Air Force, 11-12, 19, 61, 79, 84, 142
  13th Air Force, 26, 61
Allied command structure, 4-5
Allied troop strength, 26, 27, 41, 59, 64, 85-86, 95, 196
Ames, Colonel Evans, 102
Arty Hill, 195
Ashmun, Capt. George, 144
Asitivi mission, 138
Austin, Cmdr. B.L., 81, 83
Australia: air operations, 195;

casualties, 201, 203, 206, 208, 210; tactics, 4, 5-6, 191, 192-93, 194, 196, 208, 209
—army units, 4, 5-6
II Corps, 191
3d Div., 188, 193, 195
7th Div., 10
7th Brig., 191, 193, 205
11th Brig., 191, 194, 197
15th Brig., 191, 194, 205, 206
23d Brig., 194
29th Brig., 190, 191, 194, 195, 201, 206, 209
2/4 Armored Reg., 205
9th Bn., 195, 203
15th Bn., 201
24th Bn., 206
25th Bn., 202, 203
26th Bn., 208
47th Bn., 201
31/51st Bn., 197
57/60 Bn., 206, 207
New Guinea Bn., 201
2/8 Commando, 193, 194
58/59 Commando, 206, 207
Company B, 25th Bn., 197
Company D, 25th Bn., 196
Averill, Lt. Gerald, 48, 51, 57-58

Baanga, 30-31
Bairoko Harbor, 27, 30
Ballale, 20, 33
Barrett, Maj. Gen. Charles, 36-37

Index

Bataan, 8
Beans, Lt. Col. Fred, 68, 69, 100
Beightler, Maj. Gen. Robert, 29, 37, 150, 164, 165, 170, 175, 178
Berndtson, Lt. Arthur, 56
Bigger, Maj. Warren, 53-54, 55-56, 57
Bismarck Archipelago, 63
Bismarck Sea, 19
black troops, use of, 6, 172-74, 176, 182-83
Blamey, Gen. Sir Thomas, 4, 191, 193, 196
Blanche Harbor, 39, 40, 43
BLISSFUL plan, 47, 48, 49
Bonis Peninsula, 62, 196, 199, 207-8
Bougainville, 2, 3, 4, 6, 13, 31-33, 34-36, 39, 43, 45, 47, 59; airfields (Allied), 129-31, 140, 145, 149, 189; airfields (Japanese), 20, 31, 33, 36, 61, 62; beach defenses, 69-70, 72-73, 74; coastwatchers, 35-36, 46, 199; earthquake, 117; guerrilla forces, 199-201; health conditions, 121-26; Japanese defenses (see individual headings); maps of, 36, 102, 104-5; terrain features, 34-35, 36, 117, 125-26, 150; U.S. invasion of (see individual headings); weather conditions, 122-23, 202, 209-10
Boyd, Brig. Gen. Leonard, 181
Boyington, Maj. Gregory, 129-30, 144
Brady, Maj. John, 98
Bridgeford, Maj. Gen. William, 191, 206
Brodin, Sgt. Ralph, 178, 179
Buin, 35, 39, 40, 61, 209
Buin Road, 202, 203, 205, 207
Buoi Plantation, 207
Buka, 13, 20, 35, 61, 92, 142, 192
Buka Passage, 62, 63
Buna, 10, 12, 19, 192
bunkers (pillboxes), 70, 72, 73, 120, 134, 150-51, 152-53, 154-55, 171, 178
Buretoni Plantation, 70, 76
Burke, Capt. Arleigh, 81, 83, 84, 92
Bush, 133
Butler, Lt. Col. Arthur, 118

Caldwell, Cmdr. Henry, 87
Callaghan, Rear Adm. Dan, 18
Cannon Hill, 150, 151
Cape Esperance, 17
Cape Gloucester, 34, 132, 142, 184

Cape Moltke, 136, 170
Cape St. George, 92
Cape Torokina, 2, 3, 6, 20, 36, 37, 57, 61, 63, 64, 65, 72, 74, 78, 80, 85, 87, 99, 101, 114, 130, 132
Carney, Rear Adm. Robert, 34, 86
Caroline Islands, 71
CARTWHEEL plan, 25, 31
Central Pacific Command, 11, 25, 174, 184, 190
CHERRYBLOSSOM plan, 37
Choho Ridge, 194
Choiseul Island, 2, 34, 38, 46-59, 63, 113, 141
Cibek, Lt. Steve, 105-7
Cibek Ridge, 107, 108, 112
coastwatchers, 35-36, 46, 199
coconut grove battle, 102-5
Collins, Maj. Gen. J. Lawton, 29
Commando Road, 205, 206, 207
COMSOPAC, 39, 45, 46, 85
Congressional Medal, 73-74, 100, 139, 144
Coral Sea battle, 9-10, 12, 78
Corregidor, 8
Cox Creek, 161, 162, 164
Craig, Col. Edward, 99, 101, 163
Cross, Lt. Charles, 138
Curran, Capt. James, 178, 179
Cushman, Lt. Col. Robert, 100, 124

Daehler, Maj. Raymond, 159
Davenport, Lt. Oscar, 180
de Zayas, Lt. Col. Hector, 105, 107, 108
Drowley, Staff Sgt. Jesse, 139
Duncan, Lt. Rea, 55

Eagle Creek, 156
East-West Trail, 35, 101, 102, 104, 105, 112, 115, 147, 181
Edson, Col. Merritt, 16
Edwards, Sgt. Eugene, 123
Eichelberger, Lt. Gen. Robert, 194
ELKTON III plan, 24, 25, 31
Emmons, Lt. Gen. Delos, 174
Empress Augusta Bay, 2, 34, 35, 39, 59, 61, 63, 64, 76, 79, 81, 82, 96, 113, 127, 133, 171, 175, 176, 193
Enogai Point, 27
Erventa, 209
Espiritu Santo, 16
Europe First doctrine, 11

Index

Fagan, Maj. Richard, 113, 114, 115
Falami Point, 39, 40, 43
Fiji Infantry Regiment, 136, 137-38, 166, 171, 172, 177
Fiji Islands, 11, 40, 133
Finschaven, 8
Fitch, Vice Adm. Aubrey, 26
Fletcher, Vice Adm. Frank Jack, 12, 15
Fogge, Pvt. Wayne, 178
Fort, Rear Adm. George, 37, 40
Frederick, Col. John, 161, 162, 163
Freeman, Lt. Orville, 122-23
Freer, Col. George, 154
Fry, Col. Ernest, 98
Fukudome, Vice Adm. Shigeru, 79, 85

Garvin, Col. Crump, 133
Gazelle Peninsula, 142
Geiger, Maj. Gen. Roy, 37, 93, 108, 110, 113, 114, 115, 118, 119, 132
Genga River, 197
Ghormley, Vice Adm. Robert L., 13, 15, 16
Gilbert Islands, 60, 62, 91
Gillman River, 199
Gona, 192
GOODTIME plan, 40, 45
Green Islands, 142, 143, 184
Grenade Hill, 112
Griswold, Maj. Gen. Oscar, 20, 30, 119, 132, 133, 135, 139, 141, 147, 152, 157, 159, 163, 169, 170, 175, 176, 177, 178, 180, 185, 191, 193
Guadalcanal, 1, 4, 10, 12, 13-19, 20, 21, 23, 33, 35, 38, 41, 62, 63, 76, 114
Gurke, Pvt. 1st Class Henry, 100
Guppy Island, 54, 58

Halsey, Vice Adm. William F., 2, 5, 16-17, 23, 24, 25, 26, 30, 31, 54, 60, 62, 79, 85, 86, 87, 88, 89, 132, 184, 185, 191
Hannafin, Sgt. D.O., 144
Hanson, Lt. Robert, 144
Harmon, Lt. Gen. Millard, 24, 26, 29, 126, 132, 174, 176
Hellzapoppin Ridge, 117-18, 119, 120
Henderson, Maj. Frederick, 70-71
Henderson Field, 15, 49
Hester, Maj. Gen. John, 26, 27
Hill 155, 171
Hill 165, 165, 171
Hill 205, 170

Hill 250, 136, 178, 179, 180, 186
Hill 260, 149, 152, 156-61, 177
Hill 500, 115, 171, 177
Hill 501, 170-71, 177
Hill 600, 115, 119, 132, 136, 147, 149, 170
Hill 600A, 132
Hill 608, 140
Hill 700, 134, 140, 145, 150, 151-55, 161
Hill 1000, 115, 117-18, 136, 140, 170
Hill 1111, 136, 140, 147, 170
Hiru Hiru, 202
Hodge, Maj. Gen. John, 133, 138, 142, 157, 159, 169, 170
Hollandia, 184
Hollywood entertainers, 187
Homma, Gen. Masaharu, 8
Hongorai River, 202, 205, 206, 207
Horaniu, 60
Horii, Lt. Gen. Tomitaro, 10, 13, 16
Horseshoe Ridge, 181
Hundley, Lt. Col. Preston, 102
Huon Peninsula, 9, 24
Hyakutake, Lt. General Harukichi, 16, 17, 78, 96, 99, 131, 140-41, 143, 144, 145, 147, 164, 166, 167, 168, 169, 170, 185-86, 196

Ibu, 137, 138
Ijuin, Rear Adm. Matsuji, 80
Imamura, Gen. Hitoshi, 13, 166
Inouye, Vice Adm. Shigeyoshi, 9
Iwasa, Maj. Gen., 99, 101, 151, 155
Iwasa unit, 144-45

Jaba River, 195
Japanese: air operations, 7-8, 9, 12, 16, 63, 67-68, 79, 84, 87, 90-91, 92, 95, 101, 104, 142, 143, 144; casualties, 17, 18, 19, 30, 45, 46, 53, 58, 74, 94, 98, 100, 101, 104, 105, 111, 113, 115, 118, 136, 138, 143, 152, 153, 155-56, 161, 164, 166, 188, 190, 201, 204, 209, 211; food supply, 167, 185, 196; health care, 167, 196, 204; naval actions, 1, 2, 3, 7, 8, 9-10, 12-13, 15-16, 17-18, 19, 30, 60, 71-72, 78-79, 80-84, 91-92; navy, 2, 3, 7, 9-10, 12-13, 15-16, 17-18; ship losses, 78-79, 83-84, 88, 89-90, 91-92, 143, 144; surrender, 4, 210-11; tactics, 2, 3, 4, 7, 10, 12, 15-19, 96-97, 149, 168, 185-86, 201-2, 203-4, 205, 206, 209; troop strength, 16, 20, 21,

232 Index

27, 33, 40, 59, 96, 145, 147, 168, 196, 197, 206, 211
—army units:
8th Area Army, 9, 166, 210
17th Army, 16, 141, 168, 186
11th Air Fleet, 20
Iwasa Force, 144-45, 152, 156, 161, 169
Magata Force, 145, 147, 161, 169
Muda Force, 145, 152, 156-59, 168, 169
6th Div., 20, 139, 166, 167, 168, 195
13th Div., 144, 156
17th Div., 96, 99, 140
51st Div., 19
2nd Air Squad., 143
4th South Seas Garrison, 10, 166, 169
6th Cavalry Reg., 166, 169
13th Reg., 145, 161, 164, 202, 203
23d Reg., 99, 111, 117, 150, 164, 204
45th Reg., 145
53d Reg., 140
81st Reg., 145
2/13, 140
2/23, 151
3/23, 151
1/45, 162
45/45, 162
1/53, 140
3/53, 140
—naval units:
Combined Fleet, 63, 78
Southeast Area Fleet, 13
2nd Fleet, 85, 88
4th Fleet, 9
8th Fleet, 141
3rd Naval Landing Force, 10
Johnson, Lt. Sam, 56

Kahili, 4, 33, 61
Kanda, Lt. Gen. Masatane, 140, 144, 147, 160, 186, 201, 202, 203, 204, 205, 209, 210-11
Kara, 62
Karina, 190
Kavieng, 87, 132, 143
Kawaguchi, Maj. Gen. Kiyotake, 16, 19
Kawano, Lt. Col., 204
Kennedy, Lt. John F., 57
Kenney, Lt. Gen. George, 8, 9, 11, 24, 61, 79, 86, 90
Kieta, 20, 35, 36, 61, 201, 209
Killen's Track, 207
King, Adm. Ernest J., 13, 15, 23, 25
King, Lt. Col. Ralph, 105, 108

Kingori, 207
Kiriwina Island, 24, 25
Kirk, Capt. L.J., 44
Kiviri Point, 138
Koga, Adm. Mineichi, 13, 60, 62, 75, 79, 91, 92, 143, 144
Koiari, 113-15
Kolombangara, 2, 20, 29, 30, 31, 60, 79
Kokoda Trail, 10, 192
Kondo, Vice Adm. Nobutake, 17, 18
Koromokina River, 69, 96, 97, 98, 101, 121, 127, 161
Koror, 144
Kreber, Brig. Gen. Leo, 133, 165, 181
Kruger, Lt. Gen. Walter, 192
Krulak, Lt. Col. Victor, 46, 47, 48-49, 52-54, 55, 58-59, 113
Kula Gulf, 27, 29, 81
Kunamatoro, 197, 199
Kuraio Mission, 194, 197
Kurita, Vice Adm. Takeo, 85, 86, 143
Kusaka, Vice Adm. Jinichi, 13, 63, 79, 85, 87, 90, 91, 95, 96

Lae, 8, 9, 22, 194
Laiana Beach, 27
Lakunai Airfield, 90
landing craft, 67, 72, 74-75, 88, 95, 114, 127, 133
Laruma River, 36, 68, 94, 96, 97, 139, 170, 177, 181, 188-90
Lee, Rear Adm. Willis, 18
Leyte, 194
Little George Hill, 194-95
Liversedge, Col. Harry, 27
Logan, Maj. G.W., 41
Logan Force, 43, 44
Long, Col. William, 133, 157
Lowry, Lt. Col. Dexter, 157
Luzon, 8

MacArthur, Gen. Douglas, 2, 4, 5, 11, 13, 15, 21, 22, 23, 24, 25, 31, 34, 39, 60, 79, 89, 142, 173, 184, 185, 191, 192, 196
McCain, Rear Adm. John, 12
McClelland Road, 151, 152
McCloy, John J., 182
McClure, Maj. Gen. Robert, 170
McCulloch, Brig. Gen. William, 160
McHenry, Col. George, 104
McNair, Lt. Gen. Leslie, 174
McNarny, Lt. Gen. Joseph, 174-75

Index

Magata, Col. Isashi, 145, 147, 160, 161, 162
Magata Unit, 145, 147
Magine Islands, 139, 171
Makin, 33, 87
malaria control, 124-26
Malasi, 43, 44
Malaya, 7
Manchester, Capt. Robert, 52
Manus, 194
Marabie River, 170
Mariana Islands, 184, 190
Marshall, Gen. George C., 6, 24, 173, 176, 182
Marshall Islands, 60, 63, 71, 78
Mason, Lt. Col. Leonard, 72, 73
Mason, P.E., 201
Mavavia River, 139, 177
Mawareka, 35, 145, 195, 201, 202
medical care, 120-22, 128, 134
Merrill, Rear Adm. Aaron, 37, 62, 81, 82, 83, 96
Midway Island, 1, 9, 12-13, 19, 78
Mikawa, Rear Adm. Gunichi, 15
Mitchell, Maj. Gen. Ralph, 37, 143
Mitscher, Rear Adm. Marc, 26, 144
Mivo River, 207, 209, 210
Mono Island, 39-40, 43, 45
Monaghan, Brig. Gen. R.F., 201
Montgomery, Rear Adm. Alfred, 89, 90, 91
MO operation, 9
Mosigetta, 35, 145, 195, 201
Mosina, 195
Motupena Point, 201, 202
Mount Bagana, 34
Mount Balbi, 34, 138
Mount Nampei, 147
Muda, Col. Toyhorel, 145, 147, 156, 157
Muda Unit, 145
Munda, 2, 20, 25, 27, 29, 30, 31, 130
Murray, Maj. James, 45

Nagumo, Adm. Chuichi, 7, 8, 9, 12
Nanking, 140, 168
Neston, Vice Adm. John, 185
New Britain Island, 2, 3, 9, 20, 21, 91, 92, 142, 143, 192
New Caledonia, 11, 175
New Georgia Island, 2, 20, 21, 23, 24, 25, 26-30, 31, 33, 37, 47, 60, 65, 90, 174

New Guinea, 2, 3, 4, 8, 10, 12, 21, 22, 23, 63, 90, 191, 193
New Hebrides, 40
New Ireland, 13, 92, 142, 143
New Zealand: air operations, 202, 206, 207, 211; casualties, 45
—army units:
 3d Div., 33, 37, 142-43
 14th Brig. Group, 40, 143
 1st Brig., 37
 8th Brig., 37, 40
Nimitz, Adm. Chester W., 11, 12, 13, 23, 24, 25, 61, 62, 78, 86
Nip Hill, 189, 190
Nissan, 142-43
North Knob, 156-58
Noumea, 2, 11, 13, 185
Nukiki, 54, 55, 57
Numa Numa Trail, 99, 101, 102, 105, 161, 169, 170, 194
Numa Numa Village, 34, 35, 199, 209

O'Bannon, Sgt. Wilcie, 94-95
Omori, Vice Adm. Santaro, 80, 81-83, 96
Oso River, 207
Osugi, Rear Adm. Morikaze, 80
Owens, Sgt. Robert, 73
Owen Stanley Mountains, 9
Ozawa, Vice Adm. Jisaburo, 79, 92

Pacific Military Conference, 23-24
Palau Islands, 191
Patch, Maj. Gen. Alexander, 18, 19
patrolling, 134-35, 136-37, 138, 170-71, 172, 177, 185, 188, 190, 194, 209
Pat's Nose, 151, 153, 154
Pearl Harbor, 7, 8, 12, 78, 173
Pearl Ridge operation, 196-97
Peko, 147
Peperu, 207
perimeter defense, 129, 134-35, 138-39, 140, 149-64, 185, 191
perimeter development, 186-87
Piaterapaia, 194
pillboxes. See bunkers
Pipipaia, 138
Piva Forks operation, 99-101, 102, 107-11, 127, 131
Piva River, 94, 105, 107, 127
Piva Trail, 94, 99, 101
Piva Uncle airfield, 130, 145, 149
Piva Yoke airfield, 130, 145, 149

234 Index

Philippine Islands, 4, 168, 184, 192
Poro Poro, 199
Port Moresby, 2, 8, 9, 10, 13, 16, 192
Porton Plantation, 207
Pratt, Capt. Spencer, 53
PT Boats, 47, 57, 131, 143
Puller, Lt. Col. Lewis, 17
Puruata Island, 64, 68-69, 95, 98, 126
Puruata River, 202, 203

Rabaul, 2, 3, 6, 9, 20, 21, 23, 25, 31, 34, 60, 61, 63, 65, 79, 80, 84, 85, 86, 87, 88, 90-91, 92, 130, 131, 140, 142, 168, 184, 210
Rapapo airfield, 61
Reifsnider, Commo. L.F., 64, 85
Reini River, 177, 188
Rendova Island, 26, 27, 38, 64, 85
Rice Anchorage, 27, 29
Richards, Lt. John, 54
Richardson, Lt. Gen. Robert, 5
Riley, Col. William, 34
RO operation, 63, 91
Row, Brig. Gen. R.A., 40, 41
Rukussia, 197
Rusei, 207
Russell Islands, 19, 37

St. Georges Channel, 87
Salamaua, 8, 9
Samejima, Vice Adm. Tomoshige, 80, 85, 210-11
Sangigai, 47, 51, 52, 53, 54, 58
Santa Isabel Island, 20
Santa Cruz Island, 17
Sasake, Maj. Gen. Noburu, 27, 29, 30-31
Saua River, 171, 172, 182
Savek River, 43
Savige, Lt. Gen. Sir Stanley, 4, 25, 191, 193, 194, 195, 196, 199, 201-2, 205, 206, 209, 210-11
Savo Island, 15
Seabee Creek, 125
Segei Point, 26
Seton, Capt. C.W., 46, 47, 48, 49, 201
Shapley, Maj. Alan, 100
Sherman, Rear Adm. Frederick C., 37, 62, 63, 86, 87, 88, 89
Shortland Islands, 20, 33-34, 59, 62, 205
Simpson Harbor, 20
Sisive, 194

Slater, Pvt. C.R., 202
Slater's Knoll, 202-4, 206
Smith, Lt. Gen. Holland M., 5, 102, 103
Smith, Pvt. J.E., 44
Smoak, Lt. Col. Eustace, 102, 103
Soanatalu River, 10, 41, 45
Solomon Islands, 1, 2, 5, 9, 10, 13, 21, 22, 23, 35, 38, 63, 143, 191
Somerville, Adm. James, 7
Soposa Island, 199
Soraken operation, 197-99
South Knob, 156, 157, 158
South Pacific Theater, 2, 4, 10, 22-23, 24, 132, 174, 184
Southwest Pacific Theater, 2, 4, 11, 22-23, 181, 184, 192
Spruance, Adm. Raymond, 12, 144, 184, 190-91
Stevenson, Brig. Gen. J.R., 197
Stimson, Henry L., 174, 182-83
Stirling Island, 39-40, 43, 45
Sutherland, Maj. Gen. Richard, 24, 192

Taiof Island, 99
Tanaka, Rear Admiral Shimishi, 18, 19
Tanikawa, Maj. Gen. Kanzuo, 166
TA operation, 140-41, 144-47
Tarawa Island, 33, 87
Tassafaronga Island, 17-18
Tavantu, 188
Taylor, Lt. Col. J.B.K., 137
Taylor Creek, 161, 162
Tenekau, 20
Thomas, Lt. Col. John, 175
Thorn, Col. Hamilton, 175
Tobera Airfield, 61, 90
TOENAILS plan, 25, 26, 31
Toko, 202
Tongatabu, 11
Tonlei, 205, 209
Torokina Airfield, 129-30
Torokina River, 94, 113, 115, 134, 138, 139, 140, 156, 179, 181, 188
Treasury Island operation, 34, 37, 38, 39-45, 51, 63
Truk, 20, 63, 78, 79, 85, 87
Tsimba Ridge, 197, 199
Tsurutai, 205
Tulagi Island, 13, 15, 22
Turnage, Maj. Gen. Allen, 67, 93, 95, 100, 102, 111, 133

Index

Turner, Rear Adm. Richmond K., 5, 15, 26, 27, 31
Twining, Maj. Gen. Nathan, 26, 31, 65, 86

United States: casualties, 30, 33, 53, 55, 58, 97, 99, 100, 101, 104, 111, 113, 115, 118, 122, 136, 137, 149, 152, 153, 154, 157, 161, 164, 177, 180; naval actions, 2, 3, 7, 9-10, 12-13, 15-16, 17-18, 19, 30, 60, 71-72, 78-79, 80-84, 91-92, 144
—Army units:
  6th Army, 192, 194
  8th Army, 194
  X Corps, 194
  XIV Corps, 18, 29, 119, 128, 132, 133, 166, 168, 169, 171, 172, 175, 187, 191, 195
  XXIV Corps, 170
  Americal Div., 3, 4, 11, 18, 26, 37, 119, 128, 130, 132, 133, 134, 135, 136, 138, 145, 147, 149, 152, 156, 159, 160, 167, 169
  25th Div., 19, 29, 31, 33
  32d Div., 10, 11
  37th Div., 2, 3, 4, 11, 26, 29, 33, 37, 64, 95, 104, 107, 108, 111, 126, 127, 128, 133, 134, 135, 136, 137, 138, 144, 147, 149, 150, 152, 160, 161, 165, 167, 169, 170, 175, 181, 186, 187, 188, 189, 193, 194, 195
  41st Div., 11
  43d Div., 19, 20, 26 27, 29, 30, 33, 176
  92d Div., 174
  93d Div., 6, 169, 172, 173, 174-75, 176
  24th RCT (Regimental Combat Team), 172, 175, 176
  25th RCT, 6, 176, 177, 180, 181, 182
  27th RCT, 30, 31
  129th RCT, 128, 135, 145, 149, 153, 161-65, 166, 167, 170, 175, 193
  132d RCT, 133, 134, 159-60, 170, 171, 177, 181, 190
  145th RCT, 29, 134, 136, 137, 150, 152, 154, 155, 193
  147th RCT, 11
  148th RCT, 29, 86, 95, 103, 111, 153, 165, 170, 175-76
  161st RCT, 29, 95, 104, 107, 111
  164th RCT, 17, 133, 134, 170, 177, 178, 188, 194
  169th RCT, 27, 30
  172d RCT, 27, 30
  182d RCT, 133, 136, 145, 156-61, 177, 178, 182, 188, 190, 195
  368th RCT, 176
  369th RCT, 176
  131st Engineering Reg., 128
  1/24, 154, 171, 175, 176, 177, 181
  2/24, 175
  3/24, 175
  1/25, 171, 177, 181
  2/25, 170, 177, 178, 181
  3/25, 178, 181, 182
  1/27, 30
  1/129, 162
  2/129, 162, 163
  1/132, 159, 177
  2/132, 134, 177
  3/132, 177
  1/145, 111, 151, 152, 153
  2/145, 136, 152, 153
  2/148, 154
  3/148, 27
  1/164, 133, 134, 136, 189-90
  2/164, 189, 190
  3/164, 133, 189, 190
  1/182, 177
  2/182, 156, 157-58
  57th Combat Engineer Bn., 128
  117 Combat Engineer Bn., 128, 152
  6th Field Artillery Bn., 149
  245th Field Artillery Bn., 133
  246th Field Artillery Bn., 156, 159
  247th Field Artillery Bn., 171
  593d Field Artillery Bn., 176, 178
  2d Bn., 54th Coast Arty., 175
  49th Coast Arty. Bn., 181
  754th Tank Bn., 138, 163, 164, 177
  21st Recon. Troop, 139
  A Co. 1/25, 171
  F Co. 2/25, 178
  K Co. 3/25, 178-80, 180-81, 182, 183
  L Co. 3/25, 180
  A Co. 1/32, 159, 160
  B Co. 1/132, 160
  C Co. 1/132, 138-39
  C Co. 1/129, 162
  E Co. 1/129, 162
  F Co. 2/129, 162, 164
  G Co. 2/129, 162
  K Co. 3/129, 165
  C Co. 1/145, 152
  E Co. 2/145, 150, 151, 154

236 Index

—Army units (continued):
F Co. 2/145, 150, 152, 154
G Co. 2/145, 152, 153, 154
A Co. 3/145, 136
B Co. 3/145, 153
C Co. 2/164, 189
E Co.2/164, 189
B Co. 1/182, 157, 158, 159
E Co. 2/182, 157-58
F Co. 2/182, 157-58
G Co. 2/182, 156-58
—Marine Corps units:
1st Marine Amphib. Corps (IMAC), 37, 40, 41, 45, 48, 70, 93, 112, 113, 128
1st Div., 15, 25, 132, 184
2d Div., 18, 33, 132
3d Div., 2, 26, 33, 36-37, 64, 73, 110, 119, 132, 133, 211
1st Parachute Reg., 47, 77, 115
2d Raider Reg., 37
1st Marine Airwing, 61
2d Marine Airwing, 61
VMF 214, 129
VMF 215, 144
VMF 216, 129, 130
3d Marines, 64, 68, 93, 97, 101, 104, 105, 107, 108, 111, 112
5th Marines, 15
7th Marines, 15, 17
9th Marines, 64, 65, 68, 69, 74, 76, 93, 99, 101, 102, 104, 107, 111, 117, 121, 133
12th Marines, 74, 75, 100, 108, 113, 125
21st Marines, 85, 95, 102, 107, 111, 113, 115, 118, 121, 133
1/3, 70, 74, 76, 98, 104, 107, 108
2/3, 70, 95, 104, 108, 109, 110
3/3, 70, 95, 104, 105, 108, 109
1/9, 95, 97, 101, 111, 112, 113, 118
2/9, 95, 97, 100, 101, 115, 124
3/9, 95, 97
1/21, 98, 102, 103, 104, 105, 107, 118
2/21, 102, 104
3/21, 104, 107, 118, 119
1/1 Parachute, 49, 113
2/1 Parachute, 47, 48, 49
3/1 Parachute, 115-18
2/2 Raider, 64, 70, 94, 99, 100, 111, 112, 113
3/2 Raider, 64, 94, 99-100, 101, 105

3d Defense Bn., 37, 64, 74, 94, 113, 114
3d Tank Bn., 97, 100
3d Service Bn., 74
3d Amphib. Tractor Bn., 75, 127
A Co. 1/3, 73
B Co. 1/3, 73, 98
C Co. 1/3, 73, 98
I Co. 3/3, 110
K Co. 3/3, 110
L Co. 3/3, 109, 110
A Co. 1/9, 112
B Co. 1/9, 112
C Co. 1/9, 112
K Co. 3/9, 97, 98
E Co. 2/21, 102, 103
F Co. 2/21, 103
I Co. 3/21, 119
K Co. 3/21, 119
E Co. 1/1 Parachute, 52, 53, 54
F Co. 1/1 Parachute, 52, 53, 54
G Co. 1/1 Parachute, 54, 56
E Co. 2/3 Raider, 99, 100
F Co. 2/3 Raider, 100
G Co. 2/3 Raider, 99
K-9 Co., 94
—naval units:
5th Fleet, 190-91
TG (Task Group) 50, 3, 89, 90
TF (Task Force), 31, 37, 38, 63
TF 32, 26, 31
TF 33, 26, 37
TF 38, 62, 86, 87, 89-91
TF 39, 37, 62, 63, 81
TF 58, 144
TF 72, 37
Cruiser Div. 12, 37
Destroyer Div. 23, 37
Destroyer Div. 45, 81, 82, 92
Destroyer Div. 46, 81, 92
25th Construction Bn. (Seabees), 75
36th Construction Bn., 130, 131
71st Construction Bn., 75, 125, 129
75th Construction Bn., 75, 130
United States Joint Chiefs of Staff, 2, 5, 11, 13, 22, 23-24
Upton, Maj. Gregory, 137
USO shows, 187

Vandegrift, Lt. General Alexander, 15, 16, 18, 37, 45, 57, 64, 67

Vella Gulf, 30
Vella Lavella, 2, 31, 38, 41, 52, 53, 54, 57, 58, 60, 61, 64, 87, 115, 121, 130
Vila Airfield, 31
Viru Harbor, 26
Vogel, Maj. Gen. Clayton, 26
Voza, 46, 51, 52, 53, 54, 55, 57, 58
Vunakanau, 61, 90

Waddell, Charles J., 46
Warrior River, 54, 55, 56, 58
WATCHTOWER plan, 13
Watson Island, 43
West, Captain Frazer, 117, 123, 124

Whitcomb, Lt. Col. Cecil, 136, 151, 152, 154
Wickham Anchorage, 26
Wilkinson, Rear Adm. Theodore, 31, 37, 45, 62, 65, 74, 76, 78, 93
Williams, Lt. Col. Robert, 47, 115, 117
Willoughby, Maj. Gen. Charles, 196
Woodlark Island, 24, 25

Yamamoto, Adm. Isoruku, 8, 9, 12, 13
Yamashita, Gen. Tomayuki, 7
Yon, Col. Everett, 182

Zanana Beach, 27